DISCIPLINE with DIGNITY

Richard L. Curwin
and Allen N. Mendler

Association for Supervision and Curriculum Development

To my wife Barbara for her love and friendship and sharing in the daily challenge of parenting; and to my wonderful sons Jason and Brian, whose love and achievements affirm the virtue of raising children with dignity and respect.

Allen Mendler

For my mother Ann for a lifetime of support and love, who taught me the true meaning of dignity; and for three of her grandchildren—David, Andy, and Danny Curwin—to whom I hope to teach the same.

Rick Curwin

Whose school is this, anyway?

Is it the principal's?
Is it the teachers'?
Is it the smart kids'?
Is it the shy kids'?
Is it the pushy kids'?
Is it the popular kids'?
Is it each kid's equally?
Is it the kids', the principal's, and the teachers' equally?

Who decides what goes on in here?
Who does it go on for?
Does it go on for the kids who go to college?
Does it go on for the kids who go to work?
Does it go on for the kids who have nowhere to go?
Does it go on for all kids equally?
Does it go on for the teachers?
Does it go on for the principal?
Does it go on for the teachers, the kids, and the
   principal equally?

Who tells whom what to do?
Who makes the rules?
Who are the rules for?
Who must follow the rules?
Who must see that the rules are followed?

Whose school is this, anyway?

Richard Curwin is an assistant professor of education at San Francisco State University. He has been a junior high school teacher and has conducted workshops for ASCD for 15 years. He is also the author of *Discovering Your Teaching Self*.

Allen Mendler is a school psychologist and a psychoeducational consultant in Rochester, N.Y. He has worked extensively with children and teachers at all grade levels and among special needs populations.

Curwin and Mendler have coauthored two earlier books on discipline.

Copyright 1988 by the Association for Supervision and Curriculum Development.

ASCD publications present a variety of viewpoints. The views expressed or implied in this publication are not necessarily official positions of the Association.

Typeset by Scott Photographics

Printed by Edwards Brothers, Inc.

ASCD Stock Number: 611-88166

Library of Congress Cataloging-in-Publication Data
Curwin, Richard L., 1944-
 Discipline with dignity/Richard L. Curwin and Allen N. Mendler.
  p. cm.
 Rev. ed. of: Taking charge in the classroom/Allen N. Mendler,
Richard L. Curwin.
 Curwin's name appears first on the earlier edition.
 Bibliography: p.
 ISBN 0-87120-154-2
 1. School discipline. 2. Classroom management. I. Mendler,
Allen N. II. Mendler, Allen N. Taking charge in the classroom.
III. Title.
 LB3011.C887 1988   88-39922
 371.1′024—dc19
Price: $9.95

Discipline with Dignity

Acknowledgments

When the Association for Supervision and Curriculum Development asked us to revise our book *Taking Charge in the Classroom*,[1] we were both professionally and personally delighted. The personal joy came from the opportunity to work together once again as friends and colleagues on a project that is just as relevant today as it was when we first began our work in discipline 10 years ago. Professionally, it provided us an opportunity to apply what we had learned since we wrote *Taking Charge* in 1983. This new version, *Discipline with Dignity*, is significantly different. Some of our earlier thoughts no longer seem as valid, and many new ideas, principles, concepts, and strategies have been added.

Significantly, we see the need for "disciplining with dignity" as even greater now. School staff members seem to feel the need to get tougher, to send the message that misbehavior will no longer be tolerated. The fabric of society is changing rapidly. This change significantly affects children, and the schools are having trouble keeping up. Changes in the family, in early child education, in the demands that society has placed on the schools, and the information

---

[1] Allen Mendler and Richard Curwin, (1983), *Taking Charge in the Classroom* (Reston, Va.: Reston Publishing Co.).

explosion have all made a powerful impact on the way students perceive school and their role as learners.

Now, more than ever, we must take a good look at what we are teaching our children by the way we treat them. Controlling their behavior is simply not enough. We must help them become decision makers and critical thinkers. We must help them feel that they can contribute to society, and we must enhance their joy for learning. *Discipline with Dignity* was written to achieve these goals.

We wish to thank the following individuals for their assistance, support, insights, and encouragement: Ron Brandt, Raymond Wlodkowski, Millie Ness, Marian Leibowitz, Alan Fibish, Bernard Palmer, Betty Osta, Pat Bourcy, Jake Clockedile, the teachers and administrators at Tam High School in Mill Valley, California, Jefferson High School and Westmoor High School in Daly City, California, Oceana High School and Terra Nova High School in Pacifica, California, Nancy Modrak, René Townsley, and the ASCD staff, and the many participants in ASCD conferences and NCSIs who have asked many difficult questions and added many suggestions, refinements, and on-site validation.

RICHARD CURWIN
ALLEN MENDLER

Foreword

School staffs searching for ways to enhance their discipline practices will find this book filled with practical, tested, and worthwhile school and classroom techniques. Working together, parents, administrators, and teachers of all grade levels and subject areas can develop a common agreement on ways to handle behavior problems in a manner that helps students consider their own actions, examine rational consequences, and decide for themselves which results they will choose.

The guidelines Curwin and Mendler offer can help teachers develop a repertoire of practical consequences to use when students forget or don't know how to perform the behaviors agreed upon in their social contracts. They suggest a range of strategies for creating additional consequences and encourage treating students in fair and individualized ways.

Curwin and Mendler respect students' individuality and make an eloquent distinction between consequences and punishment. Thus, the processes and strategies presented are intended to enhance student self-esteem, to invest social problem solving and self-regulation as serious components of curriculum and instruction, and to cast teachers as professional educators—mediators of learning— rather than policemen.

Discipline With Dignity implies not only dignity for the student but for the teacher as well. Not only do both parties enter and leave a problem situation with their dignity enhanced, but the process they engage in dignifies the problem itself. Thus, learning how to behave in responsible ways is accomplished not only in the context of classroom life, but is applied to social problem solving in other life situations as well.

We are increasingly aware of the demands of living in a future society in which compassion and cooperation, problem solving and creativity, and communications and internal responsibility will be paramount. Curwin and Mendler have given yet another means of aligning our discipline policies and procedures with those larger, long-range educational outcomes.

I strongly urge educators to consider the theoretical and practical suggestions presented here; to test their validity in each community, school, and classroom setting; to gather evidence of their effects over time; and to generate additional discipline strategies consistent with this philosophy.

ARTHUR L. COSTA
ASCD President,
1988-89

1
Discipline

n 1907, William Chandler Bagley of the University of Illinois wrote, "Absolute fearlessness is the first essential for the teacher on whom rests the responsibility for governing an elementary or secondary school. This fearlessness is not alone or chiefly the expression of physical courage, although this must not be lacking. It is rather an expression of moral courage; daring the sometimes certain interference of parents, officious trustees [administrators] and others of like character; standing firm in one's convictions even though the community may not approve. And, after all, it is this sort of courage that is the rarest and, at the same time, the most essential."[1]

In 1988, Heather D. Osborn, a high school senior from Houston, Texas, wrote the following poem about her experiences in school.

Silent Defiance
I'm the one who watched,
As you laughed;
I'm the one who listened patiently,
While you talked unceasingly;
I'm the one who sat silent,
As your shouts grew louder,

I'm the one who always came,
While your chair sat empty;
I'm the one whose dreams were hidden,
as yours were fulfilled;
I'm the one who cared,
while you butchered knowledge;
I'm the one who watched your petty wars
over something you couldn't understand;
I'm the one who reasoned,
as you discussed,
I'm the one who will remember
when all of you will forget.

Dedicated to Laura—who understood.

For at least the eight decades between the writings of Dr. Bagley and Heather, teachers and students have needed courage to face each other. School is a battleground for too many participants, a place where major confrontations and minor skirmishes occur daily. Why must this be so? Teachers and students share the same space, time, goals, and needs. They spend most of the day communicating with each other, thinking about each other, scheming against each other, and judging each other. When they are antagonistic, they expend as much if not more time and energy trying to outsmart each other and win, or at least achieve a standoff. If things get bad enough, they have the power to ruin each others' lives. When things go well, they share tender moments, meaningful triumphs, and genuine respect and love. Regardless of how it goes, teachers and students never forget each other.

We contend that it is essential to replace competitive metaphors in schools with new images of cooperation, mutual respect, and commitment to common goals for the good of everyone in the classroom. Courage must always be a part of the learning process, but we prefer courage to be used to explore new worlds or to make meaningful changes in perceptions and behaviors.

For most teachers and students, a main battlefield revolves around discipline. Much has been written about discipline over the years, and many programs and methods have been tried and retried with new names. The issue will always be an integral part of school because students will always learn more than the content of the curriculum. They will learn about their behavior, their choices, and their impact on others. Instead of trying to solve the discipline problem, it might be wiser to try to positively affect the lives of children. We strongly advocate a model of discipline based on a positive value system and suggest many practical methods to implement such a system in the classroom. One of our goals is for all the suggestions in this book to be consistent with what we believe to be best for children.

In this book you will learn strategies for developing a philosophy about behavior management based on sound educational, psychological, and commonsense principles:

- Developing a comprehensive classroom discipline plan.
- Stopping misbehavior when it occurs without attacking the dignity of the student.
- Resolving problems with students who chronically disrupt the learning process.
- Reducing student stress as well as your own.
- Using special guidelines for rules and consequences that work.

Few would argue that maintaining good discipline is a necessary precondition to establishing a school or classroom climate that is conducive to learning. James Coleman, the controversial University of Chicago sociologist, recently studied the effects of private versus public school education. After surveying 58,728 sophomores and seniors in 1,016 high schools, he concluded that private schools do a better job of educating than public schools.[2] Coleman pointed to the ability of private schools to maintain better discipline and provide more challenging academic demands. He found that public school sophomores appear twice as likely to disobey, fight, or commit acts of vandalism than their private school counterparts.

While one may question Coleman's ability in light of his 1966 study, which found that schools make little difference in educating students, it is unlikely that contemporary educators will argue against the notion that discipline problems in schools throughout America are on the rise in scope and intensity.

The many problems in schools today can generally be categorized with out-of-school or in-school causes. In discussing today's student, Dillon notes:

> Teachers today are working with a different kind of student. . . . Parents more and more frequently admit that they cannot control their children. Many even abandon them. Many students act as free agents. They do not live at home

and are responsible to no one. They have few personal restraints. . . . The number of students placed on permanent suspension from school for misbehavior or maladjustment is increasing. The age of those being suspended is decreasing. Growing numbers of elementary students are out of school because they are disruptive to the teaching-learning process. The growing clarity of student rights and due process has taken away traditional discipline strategies in which many teachers found security; and many teachers are without skills to replace them.[3]

In schools that "care," it is common for a disruptive student to be referred to guidance, mental health, and administrative resources for an evaluation. Following the evaluation, a conference is called to inform the teacher about the student's background, home situation, test results, and other descriptive information. The teacher already knows most of this information, but using it to take concrete and specific action is rare. The teacher, while filled with empathy, often feels incapable of responding differently because he views these recommendations as not feasible for a regular class setting. But he does not want to appear rigid and uncaring, so he simply nods his head in agreement with the recommendations and proceeds to do the best he can.

Psychologists or social workers, well-trained in counseling, are often unavailable for needed intervention because of their limited time and excessive caseloads in most schools. Instead they meet with the child's parents, suggest the need for individual or family counseling at the local child guidance clinic, and write their reports; perhaps 9 times out of 10, no further action ensues. The administrator, wanting to support the teacher, makes himself available for crises, which occur with frequency, and often elicits a series of temporary promises from the student to try harder and behave better. The overall effects of this process: a lot of understanding and very little change!

Much of this book addresses what can be done about discipline problems, but it is first necessary to consider those factors responsible for the alienation experienced by too many youths in schools. The causes of discipline problems are discussed *briefly* because it is our belief that schools waste far too much time and energy trying to understand why students misbehave when they should be trying to change their pattern of misbehavior.

Schools do not exist as isolated institutions untouched by the social events surrounding them. Schools are both a mirror image of what transpires in their communities and a force that attempts to convey and shape the values, beliefs, and attitudes of students. Being both a mirror image and a dynamic force makes it essential that we understand how factors that occur both within and outside the boundaries of schools interact to create discipline problems. Once the context is understood, teachers can learn how to act upon those factors that are within their control and how to live with those that are not.

Out-of-School Causes of Discipline Problems

Violence in Society

Without belaboring the social ills of our world, the fact is that we live in a society where resolving problems through shootings, knifings, fist fights, extortion, and threats of injury is commonplace. Every day we pick up the newspaper and learn of another violent death. People's inhumanity to one another is not news. Children are constantly exposed to violence and have become insensitive to it. Shortly after the assassination attempt on President Reagan, we interviewed school-age children to learn of their reaction. We were astounded by the near absence of emotion to the event. That *absence* of shock is a sad commentary on how easily we seem to accept violence as a natural way of life.

Effects of the Media

Television has often been blamed, with justification, for the increase in violence among children. We recently noted at least 50 acts of violence during a half-hour broadcast of a well-known, daily cartoon show. Try observing children's television and notice how the most popular shows glamorize and glorify anti-authority protagonists as they behave irresponsibly.

A recent study that reviewed a decade of research concerning television and youth concluded that children will have viewed approximately 18,000 acts of television violence by the time they enter adolescence.[4] Although it is impossible to know the full extent of the influence of standard programming, we believe that television and other media have a potentially damaging effect on children. And kids with special needs seem particularly at risk. Sprafkin, Kelly, and Gadow (1987) found that emotionally and learning-disabled children are less able to distinguish between fantasy and reality on television programs and commercials.[5]

In *Media Sexploitation* (1976) and *Subliminal Seduction* (1973), Wilson Bryant Key points out how violent and sexual messages are implicitly and explicitly built into television and print advertisements. His studies show that people become agitated when confronted with these messages, which are really selling sex, death, and violence.

"Me" Generation

The absence of emotional nourishment for many of our children, in a nation still reeling from the values permeated by what Christopher Lasch calls the "me generation," is another external cause of school discipline problems. We have become a throw-away society that discards husbands, wives, children, and things. Rightly or wrongly, many people seek refuge from unhappiness and depression in ways that leave little time and commitment for their children.

Recent statistics have suggested that between 35 and 50 percent of all school-age children will experience significant shifts in their family constellation before they complete school.[6] Twelve of 100 children in 1986 were born to unmarried parents, 40 were born to parents who will divorce before the child is 18, 5 have parents who will separate, and 2 have parents who will die. In all, only 41 percent will reach their 18th birthday in "traditional" family units.

It is no secret, therefore, that many students come to school more concerned for their basic security needs than for learning their times tables. The loss of reliance upon parents for basic security has created a large group of children who are desperate for help in healthy emotional development. Many students have adopted the me-generation attitude of, "Meet my needs first. I do not intend to wait. I come first."

Lack of a Secure Family Environment

Perhaps the largest single influence on children is the quality of their home life. Throughout the last century, our society has undergone major shifts in values and traditions. The extended family has been replaced by smaller nuclear units in a multitude of configurations. Single-parent families, two working-parent families, and one- and two-child families are all common. The divorce rate has steadily risen so that some states have more divorces than marriages. All those changes, while neither good nor bad in themselves, have made it increasingly difficult to raise children in the traditional ways. And because we have not been as successful in developing family systems that match these shifting life styles, many parents have no new options for providing a secure family structure.

Much research shows that how parents respond to their child's misbehavior has major consequences for the child's future development. For example, Holmes and Robbins (1987) found that unfair, inconsistent, and harsh discipline by parents predicted later alcohol and depressive disorders.[7] Self-concepts are first developed and most strongly influenced in the home, and parents need to learn more skills for helping children develop amid constantly shifting family patterns.

Difficult Temperament

Some recent studies (Maziade et al. 1986) have found children's temperaments to be more "plastic" than formerly believed. Particularly at the extreme ends of the continuum, children who are very easy or very difficult to deal with are likely to remain that way for years. Clearly, some children are difficult to manage despite adequate parenting and relative absence of all the psychosocial factors already mentioned. But parents can influence such children to change in "desirable" ways when a firm, consistent, and loving approach to discipline is offered.

In-School Causes of Discipline Problems

Student Boredom

Teachers have spent many years accumulating a body of knowledge that they value, and they are excited with their work when they feel their students are enthusiastic about what is being offered. Nobody wants to have students in class who appear uninterested, do not participate, and do not do their assignments.

Some students do not present themselves as discipline problems because they have developed good classroom etiquette. They sit up straight, appear attentive by making eye contact, nod their heads every so often, and present themselves as interested and somewhat involved, even when they are downright bored. But there are some students who don't have (or won't develop) these survival skills. Instead they act out to satisfy their needs. They have no desire to hide their boredom, and they appear unconcerned with the consequences of poor grades, a trip to the principal's office, or a phone call home. Most teachers feel fed up and angry with such students, and they view them as a waste of their time. Such students derive pleasure from making the teacher angry, and their teachers derive a measure of satisfaction in catching them being "bad." When this interaction continues, conflict ensues. The teacher will often resort, consciously or not, to labeling the student negatively, and the student will then accuse the teacher of picking on him unjustly. A discipline problem has occurred, and both are responsible!

Powerlessness

Powerlessness is another factor in school and classroom discipline problems. Some students rebel as a way of voicing their dissatisfaction with their lack of power. In most schools, students are told for six hours every day where to go, what time to be there, how long to take for basic biological necessities, which learning is relevant, what to learn, and how their learning will be evaluated. These decisions are often made by the local school board or by the school administration in consultation with members of the school community. Student participation in decision making is often excluded. The result is that one group develops rules and procedures that define behavioral standards for another group that has had little or no input. More than one revolution has been precipitated by a similar division of power. Schools that exclude students from school or classroom policy-making committees run a major risk of widespread dissatisfaction with rules that are perceived as arbitrary and unfair. Students show their dissatisfaction by acting out when they perceive themselves as having no say in how the classroom is run. "Powerless" students have more power than many school personnel give them credit for, and many students are more than willing to show just how much power they really have.

Unclear Limits

At the very least, teachers and administrators must clearly and specifically inform students of the standards of acceptable behavior *before they are violated* and what will happen when these standards are violated. At best, students are often presented with unclear rules and less clear consequences. In most schools, students are unwittingly encouraged to break rules because they are not informed of them in advance. When limits are unclear, students will test the system to find out what they are. The following case illustrates the necessity for clear rules and consequences.

A junior high school we recently worked with was having a problem with student fighting. We discovered that a no-fighting rule existed in the student handbook, but no mention was made of consequences. An interview with the principal revealed that the actual, unwritten consequences ranged from teachers not even referring the student, to a talk with the student, to a one-day suspension. Because fighting had become a serious problem, we suggested an immediate, short-term solution to the problem—a solution that reveals one of our biases. We met with faculty members, and they agreed that any student who fought on school grounds would be suspended from one to five days, depending on the severity of the infraction. The student would not be allowed to return to school until he had developed a written plan for how he would behave if the circumstance happened again. In addition, a parent conference was mandatory before the student could return to school.

The principal was initially uncomfortable with the recommendation because he believed that suspension was an ineffective response to student misbehavior. He believed it would not help to give the offender a sanctioned vacation. We believed that if all teachers agreed on the procedure, it was worth trying. Furthermore, we felt that all students (and teachers) have a right to attend school without concern for their own safety. If people are fearful, their ability to learn (and to teach) is adversely affected. If a student chooses to fight, then he is violating the safety rights of others and is choosing to be temporarily excluded from school.

Feeling desperate, the principal reluctantly agreed to try the plan. He next met with every faculty team, and they presented the plan to the students. In short, the principal specified the rule, solicited support from his staff members, and told students *in advance* what would happen if fighting occurred. Fighting increased during the first few days after the plan was implemented. But after one week, the incidence of fighting dropped to near zero. Students needed to test the rule, and when they found out that the rule would be strictly enforced, they stopped.

Lack of Acceptable Outlets for Feelings

Another source of discipline problems is the lack of acceptable outlets for expressing feelings. Don't run. Don't fight. Don't throw food. Most teachers have rules so students know what not to do, but we rarely teach students what to do instead. We assume that they know how to behave properly and forget that it requires skill and training to learn what to do instead of fighting. Students need emotional, behavioral, and intellectual skills for following rules. Books have been written that purport to teach people how to "fight fair." Other books have been written to help people learn how to identify their feelings and how to communicate them to others assertively. We have found in our extensive training that schools that provide substitute outlets for the feelings that motivate misbehavior have less misbehavior. (This theme will be discussed further in Chapter 5.)

Attacks on Dignity

Finally, and most significantly, most students with chronic behavior problems believe that they cannot and will not be successful in school. Such students often appear to give up before they have even tried. They do not believe they can receive the attention and recognition they need through school achievement. They see themselves as losers and have ceased trying to gain acceptance in the mainstream. Their self-message is, "Since I can't be recognized as anything other than a failure, I'll protect myself from feeling hurt. To do nothing is better than to try and fail. And to be recognized as a troublemaker is better than being seen as stupid."

Related to the issue of self-concept is maintaining student dignity. When a student's dignity is attacked, he will protect himself in whatever way he can, even at the cost of his relationship with the teacher and possibly his education. We will discuss the issue of dignity in greater depth in other chapters.

Schools Do Make a Difference

While there is little question that family instability, violence in society, low-quality television, confused values, lack of positive self-concepts, powerlessness, boredom, and unclear limits are significant contributing factors to discipline problems in the school, the fact is that schools vary widely in their ability to maintain and promote effective systems of discipline.

Rutter and associates conducted a longitudinal study of secondary schools in Great Britain and concluded that the school does make a difference in student behavior and achievement even when factors such as socioeconomic status, location of the school, and family background are controlled. (He studied mixed comprehensive schools, the English equivalent of American public schools.[8])

Many of the findings of that study have important implications for teachers and administrators in regard to discipline because the focus of the research was to identify specific factors that promote a positive or negative climate within the school. An exhaustive review of the study is beyond the scope of this book (see *Fifteen Thousand Hours* by Rutter et al.), but some of the findings that appear to relate directly to effective or ineffective discipline are:

1. High levels of corporal punishment and frequent disciplinary interventions led to worse student behavior.

2. Praise for work in the classroom and frequent public praise for good work or behavior at general assemblies or other meetings was associated with better behavior. (The use of praise will be discussed in more depth throughout this book.)

3. Schools and classrooms that were well decorated with plants, posters, and pictures were associated with better student behavior.

4. The willingness to see children about problems at any time was associated with better student behavior.

5. Better behavior was noted in schools where a high proportion of students had opportunities to hold some position of responsibility.

6. An interesting and perhaps unexpected finding was that schools with highest staff turnover often had the best behavior among students.

7. Schools with good outcomes had most decisions made at a senior level (administration) when staff members felt that their views were clearly represented in the decisions.

8. An agreed upon set of standards, consistently maintained, appeared more important in maintaining effective discipline than specific rules or a certain type of teaching approach.

9. Frequent homework and a check on staff members regarding administering homework was associated with better student achievement and behavior.

10. Very little class time (2 to 13 percent) spent in setting up equipment and materials was associated with better student behavior.

11. Starting the class on time, pacing throughout the lesson, and not ending early was associated with better student behavior.

12. A high proportion of topic time per lesson (65-85 percent) spent in interaction with the whole class rather than with individuals (when using a formal class-based teaching approach) was positively related to good student behavior.

Rutter's findings are cause for optimism in contrast to prior research by Coleman, Jenks, and Plowden. Rutter clearly suggests that despite all of the causes of discipline problems, schools can and do make a difference in affecting student behavior and achievement.

Test Yourself

If you would like to see what you have learned after you finish reading this book, try the self-administered *Behavior Management Inventory* (Appendix A). Respond to the questions in the survey, read the remainder of this book, and then answer the questions again. Compare your second set of answers with what we believe to be appropriate responses that are explained in the *Behavior Management Survey*. The changes in your answers will show you what you have learned.

Three-Dimensional Discipline

While Rutter and his associates provide optimism, there is still difficulty in translating principles of successful schooling into tangible and realistic procedures that can be implemented in the classroom. After all, discipline problems have existed for as long as schools. Any time a group of 25 to 30 people are in close proximity to each other for 6 hours every day, 10 months of the year, a variety of interpersonal conflicts occur. Three-Dimensional Discipline offers many ways to help you take charge of such conflict. The three dimensions are:

- prevention—what can be done to prevent problems.
- action—what can be done when misbehavior occurs to solve the problem without making it worse.
- resolution—what can be done for the out-of-control student.

It will help you prevent problems by acknowledging that they will occur and by providing many behavioral, interpersonal, and anxiety-management skills that will reduce the impact of misbehaving students upon the teaching-learning process.

The Need for Planning

Planning is a chance to influence the future. We strongly advocate teaching students how to plan as a way to modify their behavior.

We feel just as strongly that planning is essential for managing something as complex as student behavior. A good plan for discipline includes clear rules and multiple interventions when rules are broken. An effective plan will minimize "the system effect" (see Chapter 2) and maximize personal interaction between teacher and student. Planning also encourages clear expectations for both teachers and students and increases the opportunities for student involvement in developing classroom discipline procedures. Research by Emmer, Evertson, and Anderson (1980) and Evertson and Emmer (1982) indicates that effective teachers teach classroom rules and procedures, monitor compliance with the rules, follow through with consequences quickly and consistently, establish a system of student responsibility and accountability for work, communicate information clearly, and organize instructional activities. These outcomes are synonymous with planning, which is the best methodology for ensuring these behaviors.

Foundation of the Program

If we allow ourselves to become helpless in the face of the overwhelming causes of misbehavior, it becomes impossible to teach. Three-Dimensional Discipline is designed to help the teacher work effectively with children despite these numerous problems. We have identified 12 processes* that form the foundation of an effective discipline program.

1. *Let students know what you need.* To run the classroom, you must establish clear and specific guidelines that define rules and consequences for both you and your students (Chapters 3 and 4).
2. *Provide instruction at levels that match the student's ability.* If a student is acting out, assume that this is his defense against feeling like a failure because he cannot, or believes he cannot, handle the material. You may want to conduct some brief tests to determine academic level or have the child referred to educational specialists in your building for an assessment. If you are unable or unwilling to adapt your teaching style to lower or higher academic levels based upon the student's needs, then you are offering the student a valid excuse for acting out.

   Just as expectations that are too high lead to frustra-

---

*Our thanks to Barbara Coloroso who conceptualized some of these.

tion, those that are too low lead to boredom and the feeling that success is cheap and not worthy of effort. When we make learning too easy, students find little value in it and little pride in their achievements. It is important to increase the challenge without increasing the tedium. Higher-level thinking skills that require imagination, creativity, synthesis, and analysis are of higher value than increasing the number of boring questions.

Telling students that an assignment or school task is easy does not motivate them to try. In the long run, it discourages them from making a wasted effort.

3. *Listen to what students are thinking and feeling.* There is probably no skill more important than active listening* to defuse potentially troublesome situations. Students misbehave when they feel anxious, fearful, or angry. Teachers who learn how to identify with students who have negative feelings and who can convey understanding and empathy through reflective or active listening are usually able to short-circuit the cycle that leads to disruption.

4. *Use humor.* You are not paid to be a comedian nor should you be expected to come to class prepared with an arsenal of jokes. But many frustrating situations can be lightened by learning how to poke fun at yourself and by avoiding defensiveness.

Make sure students are not the butt of your jokes. Lou, a 7th grade student, obviously intent upon hooking Mr. James into a power struggle, announced one day in class as he looked squarely at his teacher, "You smell like horseshit!" Mr. James responded by promptly lifting up each of his armpits, smelling them, and with a puzzled look saying, "That's strange. I took a shower this morning, put on dry deodorant and a fresh shirt, and came to school. I think I smell rather good!" The class laughed, and a tense moment had abated.

Moscowitz and Hayman found that students who rated their teachers as "best" mentioned the following teacher characteristics: they listened well, they were able to focus upon the current interests of students, they avoided yelling when disciplining, and they used humor.[9]

---

*See Thomas Gordon, *Teacher Effectiveness Training.*

5. *Vary your style of presentation.* Research has shown that older children have a maximum attention span of 15 minutes and younger children 10 minutes for any style of presentation. If you lecture for 15 minutes, it helps to have a discussion for the next interval. If you have a large-group discussion, switch to small groups. Continually using the same approach will create inattentiveness and restlessness, which may lead to disruption.

6. *Offer choices.* Students should always be offered a choice and must be helped to see that the consequences are a result of their choices. For example, "You can do your assignment now or during recess." "You can borrow a pencil, buy one from me, or provide collateral." "You chose to fight and so you've chosen to go home for the remainder of the day." Coloroso suggests that the teacher offer the student "good luck" with his decision, recognizing that decisions are not easy to make, but that the student is responsible for the decision after the choices are offered.

7. *Refuse to Accept Excuses.* Once there are sensible rules and consequences established in the classroom, all misbehavior is greeted with a specific consequence. If there is a fight, it makes no difference who started it. If a student is unprepared for class, it makes no difference that his homework was destroyed by the washing machine. In short, when you allow students to explain away their misbehavior, you place yourself in the uncomfortable position of being judge and jury. Students with good excuses learn that a good excuse will avoid trouble. Students with bad excuses learn that they need some practice in improving their excuse-making. Either way, accepting excuses teaches students how to be irresponsible. If you will accept legitimate excuses, they should be included as part of the rules and stated clearly before an incident occurs.

8. *Legitimize misbehavior that you cannot stop.* If you have done everything humanly possible to stop a certain behavior and it continues, think of creative ways to legitimize it. If there are daily paper airplane flights buzzing past your ear, consider spending five minutes a day having paper airplane contests. If abusive language persists, ask the student to publicly define the word to ensure understanding. If your students like to complain chronically about one thing or

another, have a gripe session or a gripe box in which students are encouraged to deposit their complaints. If your school has chronic disruptions in study hall, then offer a game-filled, nonacademic study hall in addition to one that is quiet for those who really want to study. When certain types of misbehavior are legitimized, the fun of acting out fizzles. And if the behavior continues, it will be easier on your nerves because you will no longer have to stop it.

9. *Use hugs and touching in communicating with kids* (even junior high and high school kids). A pat on the back, touch on the shoulder or handshake can go a long way toward establishing bonds with kids. One of the biggest educational fallacies is the prohibition against using touch with older students because of sexual misunderstanding. If you are intentionally attempting to seduce a student, then don't touch! If you want to use touch only to communicate anger and to force compliance, don't touch! If you know of a student who has been physically abused, then exercise caution. If you want to communicate with human warmth, caring, and concern, words will take you only so far. Supplement your words with nonverbal displays of caring and concern.

10. *Be responsible for yourself and allow kids to take responsibility for themselves.* You are responsible to come to class on time, present your subject in as interesting a fashion as you can, return papers with meaningful comments in a reasonable period of time, provide help for students having difficulty, and end class on time. You are *not* responsible to come prepared for the student, to judge the excuses a student gives, or to do his work for him.

11. *Realize and accept that you will not reach every kid.* Some students, after all is said and done, must be allowed to choose failure because they are consistently telling you that they need more than you can give.

12. *Start fresh every day.* What happened yesterday is finished. Today is a new day. Act accordingly.

For the Administrator

The Safe School Study (1978) clearly indicated that the schools with the fewest discipline problems had the strongest administrators, especially the principal. We suggest that the first step you, the administrator, can take to improve discipline in your school is to set up an atmosphere that encourages faculty members to discuss their problems freely and openly without fear of censure. Teachers often fear that they will be considered weak or incompetent if they admit to problems with student behavior. When we do inservice training, we always ask the teachers who have discipline problems to raise their hands. Usually only one or two hands go up. But when we ask, "How many of you know another teacher in the school who has discipline problems?", every hand is raised. Once you have an open atmosphere, positive things can begin to happen.

We find that most school faculties represent a wide range of feelings, beliefs, and attitudes when it comes to discipline. Some support a great many rules, strictly enforced, with the administration being tough in every case with student violators. Other teachers feel that it is best to have few rules and that students should solve their own problems. One of your first tasks will be to generate open discussion among your faculty members, both in formal settings, such as department and faculty meetings, and in informal settings so that all teachers know where they stand in relation to others. Acceptance of different points of view is the goal, along with clarity on what agreement also exists. Build unification from the points of agreement while allowing for individual differences. Developing this kind of open communication and shared decisionmaking will go a long way in helping faculty members feel supported and ready to make specific changes in the way they discipline students.

To help focus your discussions, you can begin with the list of in-school causes of misbehavior listed earlier. Set up working groups or task forces on each of the following causes: student boredom, powerlessness, unclear limits, lack of acceptable outlets for expressing feelings, and negative self-concept. Each group should include teachers, administrators, parents, and students. Each group can develop a specific plan for your school to minimize their chosen specific cause of misbehavior.

A group in a suburban middle school tackled the issue of giving students a greater sense of power in their school. Their recommendations included:

1. A student council of "poor achievers" and "in-trouble students" (different labels were used) to help set school policy and to help modify rules and consequences.
2. Students who served detention were given the job of commenting on how school climate could be improved.

3. Students took the job of running the school for a day once a year with the teachers and administrators taking student roles.
4. Each class was required to have at least two student rules for the teacher.

Whether you like these suggestions or not, they are a clear example of how one school gave its students a feeling of more power in the school.

Task forces such as the ones suggested above will be more beneficial if they have full administrative support (this does not mean you must agree with every recommendation), especially if their goal is to develop a plan for action. Committees that study school problems and make general recommendations are usually ineffective, and faculty members think they have little worth. The plan should state what will be done, who will do it, when it will be done, and how it will be evaluated. Each member of the school community (teachers, parents, administrators, students, librarians, nurses, bus drivers) should know clearly and specifically what their responsibilities will be for the success of the plan. Strive for at least 75 percent agreement by the community on any aspect of the plan before it is implemented.

Our findings, supported by much research on effective schools, point directly to the principal as most important in establishing a climate that supports positive discipline. Your visibility, willingness to confront and tackle difficult problems, leadership as an active professional who engineers shared decisionmaking with teachers/students and who treats all with dignity makes your school a place that people want to be. You can give direct assistance to staff members by nonjudgmentally observing classes in which teachers are struggling and offering constructive feedback.

Notice the difference in the following statements taken from classroom observations.

One: Your class was boring and dull. You never changed your pace and it was obvious that your students were turned off.

Two: You lectured (presented information) for 20 minutes. You discussed the topics (asked questions of the students about the lecture) for six minutes. You used small-group discussion for five minutes, and seven minutes were used for noninstructional time (giving directions, answering questions unrelated to task, writing a bathroom pass).

By establishing an open communication atmosphere in your school, by creating task forces that work, and by gearing your classroom observations on discipline to those items most directly related to improved discipline, you will be on your way to using the structure and processes of Three-Dimensional Discipline to improve discipline in your school as a whole and in each classroom.

You can encourage your staff members to use the Behavior Management Inventory (Appendix A) as a way of testing their knowledge before and after they read this book or explore ideas based on its contents.

Endnotes

[1] W.C. Bagley, (1907) *Classroom Management*, (Norwood, Mass.: MacMillan Co.)

[2] "Can Public Learn From Private," (April 20, 1981), *Time*: 50.

[3] United States Department of Health, Education, and Welfare, "Violent Schools-Safe Schools. The Safe Schools Report to the Congress, 1978." (Eric Document Reproduction Service No. Ed 149 464).

[4] Reported in *Behavior Today*, (November 9, 1981), 12: 4.

[5] J. Sprafkin, E. Kelly, and K.D. Gadow, (June 1987), "Reality Perceptions of Television: A Comparison of Emotionally Disturbed, Learning Disabled and Non Handicapped Children," *Journal of Developmental and Behavioral Pediatrics* 8: 149-153.

[6] Reported by Joseph Corsica in an unpublished doctoral dissertation.

[7] S.J. Holmes and L.N. Robins, (May 1987), "The Influence of Childhood Disciplinary Experience on the Development of Alcoholism and Depression," *Journal of Child Psychology and Psychiatry and Allied Disciplines* 28: 399-415.

[8] M. Rutter, B. Maughan, P. Mortimore, J. Ousten, and A. Smith, (1979), *Fifteen Thousand Hours* (Cambridge, Mass.: Harvard University Press).

[9] E. Moscowitz and J.L. Hayman, (1974), "Interaction Patterns of First Year, Typical, and 'Best' Teachers in Inner-City Schools," *Journal of Educational Research* 67: 224-230.

2
Dignity and Responsibility in the Classroom

Managing student behavior is a complex task. There is a delicate balance between meeting the needs of the group by maintaining social order and meeting the unique needs of each student. Few choices work for all teachers and all students. Research has provided a wealth of knowledge about teaching and learning, but we still know relatively little in absolute terms.

We believe that the best decisions for managing student behavior are based on a value system that maintains the dignity of each student in all situations. Behaving responsibly is more valued than behaving obediently. We believe that behavior change is slow, occurring in small increments. Simply expecting that students will change long-standing maladaptive behavior on demand causes more problems than it solves. We believe that motivation is difficult to maintain and that plans for discipline must enhance student motivation whenever possible. We also believe that good teaching is holistic and discipline is an integral part of the entire teaching experience. Every decision affecting behavior management also affects instruction. We advocate a discipline model that is highly flexible yet highly structured, incorporating the best thinking of the last 100 years. We avoid the gimmicky, trendy, and simplistic approaches that stop misbehavior while reducing the student's desire and love of learning.

Models of Discipline

Every discipline program has in one form or another the following elements: goals, principles, rules, enforcement or intervention procedures, and an implicit or explicit evaluation process. Each process also provides students incidental, or secondary, learning about self-worth, handling responsibility, solving problems, controlling their lives, and affecting the consequences of their behavior. Figure 2.1 is a generic model of discipline that illustrates how most behavior management models function.

Rules

Rules are central to all discipline programs, but they can be highly overemphasized for both conceptual and practical reasons. Consequences and principles are more influential for achieving long-term behavior change. Rules maintain order for the present. Rules work best when they are behavioral and written in black-and-white terms. Students and teacher should easily see whether a specific behavior violates a rule. (Examples of rules: when you speak, raise your hand; bring your books and materials to class; be in your seat when the bell rings; touch other students' belongings only with their permission.) When rules are vague (i.e., be respectful, be courteous, be kind), students have difficulty making the connection between their behavior and the consequences.

Principles

Because principles cannot be enforced, they are often overlooked or ignored by packaged discipline programs. (Principles define attitudes and expectations for long-term behavioral growth. Principles are similar to vague rules: be respectful, care about others, be prepared.) If the teacher attempts to enforce principles, students

---

Figure 2.1
Generic Discipline Model

Goals: What the program will accomplish.

Principles: What general attitude and behavioral guidelines teachers model and students are encouraged to learn in class.

Rules: What is enforced every time it is broken.

Enforcement or intervention: What happens when a rule is broken.

Student (incidental) Learning: What the student learns as a result of the enforcement/intervention.

Evaluation: How well the program goals are being met.

---

often blame the teacher or focus on the part of the gray area that proves them right. However, an understanding of and exposure to sound principles is a crucial foundation for good rules. When rules are not developed naturally from principles, students may learn a specific action without seeing or understanding its value. For example, students may learn to be in their seat when the bell rings without knowing or understanding this to be part of a larger theme: responsible work habits. Effective discipline programs provide clear and specific rules along with guidelines for enforcement without sacrificing the higher levels of learning that principles provide.

Consequences

Practically speaking, rules are far less important than consequences for a program to be successful, and this is why programs based on punishment and teacher power can be dangerous. They are marketed as simple to learn, easy to implement, and quick with results, but their greatest attraction is their greatest weakness. To achieve their lofty claims, punitive programs must resort to power-based methods. They rely on an obedience model of discipline (Figure 2.2) because "telling students what to do" requires the least amount of work or change for the teacher. Obedience models have as their goals (1) minimal or no rule violations and (2) for students to follow orders.

Punishment is the main intervention/enforcement procedure. The results, if "successful," are fewer rule violations and less student learning about responsibility.

Figure 2.2
The Obedience Model

Main Goal: Students follow orders.

Principle: Do what I (the teacher or administrator) want.

Intervention: Punishment is the primary intervention.
  1. *external* locus of control
  2. done *to* student

Examples:
  1. threats
  2. scoldings
  3. writing "I will not _____ 500 times."
  4. detentions
  5. writing student's name on chalkboard

Student learns . . .
  1. Don't get caught.
  2. It's not my responsibility.

Incidental or Secondary Learning

Most educators agree that secondary learnings are powerful and must be carefully considered and evaluated to understand the true impact of a discipline program. For example, claims such as "program X yields an 80 percent reduction in referrals for discipline" often are misleading. If teachers do not refer students because they have gotten the message that discipline referrals mean poor teaching, then the program's success might be a result of teacher fear. If a teacher uses force to control misbehavior and at the same time destroys the natural motivation of a large percentage of the class, can the results truly be called successful? If a student shapes up after the third checkmark on the chalkboard because the fourth means a phone call home to an abusive parent, did the program improve the child's self-control or did it simply transfer the inner turmoil of a child caught in a dysfunctional family? If a group reward system is effective at reducing the total number of off-task behaviors, is the quality of relationships affected, and does the shift from internal to external rewards hurt the students' chances for self-control in the long run? If Susan's classmates think she is responsible for them losing out on a coveted marble in a jar, who assesses the subsequent communication patterns between Susan and her classmates on the playground, on the bus, or in the cafeteria?

The Obedience Model

We define obedience as following rules without question, regardless of philosophical beliefs, ideas of right and wrong, instincts and experiences, or values. A student "does it" because he is told to do it. In the short term, obedience offers teachers relief, a sense of power and control, and an oasis from the constant bombardment of defiance. In the long run, however, obedience leads to student immaturity, a lack of responsibility, an inability to think clearly and critically, and a feeling of helplessness that is manifested by withdrawal, aggressiveness, or power struggles. We would never say that students should be disobedient, although research has taught us to expect the "terrible two's," "out of bounds four," "moody ten's," and rebellious teens as times when acting out and testing limits is a sign of growth and independence. We strongly believe that the training for obedience in schools is a personal and societal risk with dire potential consequences for everyone. Obedience, even when it "works," is not philosophically, psychologically, or sociologically defensible. Obedience models are far more interested in keeping students in line rather than maintaining their dignity.

Figure 2.2 shows that the obedience model uses punishment as its main type of intervention. William Chandler Bagley knew in 1907 that punishments were to be reserved for those cases when nothing else seemed to work.

> It must be remembered that not every individual needs to be subjected to a penalty in order to ensure the inhibition of his social impulses. The infliction of a penalty is always the last resort, reserved for those cases in which all other means fail. . . . The individual must, if necessary, be sacrificed to the mass; but the sacrifice must not be made unless the necessity is clear, nor in any greater degree than necessity demands.[1]

It's ironic that the current mood of education is in some ways behind the past. The 1980s might someday be remembered as the decade when admiration was reserved for principals, cast as folk heroes, walking around schools with baseball bats, and for teachers and whole schools that systematically embarrassed students by writing their names on the chalkboard. But we do have hope that the pendulum will once again swing to the rational position of treating children as people with needs and feelings that are not that different from adults. Once we begin to understand how obedience is contrary to the goals of our culture and education, the momentum will begin to shift. Our view is that the highest virtue of education is to teach students to be self-responsible and fully functional. In all but extreme cases, obedience contradicts these goals.

Another problem common to many obedience models is the limited opportunity for teacher discretion. Some programs offer only one alternative intervention for teachers when a rule is violated. Others have a lock-step approach that requires a specific intervention for violation number one, another for violation two, and so forth. Either system removes teacher judgment from the process. This cripples the teacher's ability to examine rule violations in their broader context and demeans the teacher's capacity to be a decision maker. Faced with what may be an untenable either/or choice, or no choice at all, teachers often have no alternative but to look the other way. This is the only way they can factor in special circumstances that don't fit "the program." Over time, this creates numerous inconsistencies that ultimately doom the program. With such "teacher proof" programs, faculty members develop external locuses of control. The average teacher either subverts or redesigns the system—and almost always resents using it.

The Responsibility Model

Teaching students responsibility requires more work than teaching for obedience. We believe students should help develop the discipline plan, so planning can be more cumbersome and require more time. Sometimes progress seems slow because students are in the process of learning. The results are not always immediately apparent because more is desired than an immediate end to disruptions.

In the development process, teachers have the opportunity to see how they contribute to creating discipline problems. When teachers value their students' thoughts, perceptions, and opinions, they may, for example, learn that their students are frustrated. They may learn that failing to motivate students, offering little or no hope for behavioral or academic success, forcing students to back down in front of their peers, providing students with minimal or no choices, or denying students acceptable opportunities to express their feelings are the main ways that teachers contribute to their own discipline problems.

Models based on teaching responsibility can therefore seem more threatening to the teacher at first glance. In the long run, however, these models are more effective because they encourage improved teaching performance as well as improved learning performance. Responsibility models foster critical thinking and promote shared decisionmaking. Kids feel affirmed even though they don't always get their way. They understand that they have some control of the events that happen to them, and they get a chance to learn that teachers also have rights, power, knowledge, and leadership.

Teachers who subscribe to the responsibility model follow the adage, "If you want true power, you must give some of it away." For many years, we gave away too much control to students. Now we must be careful not to overreact and try to take *all* of it back. Students cannot learn responsibility without choices and without an opportunity to make mistakes and learn from them.

The responsibility model (Figure 2.3) is far more consistent with the current classroom emphasis on critical thinking and decisionmaking. What must students learn when the curriculum says, "Make

---

Figure 2.3
The Responsibility Model

Main goal: To teach students to make responsible choices.

Principle: To learn from the outcomes of decisions.

Consequences:
1. *internal* locus
2. done *by* the student
3. logical or natural

Examples:
1. Developing a plan describing how you will behave without breaking the rule when you are in a similar situation.
2. Practicing appropriate behavior in a private meeting with the teacher.

Student learns . . .
1. I cause my own outcomes.
2. I have more than one alternative behavior in any situation.
3. I have the power to choose the best alternative.

---

decisions based upon critical thinking skills," while they are simultaneously told, "Do what I say or else you'll have your name written on the blackboard for all to see?" The responsibility model is also more consistent with the general makeup of most classrooms.

Principles

The following principles are the structure for our discipline plan. They define the parameters of a healthy classroom that uses discipline as a learning process rather than a system of retribution.

1. Dealing with student behavior is part of the job.

We have already pointed out that teaching is more positive when managing student behavior is perceived as part of the job. After all, no matter how much you love teaching the story of Magellan, factoring binomial equations, the causes of the war of 1812, or the pluperfect tense, the lessons students learn about behavior, communication, and getting along with others make a longer, more lasting impression.

2. Always treat students with dignity.

Educators have acknowledged this need for centuries. Some call it dignity, others call it self-concept or self-esteem. The need to protect and enhance it is by now unquestionable. Mitchell found that 80 percent of children enter 1st grade with high self-esteem. By the time they reach 5th grade, only 20 percent have high self-esteem. By the time they finish high school, the number having a positive self-esteem has dropped to a staggering 5 percent.

Students will protect their dignity at all costs, even with their lives if pushed hard enough. In the game of chicken, with two cars racing at top speed toward a cliff, the loser is the one who steps on the brake. Nothing explains this bizarre reasoning better than the need for peer approval and dignity. Concentration camp victims and prisoners of war tell of their survival in terms of maintaining their dignity. They did anything possible to hold their heads high by defying their captors. In school, students must know that their dignity will always be maintained.

3. Discipline works best when integrated with effective teaching practices.

We previously used critical thinking as an example of using content in discipline. The processes of planning, making choices, evaluating, and analyzing results are all components of a critical thinking system. These same processes can be used as consequences when a child breaks a rule. In this system, students live what they learn, giving real life experience to both behavior and the mastery of content.

4. Acting out is sometimes an act of sanity.

When children act out they provide feedback to the teacher. The teacher misses the opportunity to improve if he punishes misbehavior without examining how he might have caused it. When kids misbehave because of poor teaching, it is better for all if the teacher can use that information to improve his skills rather than to hide problems.

We do not mean to imply that poor teaching is the sole cause of discipline problems. Drug use and other social problems already discussed no doubt contribute. But when we realize the importance of the relationship between good teaching and good discipline, we can prevent many problems and excite kids about learning. Squires, Huitt, and Segars (1984) found that effective classroom teachers (those whose students consistently demonstrated high levels of achievement) possessed skills in both management ("which has to do with controlling students' behavior") and instruction ("guiding students' learning").[2]

The 80-15-5 Principle

Generally speaking, there are three groups of students in a typical classroom. (While the percentages may vary from classroom to classroom, there seems to be consistency in the group structure.)

1. 80 percent: These students rarely break rules or violate principles. They come to school motivated to learn, prepared to work, and accepting of the restrictions of a classroom setting. By and large, these students have been sufficiently successful by both formal and informal standards so that they expect success in the future. Most discipline plans are either unnecessary or intrusive to these students.

2. 15 percent: These students break rules on a somewhat regular basis. They do not blindly accept the classroom principles, and they fight the restrictions. Their motivation ranges from completely on to completely off, depending on what happened at home that morning or how they perceive the daily classroom activities. Their achievement can range from high to low, depending on the teacher, the class, or their expectations for success. These students need a clear set of expectations and consequences. If they are not given enough structure, they can disrupt learning for all the other students.

3. 5 percent: These students are chronic rule breakers and generally out of control most of the time. Nothing seems to work for them. They have typically experienced failure in school from an early age and maintain no hope for success in the future. They believe they have no reason to try to behave or to learn. Some have severe learning or emotional problems and may come from troubled homes.

The trick of a good discipline plan is to control the 15 percent without alienating or overly regulating the 80 percent and without backing the 5 percent into a corner. Plans that are heavily punitive tend to control that 15 percent and thus give the illusion that they are successful. However, the seeds are sown for the out-of-control students to explode, or for some of the 80 percent to lose interest in learning. Teachers often feel trapped between their desire for consistency and the fear of coming down too hard on the rare rule violation of the naturally motivated student. They are also aware of the need to give the out-of-control student hope and some space and to make school as positive an experience for them as possible.

Most teachers believe that instruction must be matched to the ability of the student. We would all be horrified if we were asked to teach all students the same content in the same way at the same speed. It's been said that "there is nothing as unfair as treating unequals as equals." Even our government does not advocate single solutions to all problems. Judges want the discretionary powers of their office to enforce the best possible sentence for a particular crime.

Teachers need the same ability. Any plan that imposes a system at the cost of teacher judgment is demeaning and ill spirited. It is dangerous to students and teachers alike. The plan that is presented in this book is highly structured yet provides the flexibility for teacher judgment.

Locus of Control

In the last 20 years, locus of control has become a major way of looking at behavior. Simply stated, internal locus of control means that an individual perceives that he causes his own outcomes. External locus of control means that an individual perceives that powerful forces or people cause things to happen to him and he cannot control them. Generally speaking, locus of control is specific to a situation and therefore varies within an individual based on the circumstances. The degree of responsibility we take for our actions is directly related to our locus of control. The more internal we are, the more responsible.

The following examples illustrate the difference:

1. Teacher: Johnny where's your homework?
   Johnny: I did it but I left it in my jeans and my mother washed it. Now I don't have it.

   Analysis: External locus of control. His mother did it.

2. Teacher: Johnny where is your homework?
   Johnny: My dog ate it.

   Analysis: External. The dog did it.

3. Teacher: Johnny, where is your homework?
   Johnny: You never assigned it.
   Teacher: Yes I did. Every other student in class heard me.
   Johnny: You must have assigned it when I wasn't paying attention.

   Analysis: External. The teacher did it.

4. Teacher: Johnny, where is your homework?
   Johnny: I didn't do it.

   Analysis: Internal. Johnny did it. (In this case, Johnny *didn't* do it.)

5. Teacher: How come you did so well on the test?
Karen: It was easy.

Analysis: External. The test caused the high score.

6. Teacher: How come you did so well on the test?
Karen: I studied.

Analysis: Internal. Karen did it.

The following are principles of locus of control as they relate to discipline:
1. Internal is more closely related to responsibility.
2. Internal produces more guilt when a student fails.
3. Inappropriate external orientation leads to helplessness.
4. Conditions for developing internality include:
   - predictability
   - accurate, consistent, immediate feedback
   - real choices
   - planning
5. We can learn from our mistakes when:
   - Consequences are natural or logical (we learn that something happens as a result of our behavior and that it is closely related to the behavior)
   - The severity of the consequences matches the circumstances of the behavior.
   - We accept our role in creating the outcome.
   - Guilt and blame are emphasized less than planning future behavior change.

Questions to Ask to Determine the Effectiveness of a Discipline Plan

Evaluating the effectiveness of a discipline plan is not simple. As we said earlier, merely counting the number of referrals or the frequency of misbehavior gives a one-dimensional snapshot of a three-dimensional problem. A discipline plan that reduces incidents of misbehavior can be a disaster if it reduces student motivation. When evaluating the effectiveness of any discipline plan, the following questions must be included with any numerical data relating to incidents of misbehavior.

1. What happens to the student 10 minutes after an intervention? Is he angry? Is he back to the lesson? Do you see signs of passive aggressive behavior? Is he fully participating?
2. What happens to the student the next day?
3. What happens to the student a week later?
4. What happens to student motivation? Does energy for learning increase or decrease? (Good discipline plans enhance student motivation, not erode it.)
5. What happens to the student's dignity? Is it attacked? Is it maintained? Is it enhanced?
6. How is the student's locus of control affected? Does the student become more internally focused on his own behavior? Does the student become more externally focused? (An internal orientation, when appropriate, leads to responsibility. An external orientation leads to helplessness.)
7. What happens to the teacher-student relationship? Is communication improved? Is it weakened? Did the teacher win the battle (get the student to do what he wanted) and lose the war (destroy their delicate relationship)?
8. Does the student learn about his behavior in a way that provides increased choices, or does the student learn that he has no choice at all? Choices lead to responsibility.

In Conclusion

Effective discipline does not come from the quick mastery of techniques or the implementation of a packaged method. Effective discipline comes from the heart and soul of the teacher. It comes from the belief that teaching students to take responsibility for their behavior is as much the "job" of the teacher as teaching history or math and more important than simply enforcing rules. It comes from the belief that most students do the best they can, many in what they feel is an adverse environment. It comes from the belief that all students need hope. It comes from the positive energy of the teacher. Only within the framework of the teacher's internal strength and the development of a hopeful and caring classroom environment can a discipline plan be effective.

Endnotes

[1] W.C. Bagley, (1907), *Classroom Management*, (Norwood, Mass.: MacMillan Co.), 105.

[2] D. Squires, W. Huitt, and J. Segars, (1984), *Effective Schools and Classrooms: A Research Based Perspective*, (Alexandria, Va.: Association for Supervision and Curriculum Development), 10.

3
Three-Dimensional Discipline

George Nelson is a new teacher who, like most teachers, has never had a course in discipline. The topic of classroom management was covered during two class sessions in his general secondary methods course. Now he is continually finding himself making threats to his students that he cannot or will not implement. The thought of keeping the entire class after school for two months does not appeal to him one bit. Yet he finds that he resorts to escalating threats to try to get the class to follow his rules.

Sally Aldredge states very clear rules and tells her students what will happen when rules are violated. But Miss Aldredge carries out her consequences only when she is in a bad mood and usually only with the students she dislikes. When her favorite students break the rules, she reminds them if they "do that again they will have to. . . ."

Joan Stevenson took a course in behavior modification and learned how to set up a contingency program in her class. Her principal supported the concept and even brought in a consultant who worked with five teachers to set up model programs. Unfortunately Mrs. Stevenson's plan failed. No one bothered to tell her that because her value system was opposed to the philosophy of behavior modification, the plan would not work for her. One must believe in what one does in order for any approach or technique to "work." Joan felt like a failure when she was told by the consultant that behavior modification was a "proven method" that worked if correctly applied.

Tom Wilson has few problems with most of his students, but he has two students who continually drive him crazy. He has noticed an increase in the number and intensity of headaches he has when he goes home and has taken to carrying his Excedrin bottle with him throughout the day. None of the traditional approaches has worked with these two students, and because the school will not suspend them, Tom must face them almost daily. Unfortunately for Tom, these students are rarely absent.

These teachers and thousands like them all suffer from one basic problem. They do not have an established plan or system for implementing a discipline policy that is consistent with their needs and with the needs of their students. Each of these teachers has tried to control what he cannot (misperceiving external situations for ones that can be influenced internally), and each has not taken advantage of what he can control. The result is a sinking feeling of helplessness and despair, blaming students, administrators and professors of education.

Three-Dimensional Discipline is what we offer to teachers who put themselves on the line everyday. Simply stated, Three-Dimensional Discipline is an integration of many discipline approaches developed by educators and psychologists who value maintaining student dignity and teaching responsible behavior.

Because the three-dimensional approach encompasses a variety of theories and approaches, it is not always an easy process to implement. We have found that improving discipline requires hard work that involves examining and expressing feelings, gaining awareness, and establishing a structured process. It takes an integration of many ideas and methodologies to make a meaningful difference. The three dimensions are:

1. *The Prevention Dimension.* What the teacher can do to actively prevent discipline problems and how to deal with the stress associated with classroom disruptions.
2. *The Action Dimension.* What actions the teacher can take when, in spite of all the steps taken to prevent discipline problems, they still occur. Included are ways to keep simple records and how to avoid escalating minor problems into major ones.
3. *The Resolution Dimension.* What the teacher can do to resolve problems with the chronic rule breaker and the more extreme, "out-of-control" student.[1]

The Prevention Dimension

The first goal of the three-dimensional approach (Figure 3.1) is to set up an environment in which discipline problems are prevented. We think of the prevention dimension as similar to a subject curriculum. A curriculum provides teachers and students with a well thought-out plan to guide the learnings of a particular lesson or course. The best curriculums are flexible enough to allow day-to-day changes as new needs arise and to incorporate evaluations of how well the plan is working. The prevention dimension provides structure and direction but is flexible enough to accommodate both day-to-day and long-term changes as you and your students develop new needs and new awareness. Like content curriculum, our prevention dimension includes cognitive, behavioral, and affective components, blended so that awareness leads to understanding, which leads to action, which leads to awareness. The seven stages of prevention are discussed below.

1. Increasing Self-Awareness

The first stage of the prevention dimension is increasing awareness of self (teacher). We have discovered that teachers who are the

---

Figure 3.1
Three-Dimensional Discipline Overview

Prevention dimension

What Can Be Done to Prevent Discipline Problems:

1. Be aware of self (teacher)
2. Be aware of students
3. Express genuine feelings
4. Become knowledgeable of alternative theories
5. Motivate students to learn.
6. Establish social contracts
7. Implement social contracts
8. Reduce stress

Action dimension

What to Do When Discipline Problems Occur:

1. Choose best alternative consequence
2. Implement consequence
3. Collect data
4. Avoid power struggles

Resolution dimension

Resetting Contracts Negotiation with Individual Student

1. Find what is needed to prevent another problem
2. Develop mutually agreeable plan
3. Implement plan
4. Monitor plan/revise if necessary
5. Use creative approaches when necessary.

---

most effective at classroom management also have a high degree of congruence between their real and ideal teaching selves. They do what they say, and their words match their actions.

> The ideal self is comprised of values, feelings, attitudes, past experiences, influence from significant others, and self-perceptions. This ideal is not a fantasy, like childhood dreams of superhuman feats, but rather has its basis in real people as they really are. Given who people are, with all their assets and limitations, it's what they can be at their best. It is potentially within them, and is obtainable. Before they can obtain it, though, each individual must personally discover and identify his/her own unique ideal self. Each individual also has a real self, which is comprised of his/her feelings, attitudes, and behaviors right now. The real self is not static; it changes from moment to moment; and is always available for inspection by both the individual and others.[2]

There is little difference in effective classroom management between teachers who are democratic, authoritarian, or moderate. What does make a difference is knowing who you are, allowing yourself to be what you are, and permitting your students to see you as you are. Many classroom discipline problems occur because of double messages that the teacher gives the students. For example, Mrs. Jones, a 4th grade teacher, wants to be liked by her students. She has trouble understanding why her kids are so rowdy and rarely listen to her. Unfortunately, she is unaware of her soft tone of voice and non-assertive body posture when she tells students to line up or to open their books. She is afraid they will think she is mean if she raises her voice. Mrs. Jones, without being aware of it, is constantly sending double messages. Her verbal message states anger while her nonverbal message always expresses her wish for the students to like her. When incongruence exists, most students respond to the nonverbal message.

Mixed signals often lead to agitation and anxiety in students, particularly those who are already sensitive to mixed messages. Mixed signals often culminate in conflict, confusion, and classroom management problems. Mrs. Jones would be better off by becoming more aware of what she wants to be as a classroom manager.

Becoming aware of ourselves is no easy process because it requires a commitment to ongoing self-reflection. Most of us simply do not take the time from our busy schedules to indulge in such self-reflection. Yet this process need not be exhausting or particularly time-consuming. We invite you to try the experiment in Figure 3.2 to see what we mean by teacher self-awareness. It should take you approximately 5 or 10 minutes to complete.

2. Increasing Awareness of Students

The second stage of the prevention dimension is developing an increased awareness of your students. The three-dimensional approach is interactive and takes into account your students as real people in a classroom, which is a microcosm of society. Their needs and desires play a major role in developing a preventive environment. The more aware you are of your students, the more effective you will be in working with them.

Figure 3.2
R—M—L Scale (Self-Awareness)

Read the following statements and decide which you do the right amount of, which you want to do more of, and which you want to do less of. Circle the appropriate letter.

Right Amount	More Of	Less Of	
R	M	L	I encourage students to speak spontaneously, without necessarily raising their hands.
R	M	L	I expect my students to ask permission to leave the room.
R	M	L	I often threaten punishment of one kind or another for misbehavior.
R	M	L	I encourage students to work independently in self-directed activities.

Right Amount	More Of	Less Of	
R	M	L	I allow my students to make decisions about classroom management.
R	M	L	I allow my students to openly disagree with me.
R	M	L	I ignore student misbehavior.
R	M	L	I laugh a lot in class.
R	M	L	I probably let students take advantage of me.
R	M	L	I frequently touch students.
R	M	L	I sometimes use sarcasm to win a point with a student.
R	M	L	I take time to tell my students what they do that I like, and to ask them to tell me what they like about others and myself.

Now take one statement you want to do more of and list three specific steps you can take to do more of it.

I want to touch more frequently.

- I will touch Susie on her shoulder when she sits in her seat for 10 minutes.
- I will hold Johnny when he starts to fight.
- I will greet my students with a handshake at least two mornings a week.

Kathy Myers was a first-year 12th grade Spanish teacher who loved foreign languages. Before teaching her first class, she prepared all her lesson plans for her first quarter, based on her favorite college classes in Spanish. She found that all her lesson plans were useless because few of her students liked Spanish enough to commit themselves to the rigorous study Kathy thought of as fun. Soon her students were acting out to show their dissatisfaction with the class.

Bruce Johnson taught for five years in a junior high school. He spent most of his time working with the three most disruptive students in his class. After teaching for three months, he noticed an improvement in the three students, but he also noticed some of his better students acting out. When he asked why, they told him that the only way to get attention was to be bad. When Bruce denied this accusation, one student asked Bruce what his (the student's) favorite school activity was. Bruce showed surprise when he couldn't think of it, and his accuser correctly said, "But you know Bill's, Fred's, and Tom's."

There are many activities that you can use to become more aware of your students that take little time and promote a positive classroom climate. Canfield and Wells, Glasser, and Palomares[3] offer many strategies that serve both functions. We advise you to familiarize yourself with all of your students through a cursory glance at their school records. When you discover students who have had an unhappy or unsuccessful prior school experience, it becomes necessary for you to find out more about that student's interests or hobbies so that you become able to connect with him in a way that promotes positive feelings. If, for example, you know that Jimmy has been unsuccessful and disruptive in the last several math classes and you teach math, and if you discover that he enjoys baseball, you might greet him with a discussion of yesterday's baseball scores. Figure 3.3 is designed to illustrate the importance of knowing who your students are.

3. Expressing Feelings

The third stage of the prevention dimension is the expression of genuine feelings. Although this process is one of the most important steps in preventing discipline problems, it is traditionally ignored in most, if not all, teacher preparation programs, both inservice and preservice. In this stage you will learn how to genuinely express your feelings and how to use these expressions to manage your classroom more effectively.

Figure 3.3
Student Awareness Inventory

Write the name of one of your favorite students on the top of column one and the name of one of your least favorite students on the top of column two. Answer the related questions about each student as best you can.

Most Favorite Student	*Least Favorite Student*

favorite in-school activity:

favorite out-of-school activity:

favorite hobby

favorite television show

best friend (name)

one thing this student likes about your class:

one thing this student dislikes about class:

one short-range goal

one long-range goal

one skill he is most proud of:

Questions

Which student did you know more about?
Which student do you spend more time with?
What would happen if you spent more time talking with the student whom you knew least about?
What specific steps can you take to know all your students regardless of whether they are your favorites or least favorites?

1. I will _____

_____

2. I will _____

_____

3. I will _____

_____

Do the same process for one statement you want to do less of.

1. I will _____

_____

2. I will _____

_____

3. I will _____

_____

Keep a record of how often you do your list of six "wills" for one week. See if you have changed enough to satisfy yourself. Write what changes occurred as a result of your experiences:

Change you expected:
Positive   Negative
Change unexpected:
Positive   Negative

We find that most teachers have trouble expressing feelings. Our Western culture, with its emphasis on task, outcomes, and problem solving often regards genuine expression of feelings as immature, useless, silly, or a waste of time. We are reminded of Jack Washington, a senior high teacher who always appeared uptight. When asked to speak to an empty chair to express his feelings about his most troublesome class, he laughed saying "that 'shrink' stuff won't work with me." After some moderate encouragement, including telling him that this practice was used to help major league ballplayers improve their performance, Jack tried the technique. Soon he was crying, sharing a long-standing feeling of inadequacy. After three sessions like this, Jack learned some alternative methods of expressing his feelings. Eventually he was better able to deal with his feelings of helplessness that were in direct conflict with his macho self-image. A month later he reported that he enjoyed teaching more than at any other time in his life.

Expression of feelings, especially negative feelings, is very difficult for most of us because of all the injunctions we have learned against such expressions early in our lives. And while most teacher education programs pay considerable attention to curriculum, methods, and other cognitive "how to's," it is rare that any attention is given to the feelings of the teacher. Many in our school society have become numb to their own feelings and go mechanically about their day as if feelings were not a part of teaching. It can become frightening when disruptive students refuse to follow our rules and guidelines, and these difficult students often put us in touch with feelings that we have learned through the years to value as "bad." As part of an effective program of classroom or individual student management, it is important that the teacher take care of himself by both recognizing and learning to express feelings.

To help you see the connection between expressing feelings and successful classroom teaching, try keeping a simple journal for one week. The following sample questions and answers can serve as a model for this experiment. Take two or three minutes each morning before your first class, just before lunch, and immediately after your last class to answer the questions.

Monday:

Morning: Right now I feel (fill in any four words).

1) _____ 2) _____ 3) _____ 4) _____

Circle the strongest feeling.
Write one sentence about the strongest feeling.
    Noon: (Repeat format)
    End of day: (Repeat format)

Tuesday:
                 (Repeat format)

Friday:

Once you have completed your format for one week, answer the following questions.
1. How many words would you classify as positive? How many as negative?
2. How many of your circled words would you classify as positive? How many as negative?
3. Were your feelings more positive in the morning, afternoon, or at the end of the day?
4. Do you see any patterns in your feelings?
5. What methods do you use to express, acknowledge, or deal with your positive feelings about your teaching? Be specific.
6. What methods do you use to express, acknowledge, or deal with your negative feelings about your teaching? Be specific.

7. Are you satisfied with your pattern of feelings?

8. If not, what can you do to change it to one you prefer?

4. Discovering and Recognizing Alternatives

The fourth stage of the prevention dimension is discovering many different alternatives or models of behavior, theories of discipline, and some of the research into psychology and education as they apply to discipline. This knowledge alone will not make you a better classroom manager, but knowledge can generate alternatives. Once you have personal awareness, you can use the work of others in your own way. It is most important to remember that the only approaches that will work for you are the ones that are congruent with your values, attitudes, and experiences as they relate to your professional and personal self.

5. Motivation to Learn

Many motivation problems at first glance look like discipline problems. However, using a discipline solution usually makes matters worse. One novice teacher asked for a discipline method to get kids to pay attention in class. Our answer: "Teach in a way that is either interesting or meets students' needs as learners." He responded, "But I can't always be interesting or meet their needs. Sometimes, I am either boring or just plain bland." Our answer, "Then sometimes your students won't pay attention."

It is impossible to force students to learn. We can quiet them down or stop them from disrupting others, but discipline will never replace motivating activities or effective teaching methods. Students who are highly motivated rarely become discipline problems, and when they do, they are more easily brought back to learning. By connecting to the natural motivation of students, teachers can prevent many discipline problems.

6. Establishing Social Contracts

The sixth stage of the prevention dimension involves establishing social contracts with your class. A social contract is a list of rules and consequences governing behavior, either in class or schoolwide. You will make a list of rules and consequences for your class and then ask your students to develop a list of rules and consequences for you. Students also develop rules and consequences for each other. Some teachers resist the use of the world "rule" because they see it as conceptualizing a rigid classroom structure that constricts the development of humanistic teacher-student relationships. To us the word "rule" means an agreed upon standard of behavior intended to facilitate an understanding of the limits that are necessary to meet individual needs and those of the group. The lists are discussed and evaluated by the total class, and when agreement is reached, the list of rules and consequences becomes the classroom social contract. Thus, your class will be involved in a process of setting rules and consequences and will feel that the contract is theirs. This process is explained more fully in Chapter 4.

7. Implementing Social Contracts

The seventh stage of the prevention dimension involves a transition into the action dimension. By implementing the social contract, you will set up a classroom environment that is governed by the rules, and when misbehavior occurs, a consequence is implemented or acted upon.

8. Dealing with Stress Associated with Disruptive Students

Stress management could fit into the Three-Dimensional Discipline model in the action dimension (the discussion of which follows this section) because teachers feel stressed when students break rules. Our bias, however, is to teach stress management strategies as part of prevention. We feel that by practicing stress reduction activities before you encounter problems, the greater your results will be in effectively dealing with your problems.

Stress reduction involves two components. The first involves strategies for solving problems so that minimal stress is experienced. The prevention dimension is mostly based on a problem-solving orientation (with the exception of expressing feelings). However, there are also many activities, both structured and unstructured, designed to reduce or prevent stress produced by the following conditions: problems that cannot be solved, the time needed to solve problems is not available, or the process of solving the problems does not reduce stress immediately. Stress reduction will offer activities and strategies for both components.

The Action Dimension

Despite all your efforts (and those of your students) to prevent discipline problems from happening, conflicts will inevitably occur in any setting in which 20 to 30 people are expected to be together over an extended period of time. The purpose of the action dimension is twofold. When a discipline problem occurs, somebody (usually the teacher) needs to do something to stop the problem as quickly as possible. This requires action. The first step is to implement the consequence associated with a rule violation, as stated in the social contract. However, there is more to implementing consequences than saying, "Nancy, there is no gum chewing in this class and because you are chewing gum, you must stay after school and clean all the desks. Don't argue! You agreed with this rule and consequence last September." The method of implementation is at least as important as the consequence itself. Tone of voice, physical distance from the student, body posture, use of eye contact, and other nonverbal gestures determine the effectiveness of a consequence as much or more than the actual content of the consequence itself.

However, merely implementing consequences as rules are broken can become mechanical and dehumanize the whole three-dimensional approach. For simple violations of rules, consequences can be implemented quickly and without a great deal of fuss. Nevertheless, rule violations provide the teacher an students a chance to interact in positive ways. By terminating the conflict using the consequences and positive interaction, your class can realize its full energy and aliveness.

The second purpose of the action dimension involves the monitoring of the effectiveness of your class' social contract. The social contract is not to be seen as a series of fixed, inflexible sequences, but rather as rules and consequences that govern classroom or school behavior at any given time. This means that contract modification and rewriting can and should occur if the current social contract is not effective. Your needs and those of your students may change during the school year. For example, if you notice that one of the rules is being violated with considerable frequency by a number of students, then we suggest that you consult with your class and possibly rewrite this part of the social contract. The prevention and action dimensions take care of most classroom discipline problems. Only the more troublesome and chronic problems will occur once the first two dimensions are implemented.

The Resolution Dimension

The resolution dimension is comprised of activities designed to reach the out-of-control student. Most of these students have already lost hope and have been overexposed and desensitized to many school and classroom discipline interventions. If you threaten them with detention, they say, "So what? I already have five years of detention that I'm not serving already." If you warn them that they will fail the test if they don't study, they'll laugh in your face, having failed most of the tests they have ever taken. They expect to routinely get kicked out of class, sent to the principal's office, or suspended.

Reaching these students requires a great deal of effort with little assurance that there will ever be a payoff. Is it worth the effort to even try, given the disproportionate time they consume? Obviously, every teacher must decide how much energy to invest in the "out-of-control" student. We offer some creative alternatives that have the potential for reaching those out-of-control students who are willing to be reached. These strategies have been adapted from cognitive psychology, Logotherapy (Victor Frankl), standard negotiation techniques modified for classroom application (Positive Student Confrontation), adolescent psychology, and the creative work of many teachers.

One payoff for the teacher who is willing to try creative approaches is the opportunity to experiment with techniques that are generally considered too radical for the mainstream. Eventually, many of these techniques expand the teacher's awareness of possibilities to teach all children, and generate new energy because of the challenge of experimenting with the unexpected. Those who have developed their ability to reach out-of-control students often become master teachers.

For the Administrator

Three-Dimensional Discipline is a broad-based program flexible enough to fit any teacher's unique teaching style. As the administrator in your building, it is important for you to accept that your faculty is diverse, has a variety of values, and uses a multitude of strategies when managing student behavior. In the same way you might suggest to a teacher to begin working with student strengths, you can begin helping your teachers by identifying their unique strengths in relation to discipline. Improvement in classroom management can be built upon these strengths.

To ensure that your teachers receive the support they want from you, ask each teacher to discuss his plans with you for preventing discipline problems from occurring. Suggest that teachers provide you with details of their rules and consequences early in the school year so that both you and they are clear about what is expected.

To facilitate the process of teachers seeing the benefits of self- and student awareness, you can present the R-M-L scale (Figure 3.2) and the Student Awareness Activity (Figure 3.3) at one of your faculty meetings. A discussion of awareness and how it can be used in relation to discipline can follow the activities.

You can also establish support groups of interested teachers so that there is a regular, sanctioned meeting time for your faculty members to express their feelings and receive collegial support for issues related to discipline. These groups can be incorporated into the regular school day or can meet after school on a weekly or biweekly basis. This time should be seen as a regular part of the job, the equivalent of a committee or other school event, and should not simply be an added on responsibility.

A discussion group of teachers who have had experiences with one discipline approach or another can be established. The group can first read about an approach and then discuss it with the teacher(s) who have experienced it in the classroom. The groups should focus on adapting each strategy in a practical way. While theoretical discussions can be fun, they rarely lead to an improvement of discipline.

To help with positive student confrontation, the administrator can practice the role of coach and be available to teachers who want to use this method. You can also help by training others in the school to act as coaches, so that teachers and students have a wide array of choices when they need a coach.

We have found that schools with the most effective discipline and strongest faculty support are those with an active principal who respects staff and student diversity. The principal is a leader who sets the tone by having clear, consistent rules and is unafraid of accountability to staff, students, and parents and who respectfully and with dignity demands the same from them. The active principal is visible in the halls, cafeteria and at the bus stop and smiles, greets his staff, and knows the names of the students. He wants to go into the classroom to spell a teacher because he wants direct, positive, instructional contact with staff and students. A "we" not "me" feeling is encouraged through listening and reacting to the individual and collective thoughts of the school community. The concept is that school is not Burger King—you can't have it your way—when that way infringes upon the rights of others to have a safe, secure school.

We have used a "School Discipline Survey" (see Appendix B) when working with faculty and staff to discover how much agreement and disagreement exists on issues related to discipline. Areas where there are large discrepancies can cause morale problems and confuse students. Areas where there is great agreement are sources of strength upon which to build. You can use the survey at the beginning of the school year or at the end of the previous year to analyze how to improve school discipline.

Endnotes

[1] For more information, see R.L. Curwin and A.N. Mendler, (1980), *The Discipline Book: A Complete Guide to School and Classroom Management*, (Reston, Va.: Reston Publishing Co.).

[2] R. Curwin and B. Fuhrman, (Sept. 1978), "Mirror Mirror on the Wall: Developing Teacher Congruency," *Humanist Educator* 17: 34.

[3] H. Bessell and U. Palomares, (1972), *Methods in Human Development*, (El Cajon, Calif.: Human Development Press).

4
The Social Contract

The Reponsibility Model described in Chapter 2 is the foundation of the social contract, which we use as the basic tool for discipline planning. The contract is an agreement between teacher and students about the rules and consequences for classroom behavior. We have observed social contracts in both elementary and secondary classrooms for more than 10 years and have seen great variety and flexibility in the way they have been adapted. Our own concept of the social contract has evolved as we have learned more about meeting competing needs in the classroom.

The basic design of the social contract is establishing rules and consequences for classroom behavior. Included in the design are methods to:

1. Involve students in the process.
2. Ensure that rules are clear.
3. Develop consequences, not punishments.
4. Develop what seems to be a paradox: predictable consequences for rule violations that allow teachers to match one of many alternative consequences to a particular circumstance.
5. Allow the contract to change with class needs.

6. Give teachers the ability to make decisions rather than have a system decide. This encourages teachers to develop an internal locus of control, which minimizes feeling helpless and out of control.
7. Give students the ability to make decisions rather than have the teacher decide. This encourages students to develop an internal locus of control, which minimizes feeling helpless and out of control.
8. Have safeguards to protect the dignity of all students.
9. Increase communication between teachers, students, administrators, and parents.
10. Integrate discipline methodology with the teaching of content.

Because social contracts are a generic tool, they can make a positive difference for teachers in urban, suburban, and rural settings; with the gifted and talented; with hard-core behavior problems; and with new and veteran teachers in large and small schools. More than any other aspect of Three-Dimensional Discipline, the social contract embodies the principles of the responsibility model.

Development of the social contract is based on democratic decision making. White and Lippitt's studies (1960) of 10- and 11-year-old children showed that an authoritarian teacher approach led to high work output by children but was accompanied by aggression directed at the teacher. Children in democratic groups that were guided by the teachers but also clearly involved in decisionmaking had nearly as high a work output, got on "best" with the teacher, and worked slightly better than the authoritarian group when the teacher was out of the room. Children with laissez-faire teachers did worst on all criteria.[1]

The System Effect

"Systems" are efficient, impartial, and necessary if complex organizations are to function successfully. But when systems govern people, individual needs are sacrificed for impartiality, and efficiency replaces common sense. Systems make the very people they were designed to serve feel helpless and frustrated by red tape, policies, procedures, and bureaucrats who avoid responsibility for decisionmaking.

Schools mirror society at large when systems are allowed to reign. There are few who live in the modern world who haven't felt enraged by policies and procedures that work well for computers but can't make allowances for complex human needs. If generally rational, responsible adults find themselves subverting "the system" when they are confronted with a robotic voice at the end of the phone, how can they expect students to behave differently?

Educators have been paying a great deal of attention to at-risk students over the last decade, but all students are at risk from the potential to feel battered by the system. Students from all social and ability groups can become cynical, unmotivated, alienated, or hostile when they perceive the system doesn't care about them. They will often take out their frustrations, either actively or passive aggressively, by striking back at every opportunity. Students like this feel gratified by beating the system, or even by the attempt, and all the reasons and rationality for maintaining order become meaningless. The more they are told by those who represent the system that they are violating policy, the more they have bolstered their dignity.

Systems are not malicious. The way people use them determines if they are helpful or a roadblock to human interaction. Let's, for example, examine the large supermarket and the small neighborhood grocer. The large supermarket offers lower prices and more choices. It has a larger staff and access to computer technology. It makes deals with large food companies that the corner store cannot. Yet, when a store loses its humanity and its ability to make customers feel that their special needs will be met, patrons are resentful. The corner store has higher prices and less selection, but the owner knows most patrons by name and takes time out of his day to ask about the family. He personally shows the customer daily specials, and even offers a sample of something new. When his customer finishes his shopping, the corner grocer says, "Come back soon," and means it. Both the large supermarket and the neighborhood store have a system. The differences are:

1. Does the system control people or do people control the system?
2. Does the system respond to individuals or are individuals required to conform to an inappropriate norm?
3. Is the system managed by caring people or cold bureaucrats?

When the classroom is perceived by students as the large supermarket, with an efficient system that processes students, they will fight back. When a classroom is perceived as the corner store, where all students are cared about without the system thrown in their face at every turn, it goes against their ethic to fight back. Nearly every school has one or two teachers who have earned the respect of the toughest kids to reach. When asked why they like these teachers, the kids say things like, "he treats me as a human," "he treats me with respect," "he cares about me as a person, not just as a student," "he listens," "he doesn't tell me what to do all the time," "he gives me the chance to make my own decisions," "he believes in me, that I can succeed." These teachers have systems, but they are under control.

The social contract is a system, but it is designed to enhance human interaction in the classroom. We have carefully built into the social contract decisionmaking opportunities for both teachers and students, the opportunity for change, and the chance to see situations in their natural complexity rather than to simplify them down to "easily manageable levels." This also builds in the potential for inefficiency and human mistakes, but in the long run, the classroom environment is enhanced by working through problem situations rather than letting a system make the decision.

Developing a Social Contract: Suggested Procedure

There is no one correct way to create a social contract. We are continually impressed with the creativity and flexibility teachers have used in adapting the social contract to fit their own styles and situation. The most successful contract typically has the following features:

- Classroom principles.
- Specific rules that are based on the principles.
- A range of consequences for each rule.
- Student input in the development process.
- A test for student comprehension.
- Input from parents and/or administrators.
- A formal and/or informal method of evaluation.
- A process for changes in the contract as the year goes on.

Sound Principles

Good principles, based on the teacher's value system, provide guidelines for classroom behavior. Principles place rules in a larger context that helps students understand why each rule is selected and needed. Principles are not designed to be enforced because they are too general. They can, however, be encouraged, supported, valued, discussed, or suggested. Examples of principles are:

1. Be respectful.
2. Be courteous.

3. Be prepared.
4. Treat others as you wish to be treated.
5. Try your best at all times.

Effective Rules

Rules are behavioral expressions of the principles. They define clearly what is and is not acceptable in the classroom.

Rules work best when they describe specific behavior. The more specific your rules, the more you have, so try to limit the number of rules by starting only with the ones you need most. You can add others later if they are needed and not bother with them if they are not.

The importance of specific rules is related to the need for predictability to develop responsibility. The more understandable expectations are, the better the students' chances of meeting them. When students must break rules to find out what they are, they begin to feel they are unable to control the effects of their behavior.

It is possible to overdo the specificity of the rule. You need not list every objectionable swear word or put down. You need not list each body part that is off limits for hitting, pinching, poking, stabbing, tickling, or punching. As long as you and the students know what is meant by the rule, it is specific enough.

Too Vague: each student must not interfere with another student's learning. (This makes a fine principle, but not a rule.)

Too Specific: Do not poke your fingers in another student's eye.

Just Right: People are not for hitting. Keep your hands to yourself.

Positive When Possible

Being positive provides more clarity and sets a constructive tone. For example, say "be on time" instead of "don't be late."

Some rules are hard to define in positive terms. For example, the positive version of "no putting down other students"—"say only nice things about each other"—obviously does not work.

Be Brief

The social contract is neither the Magna Carta nor a legal brief. Get rid of words that are unnecessary or confusing. Avoid the word "try."

Logical Consequences

The consequences are the essential part of the social contract and the most difficult to develop. The following criteria for good consequences is brief because the next chapter is devoted entirely to consequences.

Good consequences:
- Are clear and specific.
- Have a range of alternatives.
- Are not punishments.
- Are natural and/or logical.
- Are related to the rule.

Consequences also:
- Preserve the student's dignity.
- Increase internal locus of control when appropriate.
- Increase student motivation.

These four generic consequences will work for any rule:
- reminder
- warning
- practicing following the rule
- written plan

Threats are one type of punishment that often corner the threatener, especially when the threat is more severe than intended. Another type of punishment, making students write something a number of times, only teaches students to hate writing. When students are given detention, they learn school is a bad place to be because if they are "bad" they will have to stay longer. Eventually, detention subtly erodes motivation.

Student Involvement

The more students are involved in the process of developing rules and consequences, the more they feel that the plan is a part of them. Ultimately, they will follow the plan if they had a say in its development. Here are three ways to involve students.

Students Develop Rules for the Teacher. Don't accept a rule or consequence for you that you can't live with. Most teachers can find one or two student rules for them that they can follow. Typical examples are:
- Homework is handed back in three days.
- If we can't eat in class, you can't drink coffee.
- Don't be late talking to someone in the hall when the bell rings.

- Don't call my home without telling me first.

If this method is used, the teacher can break a rule and get caught by the students. The teacher then has the opportunity to model the way students should respond when they are caught breaking a rule.

Students Develop Rules for Each Other. Let the students develop rules (and possibly consequences) for each other. These rules work best when they conform to the above standards for good rules. Do not accept any rule or consequence that you will not feel comfortable enforcing.

Students Vote on Negotiable Rules. Think of some (not all) rules that you can let the student choose by vote. We recommend that 70 percent is necessary for a negotiable rule to pass the vote. Be careful not to put up for student vote any rule that you cannot live without. If you put a rule up for a vote, you will live with the students' decision.

Time Investment

Some teachers, especially at the junior and senior high school levels, view the social contract process as too time consuming. "After all," they argue, "I have 5 classes a day with 150 students and a lot of material to cover. I don't have time to do social contracts." Our response is that the full social contract takes an average of three periods per class to complete. To feel that your time is well spent, you need to answer for yourself, "If I counted the minutes and hours that I now spend in managing disruptive behavior during the course of an entire semester or trimester, would this come to at least the equivalent of three class periods?" Our experience in observing many teachers working in various schools confirms that most teachers spend far more than three days dealing with discipline. In many junior and senior high classes, 5 to 10 minutes of class time is wasted at the beginning of class trying to focus the attention of students. At least another 5 to 10 minutes is directed toward off-task behavior (students not paying attention, using put downs, arguing) during class time. This amounts to minimally 10 to 20 minutes of a 45- to 50-minute class period doing things other than what you are paid to do and want to do: teach! If your school has a 10-week grading period and you are teaching in an average situation, then you are probably spending between 10 and 20 class periods per 10-week interval reminding students to pay attention, being interrupted in the middle of a lesson, or reprimanding them for coming late to class, for fighting, for talking out of turn, and so on.

Naturally, you must be willing to believe that the three class periods used to develop the social contract will ultimately save you a lot of instructional time, and the only way to believe it is to do it!

If you are still skeptical, that's fine. But we suggest you try an experiment. Choose your worst class, or the one you anticipate will be your worst, and try developing a social contract with them. If you begin with your worst class, you have nothing to lose. The worst that can happen is that they stay as bad as they are. Perhaps your experience will parallel that of one high school English teacher who developed a social contract with her worst class. Two months later she said, "They've been terrific. It's my good kids that are driving me crazy!"

Although developing a social contract requires a commitment of time and involvement with your students, it is usually far less difficult to do (with all classes at a secondary level) than you might think. The idea of having five separate contracts (one for each class) is something sufficiently scary to your sense of organization to make you avoid the process. However, when you consider each of the steps separately, you will find that your flag rules will be the same for all classes. Your other rules and consequences are also likely to be the same for all your classes. So, steps one through three require no more effort from you for all classes than for one. We have also found that student rules closely parallel each other.

Once the contract is developed for each class, it is no more difficult for you to implement than it is for you to have two to four different lesson plans. Actually, it is less difficult because there is no preparation time needed. In the same way that you shift gears for each class, you can shift your social contracts for each period. Most teachers simply have a large sheet of newsprint that contains the contract, and they attach the new contract to the wall each time the bell rings. Others give a handout to each student for them to keep in their class notebook.

For young children and others with limited language skills, more structure is often useful. The language you use to present your rules and consequences must naturally fit the children's understanding. When it is their turn to create rules and consequences for you, teach the process through the use of examples. You might say to students, "I want to give you a chance to have some rules and consequences for me, and for each other. Now that might sound silly to some of you because usually children aren't allowed to tell grown-ups how to act. But I remember that when I was in 1st grade, I wished that my teacher would say hello to me in the morning, not yell at me when I made a mistake, let me choose which of my papers to hang in the room, and, even though I was scared, call my parents when I hit someone or call someone else's parents when they hit me. So, what I want you to do is to think about (in small groups preferably) rules that you want each other to follow."

Testing

To prevent students from pleading ignorance about the rules and consequences, test them on the social contract. (Figure 4.1 is an example of such a test.) Students need a perfect score to pass. Nothing happens if a student does not score 100 percent, and the student

---

Figure 4.1
Example of Social Contract Test*

NAME _____

Health 301

1. Besides a notebook or folder and clean, lined paper, what else do you have to bring to health class every day?
2. What do you have to bring to health class every Friday?
3. What time does your health class begin?
4. If you hand in your homework only one day late, what happens to your grade?
5. You cannot use the lav pass for the first _____ minutes of class.
6. What is the time limit on the lav pass?
7. When can you write or draw in a health book?
8. It's OK to write or draw on a desk in health.   T   F
9. If you wear a hat to health, what must you do with it?
10. It is possible to get an assigned seat in health for the rest of the year.   T   F
11. When is physical fighting OK in health?
12. For "horsing around" in health, you may eventually be put on class pass restriction.   T   F
13. In health, students must not destroy or harm the property of others.   T   F
14. When may students play a quiet game in health?
15. The free time on Wednesday is for games and talking.   T   F
16. Mrs. White can change a rule when?
17. When can't Mrs. White give homework?
18. How much notice must be given for tests and quizzes?
19. When can Mrs. White give homework for punishment?
20. If two students have a problem in health, Mrs. White only has to listen to one side of the story.   T   F
21. Mrs. White can give homework on test and quiz days.   T   F
22. When can Mrs. White be late for class?
23. Mrs. White can give homework _____ times a week.
24. Tests and quizzes must be returned by Mrs. White within _____ days.
25. When a few students are bad, Mrs. White can punish whom?
26. It's OK for Mrs. White to read students' notes to herself.   T   F
27. Mrs. White can read students' grade in front of the whole class.   T   F
28. You need _____ plusses in a row for a free day coupon.
29. If you have 6 plusses in a row and then get a minus, you start counting plusses all over again.   T   F

---

*We wish to thank Judy White from the Rush-Henrietta School District, Rochester New York, for this material.

can take the test as many times as he wants until a passing score is attained. However, all classroom privileges are earned by a passing score.

To solve the problem of students who try not to pass the test and to help promote responsibility among your students, we believe that all classroom privileges should be earned, not given. This process helps children appreciate privileges because they are earned and motivates them to pass the test.

Some examples of privileges are:
1. Going on field trips.
2. Being a hall monitor.
3. Passing out materials.
4. Going to the office with a note for principal.
5. Earning free time.
6. Getting choice of assignments.
7. Being a line leader.
8. Washing chalkboard.
9. Working in library.
10. Being a playground monitor.

Determining Rewards and Privileges

Occasionally, a teacher will have difficulty pairing the passing of the comprehension test with classroom privileges. If you cannot think of privileges in your classroom, then either they don't exist, which in itself can be a cause of discipline problems, or you are not aware of them. We have found that students are generally very adept at pointing out privileges. When groups of students are asked, "What privileges or good consequences exist in this classroom?", they often generate long lists. If they do not, then one way of discovering age-appropriate privileges is to say, "If rewards and privileges could exist in this classroom and you could determine what they would be, then what privileges would you choose?" Hold a brainstorming session, and choose those privileges that make you feel comfortable.

Sharing List of Rules and Consequences

Your list of rules and consequences should be shared with the significant people in the school community.

Parents. Parents typically become involved in discipline matters with their children once a rule has been violated. Often, a parent, teacher, and student conference is one of the consequences used in the social contract. When parents are contacted to deal with a discipline problem, some become defensive and protective of their children. Some become overly upset with their children while others ignore the event. We have found that it helps communication with parents to send them a copy of the social contract.

One method of parent communication is to write a cover letter explaining the social contract process. Include a copy of your class social contract and a return slip indicating that they have read and understood the contract. Enclosing a phone number for questions is also helpful.

Another method is to inform parents of the contract process before development and to invite parents to suggest any rules or consequences they feel might be helpful. Then include some of the parent rules when you and your class develop the contract. It is a good idea to include at least one parent rule if you use this approach to demonstrate your willingness to use parental suggestions. Once the contract is completed, you can follow the same steps as the example cited above.

A third alternative for parent communication is to use parents' night at the school to explain the contract process and to share your classroom social contract. You can mail the contract to parents who do not attend.

Once parents have seen the contract and understand how it will work, you have increased your chances of cooperation when their child breaks a rule. They understand what is expected of their children, and what consequences were agreed to by the class, and what their role is should a child break a rule. Should you find that a parent is upset with you for "doing something to his child," you can refer to the contract and explain your decision from a point of mutual understanding. If the parents are needed to fulfill a consequence, the chances of their cooperating will be strengthened if they have a prior understanding of their responsibilities.

Administrators. Administrators, like parents, should be informed of your social contract as it is developed. This is especially important if you include administrators as part of your consequences. You should reach a full agreement with administrators about any consequence that involves them. Even if they are not directly involved in your consequences, you can help yourself by informing them of your discipline plan. We find that clarity between teachers and administrators around the issue of discipline helps counteract the stress associated with feelings of isolation and lack of administrative support described in Chapter 3.

Substitute Teachers. Students' eyes often light up when a substitute takes over for an absent teacher. Armed with lesson plans left by the teacher and a "good luck" wish by the administration, substitutes must rely on patience, good humor, and a high tolerance for ambiguity as well as, in many cases, mild chaos. We have found a significant improvement when substitutes are given a copy of your social contract, so that the substitute will know exactly what is expected of your students and what can be done if your students break the rules. Most substitutes find they spend more time dealing with behavior than with subject matter. You can make life easier for them by providing classroom guidelines. If substitutes have been informed of your social contract, the administrator can then support the substitute if a student or two becomes rambunctious in your absence. It is also helpful to include a rule in your contract that stipulates that all other rules are in effect if a substitute is present.

Other Teachers. Other teachers may be having similar problems with a student. Sharing the social contract and its effectiveness with that student might be helpful in figuring ways to team up to solve the problem. Other teachers might want to try the social contract process or get some ideas on how to modify the one they have.

Counselors. Counselors may find the social contract useful in understanding the learning environment of classes attended by certain students.

Sample Social Contract

Jeanne McGlynn*, an intermediate-level art teacher, used a social contract along with a creative system of behavior management to improve student behavior in the art room. She reports:

> The following information will illustrate how I used the social contract to improve a system I employed in my classroom. The "Monitor System" was developed to structure my overcrowded art room. I wanted to cut down on movement, talking while working, and bickering over materials. The idea is based on the children's natural inclinations to choose a leader. I use this system with grades 5, 6, and 7 at Lounsberry Hollow Middle School in Vernon, N.J. Each grade level attends art classes every day for a 13-week cycle. The class periods are approximately 40-minutes long for grades 5 and 6, and 35 minutes for grade 7. The art room is set up with 6 tables that seat 5 students.

*We wish to thank Jeanne McGlynn of Sussex, New Jersey, for sharing her ideas.

Figure 4.2 is the part of the social contract that has been set up by McGlynn as flag rules. They are necessary for effective management of the monitor system.

McGlynn uses the merit/demerit system to encourage successful cooperation in the group. Each table is given a number for identification (Table #1, Table #2 instead of Bob's table or Jane's table). At the end of every class period, the table that most successfully worked together as a team gets a merit. This is indicated by a plus sign in a column in the record book. The column lists the table number and the individual members of the group. When a table receives a merit, every individual in that group receives an extra credit to be calculated into his grade at the end of the cycle. This is particularly attractive to the student who does not feel he can achieve success by his art work alone.

A demerit is received by a group that has broken the contract in any way. Demerits are not given out daily. They are given out as the last in the sequence of consequences to deter uncooperative behavior within the group. The demerit stage is seldom reached. Problems are usually settled before the group gets to this point (see Figure 4.3).

Figure 4.2
Social Contract

1. Each table group will have a monitor who is in charge of getting materials, distributing them, supervising behavior according to the classroom rules, collecting materials, and cleaning up.
2. The monitor is voted on by the members of the group based on his leadership qualities, dependability, or whatever other qualities the group feels constitutes a good leader.
3. All members of the group must cooperate with the monitor.
4. The monitor must fulfill the duties and responsibilities of his position.
5. No one else in the group may leave his seat, unless instructed by the monitor or the teacher.

Figure 4.3
Consequences for Failure to Comply with Monitor System Contract

1. The monitor verbally reinforces to the group that he is the person in charge.
2. The group reminds the monitor that he is the person who accepted the responsibility of being the monitor.
3. The group has a consultation with the teacher present to find out what the problem is and how to solve it. The teacher will act as arbitrator, or coach.
4. Failure to resolve problems through an agreeable compromise results in a group demerit.
5. If the problems continue, the group may choose to vote for a new monitor.

Social Contract Timetable

Figure 4.4 is an example of how to set up a social contract.

It may be modified in many ways. One of the most common variations is to use small groups during class time for the development of student rules for teacher and for each other. This variation works more effectively than homework for younger students. With

---

Figure 4.4
Social Contract Timetable

A. Before class starts:	Develop your flag and negotiable rules and consequences.
B. Day one (this may occur at the beginning of school, or during the year):	Explain to the class the process you will use to develop your contract. Share what makes a good rule and consequence. Assign for homework that each student develop one rule and consequence for you and for each other. Your "flag" rules are now in effect. (Approx. time: 10–15 minutes)
C. Day two:	Collect assignments. After school, organize the students' rules, eliminating duplications.
D. Day three:	Share all the rules and consequences, (including your flag rules) and negotiable rules. Discuss, role play, or define any rules that are unclear. (Approx. time: full class period)
E. Day four:	Use decision-making process to determine which remaining rules and consequences will become part of the contract. (Approx. time: 20–25 minutes)
F. Day five:	Administer social contract test. (Approx. time: 15 minutes) After school, correct test. Send letter home to parents, and inform your administration of your contract. Set up a meeting with administration to discuss any consequences that involve them.
G. Day six:	Return tests, readminister test to any students who failed to get 100%. Post the contract in class.
H. One week later:	Renegotiate any rule and consequence that is not working. Add new rules and consequences as needed.
I. Once each following month:	Hold a social contract review meeting with class. Discuss how the social contract is working. You may add or delete rules and consequences at these meetings. Your students should have the same input as they did at the initial contract development meeting on day four.

---

proper planning, a social contract can be completed in as little as two full class periods. By spending time during the first week of its development, you will find that the contract becomes an effective communication tool that will save you a great deal of time for the remainder of the year.

Examples of Social Contracts

Figures 4.5 and 4.6 are social contracts developed by teachers with their students. We have found that most of the power of the social contract resides in the process, not in the content (the rules and consequences). By this we mean that the involvement of students with the teacher in defining acceptable classroom standards and the process of reaching agreement on these standards are more important that the content of those standards. Figures 4.5 and 4.6 are intended only as examples of the end point reached by various classes in developing their rules and consequences. The content of your contract may well be quite different.

Teachers who have used social contracts tell us quite emphatically that they make a positive difference. They find that students break rules less and that they themselves can spend more time doing what they are paid to do—to teach. We encourage you to try as much of the process as you want and judge the power of the process for yourself. Ultimately, the process becomes easier and easier each time you and your students experience it. And the more it becomes internalized as part of your teaching style, the more effective you will be as a classroom manager.

Figure 4.5
1st Grade Low-Achieving Class
Partial Social Contract

RULE

We will sit together on the rug for story. Legs will be crossed, arms folded, and there will be no moving around once you sit.

Consequences:
1. Teacher places you on rug.
2. You must sit at your desk.
3. Time-out (removal out of the room).

RULE

Children will not fight, push, or scream on the playground.

Consequences:
1. Sitting on the bench.
2. The whole class goes inside early.
3. Not going out at all.

Figure 4.6
Senior High English Class
Partial Social Contract

RULE FOR STUDENTS BY TEACHER

1. Students will be in their seats no later than three minutes after the bell rings.

Consequences:
- Reminder
- Warning
- Work will be made up after school
- A meeting will be held after school to help student learn to be in class on time
- For each week of no tardiness, the students can choose any book they want (by vote) to discuss on Friday discussion time

2. Students will hand in homework on the day it is due.
   a. Homework must be handed in by the end of the day
   b. Homework must be made up after school
   c. Homework will not be accepted

3. No fooling around, which means no acting in a way which interferes with the class process; i.e., no hitting, fighting, touching, loud talking, dropping things, leaving seat without permission, making noises.
   a. Warning
   b. Discussion after class, student learns new ways of behaving including practice
   c. Discussion with parents and students
   d. Discussion with parents and principal

STUDENT RULES FOR TEACHER

1. Students can choose between at least four books for all reading assignments.
   a. Reminder
   b. No one has to read the teacher's selection (but a book must be read for the assignment)

2. Teacher must tell why something is good or bad, not only say good or bad.
   a. Warning
   b. Teacher must give up a class period and set up 5-minute interviews with each student who wants more feedback on their papers

STUDENT RULES FOR EACH OTHER

1. No copying homework.
   a. Teacher will be informed
   b. Principal will be informed
   c. Parents will be informed

2. Put-downs in class are forbidden, if you want to comment about an individual, you must say something nice.
   a. The person who made the put-down must do one nice thing for the person put down
   b. The violator will be assigned a book for the Friday discussion by the person put down

For the Administrator

Social contracts are an integral part of the Three-Dimensional Process. As the administrator in your building or district, you can be a helpful resource for teachers who wish to develop social contracts in their classrooms. You can help the teachers by reviewing their proposed rules and consequences before they are introduced to the students. Help clarify any rules that are not clear, see if the list is complete, and check to see if they are truly consequences (see Chapter 5) rather than punishments.

Clarify what your role will be when a student breaks a rule. Specify clearly what you will do if a student is sent to you and under what circumstances you will see a student who misbehaves. You can use the social contract model to develop a contract between you and your teachers related to your responsibilities about discipline.

Once the social contracts have been established you can offer support by checking to see how it's going or by teaming up teachers who have tried the social contract with those who are ready to try for the first time. You can set up classroom visits so other teachers in the school or district can observe the social contract in operation. This process can be enhanced by choosing as a model for disciplining one classroom, which you set up in close cooperation with the teacher. The model can be used for experimentation and to demonstrate the effectiveness of the social contract.

Coach your faculty in understanding the difference between a "motivation" and a "discipline" problem. Many of the problems you see are the result of poor motivation, not discipline. You can provide training and/or coaching in developing motivation skills and improved instruction techniques for those teachers who need it. The more students are motivated, the less problems the school will have with discipline.

If you wish to set up a school-wide contract for your building, begin by reaching agreement on rules and consequences with your faculty. Then once you have worked through the school-wide issues (and this will be the most difficult part of the process), you can invite student input on the rules for teachers and students. You might even encourage a rule or two for the administrators to follow. The key to the success of a school-wide contract is that everyone on the faculty agrees to honor it, even if it is not everyone's first choice. If you decide not to develop a school-wide contract, then you can check your school-wide rules for clarity and specificity and see that they state what should be done as well as what should not be done. Also examine your school-wide consequences to see that they are clear, natural, and logical and that they provide a range of alternatives. We recommend that if you do not already do so, you should give every student a test for your school rules to ensure that there is a clear understanding about what is expected from the students.

When a substitute teacher is assigned to a class, see that he is given a copy of the classroom social contract. If the teacher does not have a social contract, then at least provide the rules and consequences. Providing behavioral guidelines are equally important, if not more so, than providing lesson plans.

Finally, see that every parent in your school knows what each teacher's social contract is, what their rules and consequences are, or what their plan for discipline is. You might also see that every parent is informed about your school's rules and consequences. When a parent questions you about what is happening with his child, use the contract as a basis of mutual understanding and agreement. That way, you will always have a common ground to begin discussion, and there will be more of an emphasis on problem solving than on blaming.

Endnotes

[1]R. White and R. Lippitt, (1960), "Leader Behavior and Member Reaction in Three 'Social Climates'," in *Group Dynamics in Researched Theory*, 2nd ed., ed. by D. Cartwright and A. Zander (New York: Harper and Row).

5
Consequences

I t is possible to understand in theory the differences between consequences and punishments and still have difficulty developing effective consequences. Some difficulty occurs because a consequence can become a punishment if it is delivered aggressively. In addition, few teacher education programs discuss consequences with the depth necessary to apply them in practical situations. Much inservice training emphasizes the use of consequences, but often the training is too limited to be effective. (A one-day workshop is usually inadequate.) Some inservice programs are more punishment oriented, leaving teachers unsure of what is the right thing to do.

We have heard more than one teacher say, "If the experts can't make up their minds, then we certainly can't, not with the little time we have. We're too busy teaching to worry about things like that."

Also, long-standing cultural mores of many schools are punishment or detention oriented. Using consequences is far more effective when the administration understands how to use them and supports teachers in their efforts to change from a punishment-oriented discipline plan.

Let's review what consequences are and how they differ from punishments in more depth.

Range of Alternatives for Consequences

Consequences work best when they:

1. Are Clear and Specific.

Predictability is important to help students understand what the results of their behaviors will be. When consequences are perceived as random, students begin to doubt that they can influence their future. When a teacher accepts minor infractions while slowly reaching his breaking point, and then lashes out at one student while others are also violating the rule, students see the classroom as a game of musical chairs. The most effective time to tell the students about consequences is before a rule is broken.

2. Have a range of alternatives.

The 80-15-5 principle stated in Chapter 2 explains the need for a range of consequences. The range works best when it is not sequenced; the teacher needs discretion in choosing the best consequence to match the particular situation. Imagine the following example.

Miss Martin is a 10th grade biology teacher who has the following rule and consequence: "All homework must be done on time. If homework is not done, the student will stay after school and finish it." In early March, Susan, one of her best students who had never missed an assignment, told Miss Martin, "I'm sorry, Miss Martin, but my father was very sick last night. I had to babysit while he was taken to the hospital, and in the confusion, I didn't have time to get my homework done." Miss Martin now faces an uncomfortable dilemma. She can tell Susan that it doesn't matter what the excuse is and Susan still has to come after school and finish her homework—there are not exceptions. If she gives this consequence, Susan and other students in class will see Miss Martin as unfair and feel resentful.

Another option is for Miss Martin to accept Susan's excuse. She doesn't have to stay after school because her excuse is legitimate. This choice will teach Susan and the other students that a good excuse will get them off the hook when a rule is violated.

Neither option helps Miss Martin deal with the situation effectively on a short- or long-term basis. She is caught in the classic bind that eventually erodes any system of discipline. The situation gets worse when, the next day, Tom tells Miss Martin that he didn't do his homework and presents his excuse. Tom is a student who has been late with his homework 10 times in the last month. Now it is difficult for Miss Martin to be consistent with her policy and still deal effectively with Susan and Tom. How can she be consistent and treat Susan and Tom as separate individuals?

Our solution to this problem is to develop more than one consequence for any rule violation. Miss Martin's range of consequences might have been:

1. Reminder.
2. Warning.
3. Student must hand homework in before close of school that day.
4. Stay after school to finish homework.
5. A conference between teacher, student, and parent to develop an action plan for completing homework on time.

With this range of alternatives, Miss Martin could gently remind Susan that homework is due on time, and then discuss how her father is doing. In this way she is implementing one of the prescribed consequences, yet she is not being overly rigid with Susan. With Tom, staying after school to finish his homework would probably be more appropriate.

The range of consequences gives Miss Martin the flexibility to meet specific needs while consistently implementing consequences when a rule is broken.

One important strategy we recommend you use as part of your preventive package involves the principle "fair and not equal." Because you may use different consequences with different students, even though they have each violated the same rule, you will be accused of being unfair. It is important when you use different consequences that you make sure to explain your reasoning in advance.

We start this preventive strategy by teaching the concept that "fair is not always equal" before any issue related to that question ever occurs. This unit makes a wonderful first or second day class project for all grade levels, although it can be helpful at any point in the school year. Begin by telling your class a story similar to the following:

Imagine that I am the parent of two children. The first is a successful lawyer who has an annual income of over $100,000. He has found his dream house and needs $10,000 more than he has in savings for the down payment and asks me for a $10,000 loan. At the same time my second child, who is a college dropout and works in the local shoe factory, has decided to go back to school. He needs $10,000 for tuition and asks me for a loan. He has been accepted and is excited about getting his life together.

I have only $10,000 to loan. Who do I give the money to? Do I split it evenly, give all to one and none to the other, or make a different percentage split?

Most students choose to give most or all of the money to the second child. This leads perfectly to the concept that being fair means giving what people need, and when different people have different needs, they are given different amounts. This is fair—it is not equal. Another example of fair and unequal that you can share with your students takes place in a doctor's waiting room. Ask your students to imagine 10 patients waiting for their turn to see the doctor. One has a cold, one has a broken arm, one has pneumonia, one has poison ivy, one has a sprained ankle, one has diarrhea, one has allergies, one has chicken pox, one has a splinter, and another came in for an annual checkup. All of a sudden, the doctor comes out and announces to the patients that today is aspirin day. All patients will be treated equally and given aspirin to solve their ailments.

A lively discussion can now ensue analyzing whether the doctor is being fair although he is clearly being equal. There are dozens of other examples that you and your class can think of. Some are:

- Equal Rights Amendment.
- Affirmative Action.
- Some people are quarterbacks, others linebackers.
- Some hitters lead off, others clean up.
- Different-aged children have different chores at home.
- Homogeneous/heterogenous grouping in school.

Once the class understands this concept, you can write on the board or make a permanent sign that reads, "I will be fair, and I won't always be equal." We like the use of the conjunction "and" rather than "but" so that the second statement does not negate the first. When a student asks why you are being unfair by giving him a different consequence for the same violation, you can point to the sign and say, "Because I am being fair and I am not being equal." That usually ends the protest. If it doesn't, you merely have to repeat the phrase until the student gets the message that protest is not going to work. This strategy will work as long as you are really being fair with your inequality. If the students see you as being unfair and unequal, this strategy will backfire and cause anger and resentment. However, if you are being unfair and unequal, your students will feel resentful with or without this strategy.

Do not use the fair and not equal principle to mask unfair and unequal treatment. Keep an informal record of the number of complaints you receive about not being fair and who is doing the complaining. If you discover that you are treating certain students unfairly, then rectify the situation.

3. Are Not Punishments.

4. Are Natural and/or Logical.

5. Are Related to the Rule.

Let us examine these criteria in more depth, beginning with the last one. Much of the research tells us that punishments stop short-term misbehavior but are ineffective for long-term change. Most of us know someone who has received a speeding ticket. Usually the speeder slows down for a hundred miles or so, and then slowly builds up speed again, but is far more careful to look for police cars. Radar detectors are sold mostly to speeders who prefer taking extravagant measures to avoid getting caught again. Similarly, punishments in classroom can work well for a short time but have little effect on improving behavior over a longer period. Punishment teaches the importance of not getting caught!

Because punishments force negative behavior to go underground, it appears on the surface that the situation is improving because the teacher sees fewer infractions. This does not necessarily mean that there has been a reduction in infractions.

What is the difference between a consequence and a punishment? While they often appear to be similar, there are significant differences. The first is that a punishment is a form of retribution. Its goal is to make the rule violator pay for misconduct. Punishments have their roots in a philosophy that students will avoid bad behavior to avoid being punished. Fear is the prime motivator.

Our view is that punishments are a release of tension for the person giving them. Scolding, yelling, hitting, and feeling avenged are common releases for the anger we feel when disruptive students constantly challenge us. They make us feel frustrated, agitated, and annoyed. None of us likes being confronted, accused, or defied; nor do we enjoy being cast in the role of the "disciplinarian." We find ourselves resorting to punishments that we know are ineffective as a way of expressing the negative emotions we feel when students misbehave. Punishment is not worth the short-term pleasure of venting anger, which only creates resentment and ultimately more rule breaking. Teachers need to find nondestructive methods of releasing their anger when working with difficult students (see Chapter 3).

Consequences are directly related to the rule. They are both logical and natural, and they help the rule violator learn acceptable behavior from the experience. Their intent is instructional rather than punitive because they are designed to teach students the positive or negative effects of their behavior. Let us look at some specific examples of the differences between consequences and punishments.

Differences between Consequences and Punishments

Rule

All trash must be thrown in the basket.

Consequence	*Punishment*
Pick your trash up off the floor.	Apologize to the teacher in front of the whole class.

Rule

Tests and homework must be completed by yourselves unless group work is assigned. There is no copying other students' work.

Consequence	*Punishment*
Do the test or homework again under supervision.	Write 100 times, "I will not will not copy other students' work."

Rule

No talking when someone else is talking. If you want to speak, wait until the current speaker has finished.

Consequence	*Punishment*
Wait five minutes before speaking.	Sitting in the hall for the entire period.

Rule

You must be in your seat by five minutes after the bell.

Consequence	*Punishment*
You are responsible to get any missed information or make up any work missed while you are late.	Miss entire class sitting in the principal's office, then make up work.

The main differences between consequences and punishments in the above examples are that the consequences are simple, direct, related to the rule, logical (that is, they are natural outcomes of the rule violation), and instructive. Punishments are not related to the rule, are not natural extensions of the rule, and tend to generate anxiety, hostility, and resentment in the student. Natural and logical consequences help teach proper behavior. Effective consequences are also direct and simple.

Consequences also:

1. Preserve the student's dignity. Punishments attack dignity as a way to get the child to stop misbehaving. Sometimes it is difficult to tell whether the dignity of the student is hurt by the consequence or not. There are instances when the student will hurt his own dignity by the way he responds to the consequence. Other times the student might interpret a reminder or warning as threat, even though it wasn't meant or delivered in that way. Obviously, if the intervention includes writing someone's name on the board, there is a great chance to hurt the student's dignity. For those interventions that are hard to determine, place yourself in the student's situation and see how you would feel if the intervention happened to you. Your own feelings are usually accurate.

2. Increase internal locus of control when appropriate. Punishments increase external control because they minimize the students' feelings of control.

Good consequences enable students to respond, are future oriented (like planning), and help the student recognize that he can do things differently. Good consequences also help the student understand what is beyond his control and how to deal with what they cannot change without feeling helpless. The rule of thumb is:

- If a choice or decision is made for a student that the student can make for himself, the possible effect is a reduction of a sense of responsibility.
- If a student is asked to change what he cannot, he eventually might lose hope, feel helpless or overwhelmed, or withdraw.

3. Increase student motivation. Punishments decrease motivation because they create strong negative feelings that make learning difficult or impossible.

Keeping students motivated to learn isn't easy. There are many distractions and other interests that compete with students' attention. When an intervention for a misbehavior leaves the child with a negative attitude for a long time, their desire to learn diminishes. Some students become so angered by an embarrassing or threatening teacher that they give up on that class for the entire school year. When a student is caught breaking a rule, we do not expect them to immediately return to their schoolwork full of enthusiasm and joy. We do, however, expect them to focus on how they can improve the situation and not hold a resentment to the point of danger.

Four Generic Consequences

These four consequences can be effective for any rule. They all fit the description above for being effective.

1. *Reminder of rule.* For example, "Mary, we raise our hands before speaking. This is your reminder."
2. *A warning.* This is a stern reminder. The consequence is for the student to hear the warning. It is not a threat that something will happen later, although the assertive tone with which it is delivered should leave no doubt in the student's mind that the next infraction will result in a more active consequence. Notice these two examples: (a) "Johnny, this is the second time today that you have gotten out of your seat and bothered Mary. If you don't stop doing that, I warn you that you will have to stay after school for detention." (b) "Johnny, this is the second time today that you have gotten out of your seat to bother Mary. This is your warning." The first example is a threat that something will happen later, and the students learns that he has at least one more chance and maybe many more after that. The second message is a clear statement, not a threat that something will follow. The warning is the consequence itself. When another infraction occurs, take action. Don't threaten! Reminders and warnings work well with the 80 percent.
3. *Developing an action plan for improving behavior.* For example, "Johnny, you are out of your seat bothering Mary. I want you to write for me how you intend to stop breaking this rule. List very clearly what you will do when you want to tell Mary something."

4. *Practicing behavior.* Often students break rules because they emotionally or behaviorally do not have the skills to match their cognitive understanding of the rules. In other words, sometimes students do not know how to behave appropriately even when they know what the rule is. Even for those students who do know how to follow rules, practice with the teacher can be a helpful and effective consequence if the teacher is not sarcastic or condescending. We have seen this consequence used effectively for teaching proper lunchroom behavior, for teaching effective nonviolent strategies for expressing anger, and for teaching effective and appropriate ways to get attention. The teacher in implementing this consequence may follow this sequence:

- Role play the inappropriate behavior first, or have the student role play it.
- Demonstrate one appropriate way of following the rule.
- The student then plays the appropriate behavior.
- Finally, the student practices other appropriate behaviors (where there is more than one optional behavior) until he can do them easily.

An example of practicing behavior occurred at Valley View Elementary School, which had developed a school-wide plan for having more orderly cafeteria behavior. Built into their system was a clear statement of the cafeteria rules, which were monitored by cafeteria aides who placed a check mark next to the name of a student who broke one of the rules. There were various individual and class privileges and rewards built into the system for short- and long-term behavior, but after a student broke a rule three times in any month, the student was assigned to a before- or after-school cafeteria class. The class was designed to teach students how to behave acceptably in the cafeteria by practicing appropriate behavior. Students in the class practiced walking through the cafeteria line, getting their food, emptying their trash, and, in some cases eating with a fork (for those who threw food). After the students practiced these behaviors, they were offered a test to make sure that they understood the rules. When they received a 100 percent grade, they were graduated from make-up class. The intent of the program was instructional. School authorities needed to stop making assumptions that the children knew how to follow the rules and accepted that some might need extra help in learning these skills.

When you evaluate the results of using consequences, don't look for immediate results. Behavior change is slow, and it is helpful to both you and the student to notice small progress.

1. The plan can be considered a success even if it fails to immediately change the behavior if the student is able to figure out why the plan failed and what to do about it. Sometimes the student recognizes that it was a bad plan and writes a better one. Sometimes the student realizes that the plan was too vague. Sometimes the student understands that he didn't account for contingencies that affected the outcome. These are all valuable learning experiences.

2. The plan can be considered a success if it helps improve the behavior even if it doesn't completely solve it. Suppose a student is constantly fighting, maybe 10 times a week. He writes a plan to stop fighting, and manages to reduce it to seven times a week. Some teachers might see this as a failure because the student is still fighting, but another teacher will say, "I'm pleased that you have reduced the number of times you fight. Your plan must have been helpful. Now let's improve your plan to cut your fighting even more."

Some students don't take the plan seriously and write anything down just to finish the task. If the behavior improves, then the plan helped regardless of the way it was written. If there is no improvement, then the student will develop other plans until the situation improves. By staying with the planning process you tell the student (1) you are serious about the plan and that you will not accept a copout and (2) you believe he has the ability to change his behavior. Students may not try to write a real plan because they don't truly believe that they can change or because they have an external orientation to the problem. Your relentless belief and faith may eventually show the student that change is possible. Teachers' expectations can influence student perception and eventually student performance.

Major Causes of Teacher Failure to Implement Consequences

Regardless of how good your consequences are, they must be implemented consistently to be effective. That means every time that you ignore a rule violation or threaten rather than actually give a consequence, you are giving the message that you are not serious about your contract. You are also telling students that they have at least some chance of breaking the contract without any consequences. This will encourage them to break rules if only to define for themselves what your limits really are. Yet, there are a great many reasons why teachers do not implement consequences, even after they have gone through the trouble of developing them and reaching agreement on them with their class. Here are four of the major causes of failure to implement consequences.

1. The Consequence Is Too Harsh or Incongruent

The teacher is not comfortable with a consequence because it is either too harsh or incongruent with the teacher's style. We are reminded of the teacher who told her class that if they didn't clean the room they would be refused a chance to go on the school field trip to the circus. She made this statement out of desperation and frustration, and the moment she said it she knew she had made a big mistake. She wanted to take her class to the circus more than the class wanted to go. After her threat, she prayed that the class would clean up so she wouldn't be forced to either live with a consequence she did not want to implement or go back on her word. They cleaned up just enough for her to say, "Okay, the room's clean. Let's get on that bus."

To avoid facing this situation when your feelings are running hot after a rule has been broken, it is important to make sure that you can and will live with every consequence on your social contract. Even though you have alternative choices, you still must be willing to implement all consequences so you won't find yourself regretfully implementing an uncomfortable consequence when the stakes are high.

2. Rule Violation Occurs at an Inconvenient Place or Time

The rule violation occurs in a part of the room physically distant from the teacher or at a time when the teacher is involved with other students. Frequently it seems like a lot of work to interrupt a lesson and quietly go over to a student who has just broken the social contract. This is especially true when the teacher is working with one group and the violation occurs elsewhere. It seems almost too much to interrupt the lesson to stop loud talking from the other group. In the long run, more time and energy will be saved when the students see that you consistently implement consequences when the rules have been broken.

While we understand the difficulty of being in two places at the same time, there are ways to implement consequences that minimize disruption. Develop some nonverbal cues which can include touching (such as gently placing a hand on a student's shoulder) or giving a student a specific look that has a prearranged meaning. These cues can be the equivalent of a reminder or warning. Once the look or touch has been established as a cue, you can often use it in situations like those described above. Then it is simply a matter of catching the eyes of the students who are breaking the contract and giving them the look.

Another method that involves self-monitoring is to have each student who violates a rule write his own name on the blackboard. This can also be accomplished nonverbally by pointing to the student and then the blackboard. Yet another possibility is to keep a simple daily chart that includes each student's name with the rules and place a check mark next to the student's name when a rule is violated. You can contact students when time permits and show them the chart. No matter which methods you use, be sure to specify all of these procedures in advance! If these noninterruptive methods do not work, then it is time to stop what you are doing and go over and deliver the consequence at closer proximity.

3. Teachers Are Not Policemen

Teachers do not want the job of policeman and prefer to let students get away with minor rule violations. We agree that the teacher should not always try to catch students breaking rules, and the teacher should not perceive of himself as a policeman. The students also should not see the teacher primarily as a policeman. However, we feel that prevention is the best solution to this problem. By that we mean that the teacher should only have rules that are important to be followed. You won't feel like a policeman if you eliminate rules that you do not mind being broken and only keep those you feel strongly about.

It is also not always necessary to enforce the consequences yourself. One alternative is for your class to hold elections for sheriff and deputy sheriff. Tell your class that you need "officers" who have good eyes and ears, who are not afraid of others, and who are willing to help enforce the consequences. Make your "officers" responsible for keeping the behavioral records that are so important to an effective social contract.

It is interesting that several teachers who have used this method have reported that the elected sheriff and deputy sheriff have often been "hard to reach" kids and they (teachers) have found this to be effective in helping to manage classroom behavior and in providing an acceptable outlet for the difficult student's need to be in control. It is also a good idea to have biweekly or monthly elections so that different students share the responsibility for monitoring their peers' conduct.

4. Teachers Sometimes Lose Their Self-Control

Teachers sometimes get angry and "out of control" themselves. When they feel extremely agitated they prefer to punish as a way of releasing their feelings rather than helping a child grow by implementing a consequence in a rational way. In this situation, the teacher ends up yelling, hitting (this is rare, but occasionally happens), or making up a new punitive consequence that is not part of the social contract. These kinds of reactions happen when the teacher has lost control and needs to express feelings in a very clear and direct way. It is obvious how negative this kind of behavior can be, especially when the class looks to the teacher as a model of appropriate behavior. You can avoid this kind of action by attending to your feelings regularly. Consider it to be part of your job responsibility so that anger, resentment, hostility, and other negatively toned emotions are released in positive and constructive ways. (See Chapter 3 for suggestions on how to accomplish this.)

Developing Effective Consequences

We are continually asked by teachers to help them think of good consequences. It takes skill and practice to develop effective consequences that are not punishments and that have a range of alternatives. Two important skills are needed for the development of effective consequences: creativity and the ability to see the logical extension of the rule violation. It also helps to know your students well and to know what works with them.

Creativity is an important part of consequence development. We know of a teacher who had trouble keeping her 5th grade students from running in the halls. She tried this creative consequence: "Any student who runs in the halls will receive a kiss from me." For her grade level this was a most effective consequence, although it might not have worked for younger children who love teacher kisses or secondary students who also might love teacher kisses for different reasons. The natural and logical aspect of this consequence was stretched a bit; she said that the reason she did not want students running was that she loved them too much to see them hurt themselves, and therefore she would direct an expression of love when she found them running. The consequence was creative, nonpunishing, humorously disturbing, and, most importantly, it worked.

A junior high science teacher was fatigued by the frequent use of name calling (i.e., "your mother _____") that occurred daily. His solution was to announce that beginning immediately, anybody who said uncomplimentary things about someone else in a student's family would be required to call that person. They would have to tell that person what they said and offer an apology. One student tested the rule, the consequence was implemented, and name-calling in the classroom came to an abrupt halt. When the teacher was asked why he decided to do this, he said, "I thought it would be useful for students to learn that another human being, not a thing, is on the receiving end of a put-down."

Here are five strategies that help you create good consequences:

1. Read your rule two or three times.

Close your eyes and imagine a student breaking that rule. See it clearly in your mind. Do not think of it in words, only pictures. Now picture the result of the rule violation—watch it carefully. Often there are natural consequences that will "pop out" at you when you try this experiment. For example, one shop teacher reported that when she visualized students refusing to clean up their mess she saw that it would be impossible for students to find their tools and supplies. She then thought of the consequence of removing any supplies and tools found out of place and putting them in a large, old trunk. At the end of the week, any student who had left tools laying around but had three consecutive days of no mess would get his supplies and tools back. All work was required to be completed, and it was the students' responsibility to find new supplies and tools from home if theirs were in the "trunk."

A high school teacher visualized the problem of students breaking the rule, "People are not for hitting in this class." The purpose for the rule was that someone might get hurt. When he saw a visual image of a student coming to school with bandages and casts he had a brainstorm. He went to one of the local department stores and asked for a display mannequin that was no longer in use. He brought it in and the class named it. (The name turned out to be an acronym for the students in the class.) Every time a student hit another student, the hitter was required to bandage the part of the body he hit and then initial the bandages. For every week that the dummy had no bandages, the class was given a night of no homework.

While you may or may not like these particular consequences, you can see the process used to invent them. By visualizing the rule violation and thinking beyond the incident to what happens after, you can begin to find either symbolic or real consequences that flow naturally from the rule.

2. Collect effective consequences.

Don't hesitate to collect effective consequences from other teachers and administrators. Often teachers feel that they must do everything for themselves when it comes to discipline, although they exchange subject matter ideas more freely. Other teachers may have one or two good consequences for you, if you systematically ask them. One or two good consequences from each teacher in your school could provide you with 50 to 100 consequences depending on the size of your school. We suggest you list some of the rules you are having trouble thinking of good consequences for, each on the top of a blank dittomaster. Then send it around through your mail routing system with a cover letter asking each teacher to write in their favorite consequence for that rule, the one most effective for them. To thank them for their effort, tell them you will run the dittos off and send them each a copy. Include administrators, secretaries, nurses, librarians, substitute teachers, and anyone else in your school who works with the students. You may get better results if the responses are anonymous. You don't have to use any consequences on the list, but usually there are a few gems and many other effective ones to choose from. You might also try modifying some of the ones you reject to be more in tune with your educational philosophy so that they can become helpful to you.

3. Use the students.

Often your students can tell you the consequences that work best for them. There are three basic strategies we have used to get input from students. The first is to spend one class period brainstorming with your students for all rules that lack effective consequences. The second is to allow your students to brainstorm at least one consequence for all of your rules. Another way to accomplish this, without using class time, is to give each student the task of thinking of one or two consequences for a homework assignment. Then you can tabulate them on a ditto and give the students a booklet of their consequences as feedback for their efforts. We strongly suggest that you use as many of the student consequences as possible to show that you value their input and to give them a feeling of contributing to the classroom environment. The third method is asking students who have already graduated to help you think of consequences that would have been effective with them when they were with you. This strategy can be used by teachers at all grade levels. First grade teachers can "borrow" the 2nd graders for a class period. High school students who have already graduated can be invited back during college vacation time for an evening meeting that will also include those students who did not go to college.

We find that some of the most helpful students in this process are those who had trouble following your rules. Make sure you include your chronic problem students in your group because they will provide you with many valuable insights, providing there is enough distance from the problems to make them willing to contribute.

4. Elicit parent suggestions.

Whether through the mail, a telephone interview, or on parent night, ask your parents about the most effective consequences with their children. You can use the same ditto technique as with the faculty and duplicate all responses. These booklets can then be sent to all the parents as a way of thanking them for helping. Parents can always use good suggestions for consequences from other parents. This process also evokes good feelings on the part of the parents and helps them feel more positive about school and you as a teacher.

5. Use your own experiences.

Recall when you were a student. Imagine yourself breaking the rules you have established in your class as a teacher. What consequences would help you to:
1. Stop the misbehavior.
2. Learn from the experience.
3. Be willing to be more cooperative.
4. Not feel embarrassed, angry, or resentful.

If you were a student who never broke any rules (some teachers were like that), remember back to the time when you were the same age as the students you now teach. Picture a student from that time who was a troublemaker. Then imagine that you are this difficult student and go through the process outlined above. When you imagine breaking the rules as either yourself or another student, be as graphic as you can. Recall the actual classroom, the teacher, the other students, and the specific rules that were broken. Ask yourself, "What do I need right now to stop misbehaving?"

A variation of this procedure is to imagine yourself as a student the same age as the students you now teach. Then imagine yourself as a student in your own classroom violating one of your own rules. Again, see this as visually and directly as possible and avoid intellectualizing the process. Then think of what consequences would be effective for you.

Involving Others

If you have other people involved as part of your consequence, it is important for you to receive their support and agreement before you put the social contract into effect. We have seen consequences such as the following:

1. A meeting with the principal, student, and/or teacher to discuss the problem.
2. A meeting with the parent.
3. No library privileges for a week.
4. No school field trips.
5. The student will eat in the classroom, not the cafeteria.
6. The student will be required to make up missed work between classes.
7. The student will make up lost work during gym.
8. The student will sit in the principal's area for one class period.

Each of these consequences involves at least one or more people other than the teacher: parents, administrators, librarians, and other teachers. We find that you can avoid many problems by gaining the support and commitment from all third-party people involved in your social contract. If a principal must keep a child in his office, or be part of a meeting to discuss ways of following the rule, then he must agree prior to your telling your students of this consequence. In gaining third-party support, we suggest you ask the other people what they need from you to be most helpful in the process (usually they at least want a copy of your social contract when completed) and what you might do for them to be helpful in their dealings with your students.

Positive Consequences and Rewards

Many schools approach discipline from the perspective of stopping misbehavior by developing punishments for rule violations. This perspective, many claim, is too negative because acceptable behavior is ignored while attention is given to those who misbehave. Behavior modification researchers believe that by giving most attention to the negative, the implicit message to students is that the way to be noticed and rewarded (with attention) is by breaking rules. Further, they claim, stressing the negative makes the school a dreary place to be, setting up an adversarial relationship between students and teachers. Why should any student behave when all the implicit rewards go to the few students who drive the teacher crazy? These educators advocate the use of positive consequences, which reward students for following the rules.

Positive consequences can fit perfectly within the social contract formula. Each rule can state precisely what happens when the rule is broken and what good things happen when the rule is followed. Positive consequences can be developed for the class as a whole or for individual students who follow the rules. Some rules can have only positive consequences when followed. The loss of the positive consequence is viewed as the natural and logical consequence of not following a rule. For example, Bill Evans, a junior high history teacher had this rule and consequence in his social contract:

Rule
Paper Airplanes are not for throwing during instructional time.

Consequence
For each week of no paper airplane throwing, the class will have a paper airplane throwing contest. Each student will use his best airplane and have three tries at shooting it across the room. The longest throws will earn points. The highest point total will win a free paperback book. Any unauthorized paper airplane will eliminate the contest for that week. A second violation will eliminate it for the next week and so on.

The creative contract stopped paper airplane throwing for the entire year.

Some teachers believe that it is wrong to have positive consequences. They feel that rewarding good behavior is akin to bribing the students or paying them to do what they should do for nothing. They note that it is more important for children to learn to behave correctly and learn responsibility because it feels good intrinsically to do so. They cite studies that indicate that rewarding good behavior decreases it, rather than increases.

Which point of view is correct? Frankly our view is relatively unimportant in helping you grapple with this difficult issue. We prefer that you choose which point of view works best for you, the one which you can feel most comfortable implementing. It is our bias to have at least one positive consequence for each rule, but it has been our experience time and again that if you do not believe in what you are doing, it won't work. And as we stated before, we believe that the process of an agreed upon set of standards is the crucial factor— not the content of the consequence.

We suggest that you choose either one point of view or the other, depending on your view of what school should be teaching students, and, more importantly, what you want to teach our students. If you are comfortable with positive consequences, use many of the same techniques described earlier to think of good, clear positive consequences for each of your rules. If you do not believe in positive consequences, don't use them.

For those of you who are not sure, and we suspect that most teachers fall into this category, we suggest you experiment and see what happens. Choose one or two rules in your social contract that seem to lend themselves to positive consequences. Perhaps you can try one rule that has both positive consequences and negative consequences (unpleasant outcomes) and one rule with only positive consequences (like the airplane example above). Then keep a journal for about a month or two (shorter or longer depending upon your situation) and record how often each rule in your social contract was broken and which of the alternative consequences you implemented. Note how often you actually gave the positive consequences. Most importantly, record how you felt giving the positive consequences and how you felt giving the negative ones. See which was more comfortable for you and which was most effective. If you seemed to enjoy giving the positive consequences, pick one of the least followed rules without a positive consequence and add a couple of positive ones. Continue your journal and see if the addition of the positive consequences made the rule more effective.

Praise Guidelines

One of the most common positive consequences is the use of praise. There are many pros and cons for using praise as a reinforcer. Along with some positive change in behavior, praise also has many negative side effects, which include conformity, stereotyped choices, students downgrading themselves (so that others will build them up), bragging, and role playing.

Harmful Characteristics of Praise

Many responses encourage sharing positive feelings and support including appreciation, enthusiasm, caring, interest and sensitivity. But the kind of praise that can be harmful has each of the following characteristics:[1]

1. Praise is used so an individual will repeat behavior. By telling a person how good some actions is, you increase the probability of the person's doing it again. But this method of responding can be highly manipulative and has many harmful side effects. You're really saying, "You can have my approval only by doing what I decide is right for you."

2. It involves making a value judgment for someone else. In order to praise, unless you praise everything, you must make value judgments that reflect your value system and beliefs about right and wrong. These judgments may contradict the values of the other person, his parents, and, in many cases, his culture. For example, some teachers try to eliminate dialects by positively reinforcing only the child's "proper" use of language. By making decisions for people, praise-giving limits the opportunity for them to develop their own decision-making ability and their willingness to try new, unique behaviors.

3. Praise is in the form of *judgments*, not *facts*. Praise is a positive interpretation of factual data. Judgments reduce the student's ability to self-evaluate and eventually to make decisions. It is better to say what criteria might be used to make a judgment than to give the judgment itself. For example, you can tell your math student, "problems should be neat, show all work, and clearly indicate the answer. How do you think you did?"

It is possible to respond to our students with encouragement, support, care, and concern—without using manipulative, judgmental tactics.

Can Praise Really Be Harmful?

This is a complex question. Many teachers like to use praise because students like it. These students often respond more positively to the teacher and to school. In many cases, the students do what the teacher wants—a pleasant departure from the usual struggle that teachers often face. As praise becomes more and more addicting (the more one gets, the more one needs), students naturally behave in ways that the teacher indicates are positive, for the teacher is the source of satisfying their habit. (Teachers who reduce praise giving don't have it easy. Withdrawal symptoms are difficult to accept, and by cutting down on praise, teachers may face the hostility and mistrust of students who want praise, but aren't getting it.)

Another reason for the general acceptance of praise is a reaction against the image of the schoolmarm with the hickory stick. For many people, the image of a teacher is punitive, critical, and negative. Praise is seen as an alternative to this unrealistic picture. The other side of the coin is that praise, like punishment, is still controlling and potentially dangerous. It is like a coin, one side (praise) is heads, the other (punishment) is tails. Regardless of which side is up, it is still the same coin. It's like choosing between the carrot and the stick— two fine choices for donkeys but not for children.

People who do not need praise show certain characteristics, sometimes recognizable to only themselves:

1. They stop asking, "What does he want?" and ask instead, "What do I want?"
2. They begin to consider a wider array of choices, some of them different from the choices of those who are sources of praise.
3. They stop manipulating others for praise and no longer play praise-getting games such as downgrading themselves, bragging in a way that encourages agreement, and living by the values of others.
4. They begin to discover their own unique, creative, and individual abilities, behaviors, and attitudes. They still try to please others, but their reasons change. They do it to feel good about themselves and for more altruistic reasons, rather than to have others tell them how good they were to do it.
5. They like themselves better. In the long run, their self-concept is improved. They are better able to appreciate themselves without dependency on the approval from others.

Don't Eliminate All Praise

There are some positive effects of praise. Praise can help people master basic skills, work harder for certain extrinsic goals, and overcome extreme cases of poor self-concept.

Students with special learning disabilities, emotional problems, and other disorders that make it critical for them to master basic skills may initially need a high dose of praise so that they can learn to feel good about being able to learn.

If you use praise:

- Praise the behavior, not the child.
- Be sure that the praise is not overdone and matches the situation.
- Present the reason why something is good along with the praise. ("That was a wonderful paragraph you wrote because. . . .")

Here are some guidelines developed by Jere Brophy that can make praise more effective.

Effective Praise:

1. Is delivered contigently.
2. Specifies the particulars of the accomplishment.
3. Shows spontaneity, variety, and other signs of credibility; suggests clear attention to the student's accomplishment.
4. Rewards attainment of specified performance criteria (which can include effort criteria).
5. Provides information to students about their competence or the value of their accomplishments.
7. Orients students toward better appreciation of their own task-related behavior and thinking about problem solving.
7. Uses students' own prior accomplishments as the context for describing present accomplishments.
8. Is given in recognition of noteworthy effort or success at difficult (for this student) tasks.
9. Attributes success to effort and ability, implying that similar successes can be expected in the future.
10. Fosters endogenous attributions (students believe they expend effort on task because they enjoy it and/or want to develop task relevant skills).
11. Focuses students' attention on their own task-relevant behavior.
12. Fosters appreciation of, and desirable attributions about, task relevant behavior after the process is completed.[2]

Alternatives to Praise

An effective alternative to praise is the use of I-statements. An I-statement contains three components. It describes specifically what another person did (the behavior), it tells the other person how you *feel* about their behavior, and when possible it gives the person the *reason(s)* for your feelings. Whereas praise statements are judgmental and non-specific, an I-statement specifically says what can be appreciated about another's behavior. We believe that it is not only possible but also quite desirable to send students messages of appreciation regarding their performance.

A statement of praise would be, "Billy, you behaved very well today." An I-statement of appreciation would be, "Billy, I feel really pleased because you were able to settle your differences by talking with Mary rather than by hitting her, and you successfully completed three class assignments today." The latter message tells Billy specifically what his teacher liked whereas the former statement lacks meaningful feedback. As a way of practicing the skill of communicating with I-statements, start by considering any behavior or performance of a student and complete the following:

1. (Student's name) _____ When you did _____.
2. It made me feel _____.
3. Because _____.

It may become obvious that I-statements are appropriate not only in sharing appreciations but also as an effective alternative to yelling, scolding, lecturing, and threatening when students do things that make us feel sad, annoyed, angry, tense, or disappointed.

We suggest you think about the use of praise in your classroom, and see if you are comfortable offering appreciations and the use of I-statements instead of praise. If so, you may try to cut down your general use of praise and reserve it for situations that really need it. Indiscriminate use of praise not only increases dependency but also eventually becomes a meaningless message.

Other alternatives to verbal praise include nonverbal cues, touching, or asking for self-evaluation such as, "Steve, what do you like about the way you have been following the social contract?"

It is important to understand the delicate difference between praise as a means to manipulate and as a positive consequence—a statement of appreciation for the effort shown by students to follow a rule. Positive outcomes that are naturally and logically related to positive behavior can be an effective method of classroom management.

A Case Study

A school where we recently consulted was experiencing considerable problems in managing the behavior of its students in the cafeteria. Their plan for solving this problem illustrates the use of consequences as well as the other factors that make for an effective social contract.

A discipline committee at this mid-sized, lower middle class elementary school worked on developing a school-wide social contract based upon the principles of Three-Dimensional Discipline. The committee was comprised of two students, two parent representatives, one administrator, the school psychologist, two primary level teachers, and two intermediate-level teachers. The discipline committee identified student cafeteria behavior as the school-wide discipline problem that required attention. As a result of their work, the following plan was developed:

Cafeteria Rules
1. Students will raise their hands and are expected to receive the permission of cafeteria supervisors before they may leave their seats.
2. The cafeteria is a place to talk quietly, not to scream, whistle, or yell.
3. Food is for eating, not for throwing.
4. Fighting is not permitted under any conditions or for any reasons.
5. Each class will have an assigned table in the cafeteria. Students are to clean their area after they have finished their eating.
6. Students are to walk in the cafeteria, not run.
7. Students may go through the lunch line only once—with their class.

Consequences
1. Violation of any of the above rules results in a ✔ mark next to the student's name on a record-keeping form. (A list of names for each class is provided the cafeteria supervisors.)
2. A student's first infraction will result in a warning.
3. A student's second infraction will result in a letter being sent home to the student's parents by the student's teacher and the school principal.
4. The third infraction will require a parent-teacher-principal conference. The student will not be allowed to eat in the cafeteria until this conference occurs.

5. Each rule infraction requires the student to eat at a separate table for the remainder of his lunch period.

6. For "fighting," each infraction results in immediate loss of cafeteria privileges until a parent-teacher-principal conference occurs.

7. The class that receives the fewest violations per week gets a banner, which is presented by the principal, cafeteria supervisors, or "celebrity" guest at a school-wide assembly (two banners—one for primary and one for intermediate).

8. The class with the fewest violations per month is rewarded with a class picnic, field trip, or some other special outing.

Before this plan could be implemented, each teacher was expected to have a thorough discussion with his class. Following this discussion, a test for comprehension was administered to guarantee that each student knew what the rules and consequences were. The most common game that students who misbehave play is to claim that they were unaware of the rules. Since 100 percent is considered a passing grade, students who passed the test could no longer claim lack of knowledge.

Class privileges were tied to passing the test, and students who didn't pass could retake the test as many times as necessary.

The list of rules and consequences was posted in the cafeteria and each classroom and mailed to parents. While this school's discipline problems have not been completely eliminated, the cafeteria is certainly a more pleasant place than it used to be.

The success of this program can be attributed to the specificity of the rules and consequences; school-wide support for the program; and clear guidelines for the teachers, cafeteria supervisors, and students. Each teacher thoroughly discussed the contract with the class, administered and scored a uniform test for comprehension, posted the Cafeteria Contract in the classroom, monitored the records kept by cafeteria supervisors, and consistently implemented consequences. The cafeteria supervisors knew how to keep accurate records of student violators and shared this information with teachers. Also of significance was the inclusion of positive consequences to reward classes which were able to follow the contract.

Cafeteria Class Test (Grades 4-6)

True or
False

1. _____ Students are allowed to go through the lunch line as many times as they would like.
2. _____ Students may move from table to table as they like.
3. _____ Students are allowed to talk quietly.
4. _____ Anyone can go to the library at lunchtime.
5. _____ Students will not be allowed to leave their seats without permission.
6. _____ The cafeteria supervisors can't tell you what to do, so you may talk back to them.
7. _____ We are not responsible for cleaning up our own area in the cafeteria.
8. _____ Spitballs and throwing food are not allowed in the cafeteria.
9. _____ Pushing a classmate off a seat is fun, so it is permitted.
10. _____ Going to the lavatory more than once, except in cases of real emergency, is allowed.
11. _____ Quiet games or school work may be done during lunchtime.
12. _____ Our feet belong on the floor and not on other people.
13. _____ We may climb on the tables and seats at lunchtime.
14. _____ People caught fighting in the cafeteria automatically have to sit at the table set off by itself.
15. _____ Only your own teacher can tell you what to do in the cafeteria.
16. How do students get permission to leave their seats?
17. Name 3 cafeteria rules that must be followed by all students.
18. What happens to students who continue to misbehave in the cafeteria?
19. Is the class that displays the best behavior in the cafeteria recognized in any way?
20. How can I improve my behavior in the cafeteria?

Conclusion

Developing effective consequences is an important part of the social contract and the prevention dimension. Whatever consequences you select, you must be willing to implement them consistently when rules are broken. Effective consequences are clear and specific; they include a wide range of alternative choices; they relate to the rule as directly as possible; and they teach rather than punish.

Consequences, like rules, are not cast in stone when they are included in the social contract. They can be eliminated if ineffective and others can be added. They can be modified at any point in time *except when a rule has just been broken.* No consequence should ever be changed just before it is given to a student rule breaker. Creative consequences can be fun, instructive, and improve classroom communication between teacher and student.

For the Administrator

The following is a list of hints for you to help develop effective consequences for behavior in your school.

1. Help your teachers share effective consequences through the use of the mimeo sharing process described earlier. Collect the best consequences from all the teachers in the school and publish them for all teachers to use. You can also organize groups of students who graduated from your school to meet with teachers to help brainstorm effective consequences. Remember to include a good number of students who were in your office much of the time for disciplinary reasons. These students usually have good ideas about effective consequences.

2. Find out from all your teachers how they plan to include your presence as a consequence. If you are to play a part in any consequence, make sure that you and your teachers agree with just what your role will be. Do not agree to any role with which you are not comfortable. If you cannot support a consequence, tell the teacher about this before you actually become involved. Our general principle is that if a teacher refers a child to you, then you can chose to do what you feel is acceptable to solve the problem. However, you should have a clear, specific range of procedures that are known to the teacher and the students before you receive a referral. It is most important that you inform your teacher of your action shortly after the student is returned to the classroom.

3. Recognize that a teacher's referral is usually an expression of frustration. It is necessary for you to be a good active listener for your teachers, even when you receive referrals that you believe are unwarranted. We have found that many teachers want their administrator to be "tough" with students when

they are referred to your office. You loom as an alternative for many who would really like to open their window and drop the student from the third floor. When you talk with the student and send him back to class, some teachers view this as being "soft" and "ineffective." It is therefore essential that you understand the frustration that teachers experience in response to disruptive student behavior. They need to know that you understand, that they will have your support, and that you also have limits just as they do, which will not always make it possible for you to do as they wish. A referral to the principal is more often an emotional rather than a rational response. Act accordingly.

4. Elicit a plan of action from the referred student. After it is clear to you as to what happened that led to the referral, be sure to have the student write up what he intends to do the next time a similar situation presents itself in the classroom that will prevent trouble from occurring. Share this plan with the teacher and, if possible, include the student in this process.

5. When students are referred to you, it is important to encourage the teacher and student to solve their own problems. Act as a resource or facilitator to help each party develop the plans stated above. It is not helpful to rescue either the teacher or the student. Let them do their own work. On the other hand, you can be very helpful by allowing the teacher to remove a student who can no longer safely remain in class. If a student will not allow a teacher to teach or other students to learn, then that student should be removed from class until he is willing to cooperate.

6. Don't force teachers to use consequences that don't fit their personality or teaching situation. When teachers use consequences they do not believe in, they appear insincere and give the students a double message. Students become confused and begin to see the teacher as hypocritical. It is better to help the teacher find consequences that you both agree are acceptable.

7. Develop a "Consequence Bank." Record consequences used by different teachers, along with a brief statement regarding when and who they are effective with. Share the list with any teacher who needs to find additional consequences.

8. Set the tone for responsibility by modeling behaviors with teachers that focus on locus of control. Encourage teachers to solve their own problems if they are able to do so. Do not ask them to do what is impossible for them with the time and resources they have available. Assist them when they truly need it, and provide resources that can help them solve their own problems. Meet regularly to discuss their needs and to find ways to meet them.

9. Use the criteria listed in this chapter to check the interventions that your teachers are using. Provide the training and support needed to change punishments into consequences.

Endnotes

[1] R. Curwin, "Are Your Students Addicted to Praise?" *Instructor*, (Oct. 1980): 61-62.

[2] J. Brophy, "Teacher Praise: A Functional Analysis," *Review of Educational Research* (Spring 1981): 5-32.

6
Taking Action

O nce your social contract is established, your students should understand the classroom principles, rules, and consequences. When a rule is broken, all you have to do is choose the most effective consequence and that should take care of the misbehavior. If this sounds too simple to be true, it is. The way the consequence is implemented is as important, if not more so, than the consequence itself. For example, imagine a teacher grabbing a student by the collar, holding him against the wall, and shouting in his face, "I don't want you to talk our of turn in class ever again. Do you understand me, you little brat? This is your reminder!" The teacher did enforce a consequence, but the method was brutal.

Many factors influence the success of a social contract: the teacher's attitude toward rule violations, the consistency of enforcement, the ability of the teacher to choose the best consequence, the ability of students to develop their own consequences, the style of consequence implementation, what happens when more than one student is acting out, and what the teacher does when a student refuses to accept a consequence. In this chapter we will explore each of these factors in depth.

Teacher Attitude

Most misbehavior is not directed at the teacher. When teachers personalize rule violations, they may fight unnecessary battles and escalate a simple rule violation into a major confrontation. It is not necessary to make the rule violator an example for the rest of the class. Teachers certainly have a right to teach, and all students have the right to learn, but children also have a right to make mistakes and to behave in ways that are developmentally appropriate for them. Sometimes the demand for children to behave in a certain way is biologically and emotionally unnatural. When a rule is broken, interpret the incident as an opportunity for that child to see the effects of his behavior and that he is capable of other choices.

We do not suggest that teachers should encourage students to break rules. We find that through the social contract process, with all the limits clearly spelled out and a strong component of student decision making, teachers can minimize the occasions when students break rules. View contract violations as an opportunity for generating positive interaction and communication with your students rather than as a personal affront to your authority.

Nine Principles for Consequence Implementation

Once a rule is broken, there are nine principles that will help you convert the situation into a growth experience for you and your students.

1. Always Implement a Consequence: Be Consistent

In the previous chapter we discussed at length the importance of developing consequences that are not punishments and that offer alternatives for each rule violation. Once a rule has been broken, choose the best consequence for the situation and implement it. Your students will learn that there is an order and predictability in your classroom, and that you will honor your contract and expect them to do the same.

2. Simply State the Rule and Consequence

By remembering that the student who broke the rule was not out to get you, you will minimize your need to punish. Lecturing about why the rule is important, scolding and making the student feel guilty, and other forms of retaliation are unnecessary. They only escalate the problem by generating angry and hostile feelings in your students. All that is necessary in most cases is to simply and gently state the rule and the consequence: "Johnny, the rule in this class is that there is no talking when other students are talking. The consequence is that you will be silent for five minutes." The best time to explain the importance of the rule is when it is developed with the social contract, not immediately after it is broken. Explanations right after a rule is broken are viewed as lectures, and students generally don't listen to them.

We often forget to be concise because we want to make sure our students have the same understanding we do. Long explanations do not help the students understand better, especially right after a rule violation. If the student needs help following the rules, provide instruction after school or when you can both be alone, and demonstrate how to follow them. Then have the student practice the correct behavior. This is far more effective than long lectures.

3. Be as Physically Close to the Student as Possible When You Implement a Consequence: Use the Power of Proximity

The closer you are to a student when you calmly explain the rule and consequence, the more effective you will be. We recommend that for junior and senior high school students, you calmly go as close as conversation distance, which is about arm's length away, then move one step closer. This is a safe yet powerful distance for delivering your message. With younger children, you can move even closer, looking directly into the student's eyes as you state the rule and consequence.

4. Make Direct Eye Contact When You Deliver a Consequence

As you repeat the rule and consequence, look directly at the student and capture his eyes with yours. A gentle hand on the shoulder is an effective adjunct to eye contact. After you have finished delivering your message, maintain eye contact for a second or two and continue to maintain it as you slowly move away. Continue with your lesson.

If a student refuses eye contact, maintain your attempt for about a minute. It is difficult for a student to continue to ignore you. Once the student looks at you, lock your eyes and deliver the consequence. Don't fight the student more than a minute. If the student won't look, say the message softly without eye contact and walk away. Later you might want to talk with the student to see if he has a problem making eye contact.

Some cultures view eye contact as a sign of disrespect. In some Native American, Asian, and European cultures, for example, children do not look at adults in the eye. Be aware of cultural differences and don't force a student to behave in a way that is not comfortable for him.

5. Use a Soft Voice

Generally, the closer you are to the student and the softer your voice, the more impact you will make. In our workshops, we try the following experiment to demonstrate this principle. We ask a teacher to stand about 20 feet away from the experimenter. The experimenter shouts a consequence from that distance, then moves three steps closer and delivers the same consequence using a softer voice. This sequence is repeated until the experimenter is about conversational distance using conversation loudness. Then the experimenter goes one step closer and delivers the message in a tone that is barely louder than a whisper. Once the experiment is completed, the teacher is asked which consequence would be the most effective in stopping a misbehavior. Invariably, the closer, soft consequence is selected as the most effective. We suggest that you try this experiment for yourself with a colleague or friend. Be sure your comments are clear and slowly paced. Try being both the sender and the receiver of the consequence. In essence you want to deliver a consequence in a soft, well-modulated tone that is convincing without being intimidating.

With practice, you can deliver a message so that only the student hears it. This ensures privacy and maintains the dignity of the student.

6. Catch a Student Being Good

About every 15 to 20 minutes (2 or 3 times in a secondary class), catch a student being good. Using the same technique described above, speak softly so no other student can hear. Tell the student you like the way he is paying attention, or that he did a nice job on his homework because it was very detailed, or that the questions he is asking in class are very thought provoking. (See the discussion in Chapter 5 before using this praise.)

This strategy helps ensure the students' privacy because other students will never know if your private discussion was positive feedback or giving a consequence. The student might make the conversation public, but then it becomes his responsibility to deal with the loss of privacy.

7. Don't Embarrass the Student in Front of His Peers

One of the most significant reasons for using a soft voice and being in close proximity is that it is important to avoid power struggles that emerge when a student needs to save face with peers. Public displays of consequence implementation embarrass the student and often make it difficult for the student to hear the message. Privacy is always helpful in implementing consequences. Remember, your goal is to keep teaching, and you need to minimize words or gestures to get the message across without worsening the situation. Preventing the rule breaker from public embarrassment will give all of the other students in class the message that their right to privacy will be maintained, that their integrity will be preserved, and that they are expected to behave in class.

8. Be Firm Anger Free when Giving Your Consequence

We have seen teachers who give consequences as if they are sorry that they have to give them. These teachers are telling their students that they fear them, and the students learn quickly that this teacher is easily intimidated. Often this kind of delivery ends with the teacher asking the student to stop or a consequence will be delivered later. For example, "Oh, Johnny, please stop talking, okay? Please, because, uh, if you don't, I will have to ask you to stay after school with me. Now please, won't you just be a bit more cooperative? Okay, then?"

This is an extreme example, but when the tone of voice and the body posture of the teacher reinforce a verbal apology, the message is loud and clear that this teacher is not serious and can be intimidated by the students.

On the other hand, an overly aggressive delivery can create hostility, resentment, and fear. These are not emotions that lend themselves to setting up a growth producing interchange. Imagine a teacher pointing his index finger at a student and shouting in a loud voice, "Johnny, this is the third time today you have gotten out of your seat. Now I'll see you after school, *buddy!*" We find that the most effective delivery is neutral and devoid of either fear or hostility from the teacher. It is delivered assertively. Words are spoken slowly, and the teacher presents himself with assurance and confidence. The teacher demonstrates seriousness, caring, and support to the student.

9. Do Not Accept Excuses, Bargaining, or Whining

If you are sure that the rule was broken, implement the consequence as directly and expeditiously as possible. If the student makes excuses, simply repeat the rule and consequence, calmly and softly, until he stops.

Teacher: Roger, the rule in this class is that only one person may speak at a time. The consequence is five minutes of no talking.

Roger: But it wasn't my fault; Susie started it first.

Teacher: The rule in this classroom is that only one person may speak at a time. The consequence is five minutes of no talking. (Teacher backs away maintaining eye control.) Now class, who can tell me what the square root of 16 is?

If the student tries to bargain with you, by promising never to do it again, or by offering you something else, it is better to ignore the offer and simply state the rule and consequence again. Or you can acknowledge the offer, and then restate the rule and consequence.

Teacher: Sally, the rule in this classroom is that people are not for hitting. Your consequence is to come in after school and I will help you practice other ways of expressing your anger.

Sally: If I don't have to stay after school tonight, I promise I will never hit again, please.

Teacher: You promise never to hit again, and I'm glad. But this time, you hit Judy and the rule in this classroom is that people are not for hitting. To help you keep your promise, your consequence is to come in after school and learn some ways to express your anger besides hitting.

Younger students might whine when given a consequence. We allow students to whine as long as they want but not in a way that disturbs the class. Ask the whiner to go to your time-out area where he can whine until he has it out of his system. Most students can only whine for about five minutes, usually less if there is no reinforcement. Older students might challenge your tenacity, and you need to remain calm and firm to this challenge.

Don't Be a Victim

Often, the way we communicate nonverbally is a more powerful message than our words. Your students read the way you walk around the classroom every day, and the message you communicate reveals how much they can affect your behavior. The following was condensed from a news story that appeared in the *Boston Globe*, January 20, 1981.

It's not your age.

It's not your sex.

It's not even the mere fact of walking alone in a high-crime area that appears to make some people more "mugg-able" than others.

It's the way you walk, according to research by a New York marketing professor and a group of dance analysts, that sends out easy-to-assault or hard-to-assault cues to potential assailants.

Hofstra University marketing and communications professor Betty Grayson became interested in the fact that some police officers and many imprisoned criminals seemed able to tell at a glance which potential victims would offer the least resistance to attack.

Were the cops and muggers just using some kind of intuition? Or were there specific behavioral cues—which no one seemed able to specify—to which they were respond-ing?

Grayson began her study by using a fixed, hidden videotape camera to take frontal shots as people walked along the street. She kept the camera on each subject for about seven seconds, the length of time, she figured, it would take a mugger to size up a victim.

She and three assistants sorted the subjects into four categories of 20 people each: young women (under 35); young men (under 35); older women (over 45); and older men (over 45). Armed with the videotapes, Grayson then talked to inmates at the Rahway, N.J., prison who helped her create a scale of "muggability"—or as she puts it, like-lihood of assault.

For methodological reasons, Grayson needed two sets of inmates, the first to view the tapes and help her create a rating scale—in the criminals' own words—of "muggabil-ity," and the second group to rate the videotaped subjects on that scale.

Grayson first showed the tapes to about 60 inmates. She audiotaped their comments and listed the main reactions on the blackboard. She then asked the inmates to rank their responses in order, which ranged from, "Most assaultable, a very easy rip-off," to "Would avoid it, too big a situation, too heavy."

With this 1 to 10 "muggability" scale, Grayson then asked a second group of 53 prisoners—all convicted of violent assaults on strangers—to rate the 60 videotaped subjects on their potential "muggability."

Whenever more than half the prisoners agreed that a potential victim fell into the first three most-easy-to-mug categories, Grayson put the videotape into a special category, which ultimately contained 20 people, male and female, young and old.

With the help of Jody Zacharias, executive director of the Laban Institute of Movement Studies, Grayson analyzed the way these 20 people walked. The researchers used a movement-analysis technique created by an Austro-Hungarian dancer-choreographer, Rudolf Laban, born in 1879.

Upon analysis, the 20 most muggable people turned out to have a number of distinctive movements, five of which, Grayson says, were apparently crucial in signaling vulnerability.

The most muggable people tended to take strides that were of unusual length, either too short or too long. Instead of walking heel to toe, they walked flatfooted. Instead of swinging their left arm while striding with their right foot, they moved their left arm and left foot, then right arm and right foot together. Instead of the usual figure-eight like sway of upper body and lower body, the most muggable people seemed to move their torsos at cross purposes to the bottom half of their bodies.

By isolating the movements that seem to trigger "muggability," the researchers say, people, especially victims of multiple assaults, may be taught how to move without signaling vulnerability.[1]

Teachers, like the walkers described in this article, can communicate muggability and non-muggability. In the classroom, this means that an assertive gait and gestures communicate confidence, control, and positive feelings of esteem. When you carry yourself in this manner, you are telling your students that you feel good about yourself and feel good about being in your classroom. If you are not sure about what your body language is communicating to your students, have yourself videotaped for a 20-minute teaching segment. (If your school system does not have the equipment, you can usually work out an arrangement with the teaching department at your local school of education.)

Watch your tape and see how you walk, how you gesture, and what messages you send to your students. If you feel that your non-verbal cues are communicating muggability, change slowly. Being comfortable with yourself will help you feel comfortable with your walk. Practice breathing and muscle relaxation as described in Chapter 3. Books on assertiveness training may also be used.

Once you have learned to relax, let your walk flow naturally from a relaxed, confident position. Practice walking in this relaxed way in your classroom when no one else is present. Imagine yourself teaching, interacting with students, implementing consequences. Feel yourself in charge of your classroom. Feel the power of being in control. It is a power you demonstrate through relaxed confidence, not force. It might be helpful to work with a colleague who wants to practice the same skill. You can observe each other teaching and give each other feedback to see if you have transferred the skills from practice to real teaching situations.

Avoiding Power Struggles

One of the most troublesome problems that teachers face is "the power struggle." The typical power struggle occurs when the teacher implements a consequence and a student refuses to comply. The cycle continues when the teacher, in a more adamant tone, demands that the student comply and the student once again refuses or makes a wisecrack. The following example is a typical beginning for a power struggle.

Teacher: Bill, the rule in this classroom is to do your own work. Your consequence is to learn how to do your own work after school under my supervision.

Bill: (In front of whole class) I'm not coming, I have a job to do after school.

Teacher: (Upset and wanting to show class who is in charge) Yes, you will! Be here at three o'clock, understand?

Bill: (needing to save face in front of his peers) I won't be here at three o'clock, and you can't make me.

Teacher: (Now the pressure is really on. He feels he must win) You will be here or else.

Bill: (Aware that the whole class is watching him) I won't be here and that's final.

By the time teacher and Bill reach this point, they have both risked their pride on the outcome of this power struggle in front of an audience of students. The stakes are high, and although neither wants to lose, it is impossible for either to win. If the teacher forces Bill to come after school, Bill will make the teacher pay later. If Bill doesn't come, the teacher will feel ridiculed and will punish Bill later.

Jeffrey Z. Rubin's article in *Psychology Today* describes an activity that shows how a power struggle can become a trap.

The psychological principles of self-entrapment are very similar to those that con artists employ to ensnare others.

One devilishly simple and effective example of entrapment is a game known as the Dollar Auction, invented about 10 years ago by Martin Shubik, an economist at Yale. As his proving ground, Shubik allegedly used the Yale University cocktail-party circuit. Anyone can make some money—but perhaps lose some friends—by trying it out at a party.

Take a dollar bill from your pocket and announce that you will auction it off to the highest bidder. People will be invited to call out bids in multiples of five cents until no further bidding occurs, at which point the highest bidder will pay the amount and win the dollar. The only feature that distinguishes this auction from traditional auctions, you point out, is the rule that the second-highest bidder will also be asked to pay the amount bid, although he or she will obviously not win the dollar. For example, Susan has bid 30 cents and Bill has bid 25 cents; if the bidding stops at this point, you will pay Susan 70 cents ($1 minus the amount she bid) and Bill, the second-highest bidder, will have to pay you 25 cents. The auction ends when one minute has elapsed without any additional bidding. . . .

Several researchers have had people play the Dollar Auction game under controlled laboratory conditions and have found that the participants typically end up bidding far in excess of the $1 prize at stake, sometimes paying as much as $5 or $6 for a dollar bill. The interesting question is, of course, why? What motivates people to bid initially and to persist in a self-defeating course of action?

Thanks primarily to the extensive research of Allan Tegar, a social psychologist at Boston University, the question has been answered. Teger found that when Dollar Auction participants were asked to give reasons for their bidding, their responses fell into one of two major motivational categories: economic and interpersonal. Economic motives include a desire to win the dollar, a desire to regain losses, and a desire to avoid losing more money. Interpersonal motives include a desire to save face, a desire to prove one is the best player, and a desire to punish the other person.

Economic motives appear to predominate in the early stages of the Dollar Auction. . . . As the bidding approaches $1—or when the amount invested equals the objective worth of the prize—the tension rises. At this stage Teger has found, the participants experience intense inner conflict, as measured by physiological measures of anxiety and nervousness; about half of them then quit the game.

People who remain in the auction past the $1 bid, however, typically stick with it to the bitter end—until they have exhausted their resources or their adversary has quit. Interpersonal motives come to the fore when the bid exceeds the objective value of the prize. Even though both players know they are sure to lose, each may go out of his or her way to punish the other, making sure that the other person loses even more, and each may become increasingly concerned about looking foolish by yielding to the adversary's aggression. Teger found that this mutual concern occasionally leads bidders to a cooperative solution to the problem of how to quit without losing face: a bid of $1 by one player, if followed by a quick final raise to $2 by the second, allows the first person to quit in the knowledge that both have lost equally.[2]

We have used the Dollar Auction game in our workshops to show how difficult it is to get out of a power struggle. We have slightly modified the auction, using a $20 bill instead of a $1 bill and starting the bidding at $10. We also go up in 50 cent increments. When the bidding escalates to between $25 and $30, we stop and talk about power struggles.

Generally there are only two ways out of the Dollar Auction trap. The first is for both remaining players to stop at $20 and $20.50 respectively. Then they can share their losses and gains together so that each loses a net of $10.25. The second is for one player to stop and accept his loss (losing $20 is better than losing $40). These two options are the basis for stopping all power struggles in the classroom.

1. Be Aware of How Power Struggles Can Entrap You

Commit yourself to avoiding power struggles, even if it means initially backing down. Remember that continuation of a power struggle makes you look foolish and out of control. You must be prepared to see long-term victory (a cooperative, positive classroom climate) as more important than short-term winning. By victory we mean changing a potentially negative situation into an opportunity for positive communication and mutual trust.

2. Take Care of Yourself Emotionally

We have stated time and time again that it is critical for you not to carry anger, resentment, and other hostile feelings once a discipline situation is over. If you are angry with a student from an incident that happened the day before, you might enter a power struggle just to flex your muscles and show who is boss. Don't! Start fresh each day.

3. Ignore Students' Initiating Power Struggles

When a student tries to engage you in a power struggle, back off and ignore his attempt. Often, by simply ignoring the student's "hook," the power struggle is over before it starts.

Teacher: (Walks slowly over to Ralph.) Ralph, the rule in this classroom is that people are not for hitting. The consequence is for you to stay after school today and practice other ways of showing your anger.

Ralph: It wasn't my fault and you can't make me come after school.

Teacher: (Maintains eye contact with Ralph for a few seconds and returns to the front of the room) Now class, who can tell me who was the only president to resign from office?

In this example, the teacher listened to Ralph's protest but did not acknowledge it in any way. If the teacher has said, "Yes, you will have to stay after school!", Ralph would have had to show the teacher and all of the other students in class that he was not going to show up. By ignoring the hook, the teacher has opened the door for Ralph to comply with the consequence. Before the class was over for the day, the teacher waited by the door and said privately in a calm, yet firm, voice, "Ralph, I expect to see you here after school!"

4. Acknowledge the Student's Feelings

In the above example, the teacher simply ignored the hook put out by the student. If the student had persisted, or if the teacher preferred to interact more directly to the hooking statement, he might have acknowledged the student's feelings by active listening and reflection.

Teacher: (Walks slowly over to Ralph.) Ralph, the rule in this classroom is that people are not for hitting. The consequence is for you to come after school today and learn some other ways to express your anger.

Ralph: It wasn't my fault, and I am not coming back after school.

Teacher: (Slowly begins to walk back to resume teaching position.)

Ralph: I said I'm not coming back after school.

Teacher: (Returns to close proximity to Ralph.) Ralph, I can see that you are upset and angry, and that you feel that the hitting wasn't your fault. I understand how you might feel. However, this is not the time to discuss it, so let's get back to our lesson, and we can discuss our problem later.

By accepting that the problem was theirs and not only the student's, and by indicating that he understood Ralph's feelings, the teacher in this example prevented what might have escalated into a classic power struggle.

Becoming an active listener requires skill and practice. You must be able to step inside the student's experience and develop a sense for the feelings that are motivating the student's obnoxious behavior. Many troubling situations can be defused by listening with empathy to a student. Active listening means that you must make an educated guess about what a student is feeling and you then paraphrase these feelings by restating them to the student.

Louis, a student who demonstrated his power by loudly accusing Mr. Neilson of running a boring class, was sent to the office for such disruptive behavior. Mr. Neilson feared losing control of the class and felt a need to assert his power. Sending to the office was his solution, and it was effective in removing the source of the problem, except Louis was always back for more the next day. One day, after Mr. Neilson had learned how to actively listen, Louis did his thing. But instead of using the standard threat of classroom exclusion, Mr. Neilson approached Louis as he continued his lesson and quietly said, "Louis this class is probably the most boring, awful class you have to attend. It must be a real drag for you to be here. You probably wish you could be doing something else, and after class today, if you would like, I would be willing to discuss with you some ideas that you might have about how you could enjoy this class more." After this exchange, Mr. Neilson immediately returned to the day's lesson, and after the class, the two began a constructive process of discovering what Louis needed to be less disruptive.

5. Privately Acknowledge Power Struggles

Tell the student directly that a power struggle is developing and you want to stop it. Often, you can defuse a potential power struggle by pointing it out to the student.

Teacher: Sally, the rule in this classroom is that only one person may speak at a time. You have chosen five minutes in Siberia (time-out area).

Sally: I was just asking what the homework was. It's not fair. I can speak if I want to.

Teacher: Sally, it seems that we both can't win. You want me to know that you can talk if you want to, and I want you not to talk for five minutes to help you learn to follow the rule. I think that if we both try to prove who is the winner, neither one of us would like that very much, and in the end we would both lose. Let's calm down and talk about it later when neither one of us feels as angry as we do now.

In this example, the teacher explained to Sally what might happen if they each escalated the situation and suggested they discuss it later. This effectively ended the need on the part of the student to show her power, and in the end, both the teacher and student won.

6. Do Not Try to Embarrass Students into Submission

Keep all communication private between you and the student. Do not embarrass the student in front of his peers. Power struggles are created when two parties need to win. The stakes are always increased when the struggle is publicly displayed. The teacher feels a need to show the other students who is boss, and the student needs to show the other students that he is not intimidated by the teacher. Often, both teacher and student make statements when others are present that they are both sorry for later but are locked into with no way out. If you can keep most of your communication private, you eliminate much of the need for you and the student to save face.

If you find yourself already into a power struggle, find a way out. If there is no escape, the escalation will continue until both sides are hurt, regardless of the final outcome. Even if the student wants to stop, it is very difficult to do so; the teacher is responsible for stopping the struggle. Finding an out might simply be stopping and shaking the student's hand, saying, "Wow, we almost got into a real argument. Let's both calm down and discuss it later. I didn't mean to let this get so out of hand. How about you?"

We feel that stopping a power struggle before it starts is a strength, not weakness, but follow-up is critical. If the student still refuses the consequence, then it is critical that you not allow him back into your class until he has accepted the consequence. One rule you can include in your social contract is, "Students who do not accept a consequence will not be permitted to stay in class until they have done so." You need to check with your principal or vice principal to let them know that you intend to have this policy. Most principals will cooperate with your request and set up a system for out-of-school suspension, in-school suspension, or some other short-term arrangement. When you explain your need for this policy, make it clear that you will not abuse it by asking for suspensions from your class unless it is absolutely necessary for you to maintain control. You might also ask what you can do for your principal to help him make your new policy work from his perspective. We have found that the vast majority of principals are thrilled when a teacher provides any sensible discipline program to them, and most will be supportive.

In the example cited earlier, if Ralph had not come in after school, then he would have been met by the principal or vice principal before school the next day and informed that he could not return to Mr. X's class until he honored the consequence. Furthermore, Ralph is responsible for all of the work missed during his absence. It is now

Ralph's choice to accept the consequence and return to class or wait it out. Most students will accept the consequence and end the matter quickly. By not publicly flexing his power, the teacher has shown the other students that he will not embarrass them or allow them to hook him into a power based game. He has quietly and confidently taken charge. When Ralph did not appear in class the next day, all of the students wondered where he was. Ralph's absence made a strong statement of the authority of the teacher, one which was much stronger than if he had tried to win a verbal argument with Ralph in class.

If a student is temporarily suspended from your classroom, privately "welcome him home" when he returns. When students are suspended, they are uncertain of how the teacher and other students feel about them. It is not uncommon for them to feel stupid, resented, or outcast. Greet the student at the door and privately say something like, "I'm glad you're back. I know we had a problem yesterday, but now we solved it. It's over for me. I hope it is for you, also. Let's start off fresh and have a good class together."

There is one other strategy that is helpful for avoiding power struggles. We find that if you can identify students who are prone to engage in a power struggle, you can develop a mutual plan to deal with the problem through prevention. Meet with the student at a time when you can both be alone and when you have no problem between you. Tell the student that you know he sometimes has a problem accepting a consequence. Ask what you can do when this happens to make it easier for the student to accept it. Such students usually want the teacher to be less public and are often willing to accept a nonverbal cue, such as a head nod, so that he will know, but the other students will not. Brainstorm three or four strategies together that help both of you avoid power struggles in the future. When you must implement a consequence with the student, be sure to follow your agreed upon guidelines.

How to Implement Consequences when More than One Student Is Acting Out

So far in this chapter we have focused on situations in which the teacher has dealt with a single student who has violated the social contract. Sometimes you may be faced with three or four students who are acting out at the same time. The better you know the dynamics of your class, the more effective you will be in handling this type of situation.

The first step is to pick the one student in the acting-out group who is the one the other students respect the most, fear the most, or are amused by the most. Stop the misbehavior with this student first. Often that is enough to stop it for everyone else. If you have two opinion makers acting out at the same time, pick the more prominent one first, and stop the misbehavior with him; then go over to the second one and repeat the same process.

Occasionally, you can effectively deal with a whole group. The best time to do this is when they are in close proximity with each other, perhaps working together at a table. Walk over to the group slowly and calmly. Make eye contact with each student before you speak. Then state the rule and consequence scanning the entire group slowly with your eyes. Maintain eye contact. When you are finished, scan the group one more time with your eyes to make sure they know you mean business.

Usually, it is not effective to yell at the class as a whole. This only leads to more confusion and noise. If you continue to have problems with groups of students, it might be worth your while to have a class meeting and see if you and your students can think of any strategies for minimizing the problem.

When several students in a class are acting out, it becomes necessary for you to acknowledge a mismatch between the needs of your students and what you are doing or not doing. Sometimes a solution is as simple as walking about the whole room as you present a lesson to keep in close occasional proximity with all students. At other times you may need to substantially modify your curriculum or method of presentation for change to occur. When you are confronted with a large-group classroom discipline problem, you must maintain an attitude of calm, a security about yourself, and a willingness to explore change.

For the Administrator

Teachers and administrators need to take direct action when rules are broken. The best action is to choose the most effective consequence from the range of pre-established consequences related to the broken rule. When a rule is broken, it is not the time for lectures, scolding, bargaining, accepting excuses, moralizing, or making a public display of the student. You can be a role model for effective consequence implementation in working with both students and teachers. You may also demonstrate effective consequence implementation at a faculty meeting, or preferably at smaller group meetings such as a support group so that teachers will be less inhibited to ask questions and try role playing themselves.

When you observe your teachers in the classroom, you can use the list of nine principles for effective action as a feedback instrument. As with any observation, it is important that you share your plan with the teacher before the observation and receive agreement that this type of feedback will be helpful. If a teacher is not interested in using the list for feedback, it will not help to do so anyway. Remember that your goal in using the principles is to improve discipline not to collect information for a formal evaluation.

Help teachers learn how to handle most of their own discipline problems. Sending students to the office not only burdens you and your office staff, it weakens the teacher's leadership. Most infractions can be handled in the classroom if they do not escalate into power struggles. Once they escalate, the teacher usually has no recourse but to kick the student out of the room. Many of the problems sent to you might have been solved by the teacher if not allowed to escalate.

Teachers need to know that the administration will support them if a student fails to accept a consequence. Honor the "insubordination rule" for those teachers who need it. At the same time, set up a policy that gives students a chance to cool off and think before they are labeled insubordinate. You might use a form of this simple model:

1. Teacher gives a consequence.
2. Student refuses, insults teacher, makes a scene in class, or tries to hook the teacher into a power struggle.
3. The teacher uses a de-escalation strategy, such as:
   - Active listening
   - Ignoring attempt by student to fight
   - Speaking with student later
   - Giving student time out (providing a chance for the student to cool down)
4. Teacher gives student time to think about whether or not to accept the consequence without pressure or threat. The student already knows about the insubordination rule and the consequence.
5. If student still chooses not to accept the consequence, administration intervenes. The insubordination rule goes into effect.
6. Administrator meets with teacher later to discuss steps 3 and 4. If the teacher omitted them, provide coaching to help them learn how to include steps 3 and 4 in the future. If they were

included, see if the teacher's skill in using them can be improved. In either case, remember that teachers' main gripes about administration are lack of support with discipline. Coach without reprimanding. Defusing power struggles is not easy. Emotions run high, and the teacher may not have developed the strength to back away. Teachers need to have their dignity maintained before they can learn to maintain the dignity of their students.

You can use the Dollar Auction technique described earlier to introduce the topic of a power struggle. Once the auction is complete, discuss how various faculty handle a power struggle once they are in it, and what they do to stop getting caught in the first place.

When you see a power struggle between a student and teacher, you can serve as a "fact-finder" or "mediator" to help bring an end to a dispute. Recognize that power struggles are caused by two people having a different set of "wants" with each believing that the other is unwilling to compromise. Try to get the student and the teacher to identify their demands to each other, and then try to solicit a commitment from each to do one thing for the other. It is sometimes helpful to serve as a third person in helping to resolve such disputes.

Endnotes

[1] Judy Foreman, "How Muggable Are You? Clue is Your Walk," *Boston Globe*, January 20, 1981.
[2] J. Rubin, "The Psychology of Entrapment," *Psychology Today*, March 1981, 58-59.

7
Stress and Discipline

Discipline with dignity means dignity for the teacher as well as for the students. Unfortunately, dealing with disruptive students is a major source of stress confronted by teachers. Classroom management is improved when you remain confident, secure, and cool in the face of unruly behavior. In order to do this, you must have a variety of strategies that you can use to reduce the tension created by disruptive students. Throughout this book we will remind you to take good emotional care of yourself. This chapter offers several options to help you express your feelings, release tension, and experience a new level of inner calm.

During the last few years, the issue of teacher stress and burnout has received increasing attention. As Hendrickson points out,[1] a burned-out teacher is losing, or has lost, the energy and enthusiasm needed to teach children. Little if any joy remains in the teaching process. Coming to work becomes an unpleasant chore, and excitement focuses around how many days, hours, and minutes are left until Friday or the next vacation. The symptoms of burnout include physical, social, and emotional maladies such as headaches, exhaustion, sleeplessness, ulcers, frequent colds, chronic back pain, loss of appetite, depression, frustration, irritability, low morale, feelings of inadequacy, absenteeism, boredom, outbursts of anger, apathy, anxiety, and lack of concern for self and others as well as a loss of pride in the job.

While there are many factors that drain the energy reserves of the contemporary classroom teacher, there is no doubt that the leading cause of teacher burnout is the tiring and exhausting effects of disruptive student behavior. The National Education Association (NEA) cites a number of reasons for teacher burnout, but the big one is the pervasive sense that teachers have lost effective control of their classroom. Many teachers are faced with the daily reality of going to work and being uncertain of their own safety. The problems of the inner city have received much attention because of the increasing number of student assaults upon teachers. Many of these teachers are satisfied to avoid physical harm by yielding to the many minor disruptive events, which have a cumulative effect of leading to stress, tension, and ultimately burnout. Teachers in suburban and rural schools also find more and more of their time and energy devoted to dealing with disruptive students, who come to school unmotivated to learn and with poor self-concepts. Some students only connect with school through displays of power, which often draw the teacher into endless power struggles. To illustrate the symbiotic relationship of stress and discipline, we invite you to imagine a classroom situation in which every student was interested in the lesson, was prepared for class, did not make derogatory remarks, had no weapons, resolved disputes through talking (rather than fighting), followed the rules, and accepted the consequences when rules were broken. We maintain that were such a situation the norm, there would be few instances of teacher burnout.

What Do Teachers Say about Stress?

We recently conducted a study that was comprised of a series of interviews with teachers who represented a broad spectrum of teaching experience, type of school, and grade level taught. We asked them to describe the stressors they viewed in their work settings and what physical symptoms or emotional difficulties they attributed to teaching. In addition, we wanted to know what elements teachers would describe as the most difficult classroom problems that they deal with on a recurring basis.[2]

Teachers in our study indicated a variety of physical and emotional reactions to stress that they believed to be job-related. Among these are headaches, backaches, tension in the neck and shoulders, loss of emotional control, ulcers, emotional withdrawal, heart conditions, drug and alcohol use, lockjaw, and suicide. The scope of perceived job-related illnesses would seem to confirm the notion of Bloch's "combat fatigue" and indicates teaching is a "high-risk" profession.

Disruptive Students and Stress

The most frequently reported source of teacher stress in our study was student provocation. One teacher's comments summarize what many others said.

> Ultimately, however, the greatest stress for a teacher probably revolves around student behaviors and classroom management. Students who lie, cheat, swear, steal, cut classes, fight, vandalize, never turn in homework, are rude and disruptive or unmotivated are sources of extreme stress for teachers. Coping with difficult students within the classroom framework produces the ultimate in stress because to some degree and in one way or another, the above situations can manifest themselves almost daily. Coping effectively with these students means the difference between a successful teaching-learning situation on the one hand, and a stressful, unproductive experience on the other.

Effectively coping with such students is probably the most difficult task for the contemporary teacher. Disruptive student behavior is difficult for many teachers to cope with because the teacher must often walk a tightrope between being firm and yet unoffensive to the student, parent(s), or the administration. Many educators come to believe that they have no impact and cannot affect student behavior.

With the exception of Thoresen et al. (1973),[3] most research on stressors related to disruptive students has concluded with vague generalities. While it is useful to know that most Gallup polls in the last decade have rated "discipline" at or near the top of public concern regarding its schools, and that teachers consistently rate "managing disruptive students" to be their leading stressor, investigators have typically failed to pinpoint what the exact meaning of "discipline" is to teachers. One goal of our study was to collect data from teachers that would shed light on the important issue of specificity regarding discipline. To this end, subjects were asked to list and explain the three most difficult recurring events they face in the classroom.

A cumulative list of events follows. Although some items were mentioned more than once, this list represents items that were viewed as distinct enough from others to warrant a separate entry.

1. Belligerent and disruptive behavior regarding class failure.
2. Excuses and "song-and-dance" routines about teacher unfairness.
3. Lack of motivation on the part of students with a history of failure.
4. Lack of interest in the class (including apathy about learning, doing homework, coming to class unprepared).
5. Vandalism (writing on desks often mentioned).
6. Stealing.
7. Expressions of bigotry in the classroom.
8. Cheating.
9. Teacher harassment (verbal abuse directed at teacher).
10. Frequent and persistent talking out-of-turn.
11. Put-down or rejection of one student by another or by a group of students.
12. High noise level.
13. Chronic class cutting.
14. Not paying attention.
15. Leaving seat without permission.
16. Lateness to class.
17. Temper outbursts in class.

Five items were mentioned by 50 percent or more of all teachers.

1. Excuses and charges of unfairness.
2. Lack of interest in the class (unpreparedness, apathy about learning, not doing homework).
3. Frequent and persistent talking out-of-turn.
4. Put-down or rejection of one student by another or by a group of students.
5. Belligerent and disruptive behavior in class.

Our study offers a glimpse into the emotionally stressful lives of teachers and what they are attempting to do to cope with their stress. As you can see, many teachers are experiencing what they believe are job-related symptoms of stress that can be summarized as being caused by one or more of these problems: (1) inappropriate student behavior, (2) job inflexibility, limited professional opportunities, (3) lack of administrative support related to disruptive students, and (4) social irresponsibility. The data revealed that teachers at all grade levels identified disruptive student behavior as their leading work-related stressor.

The feelings of frustration have become deep seated among some teachers who increasingly find themselves overwhelmed by the demands of the job with little appreciation coming from administrators, students, the school board, parents, or each other. A junior high teacher's poignant comments while perhaps overstated help clarify circumstances confronting today's teacher:

> Today's youths appear to be confused and drifting away from the basic values set down from previous generations. The lack of discipline and the lying, cheating, vandalism, vulgarity, lack of interest, and aggression creates stress for the teacher in charge. This stress can make many trained professionals learn to hate their job and sometimes make them physically sick. I'd like to discipline with dignity, but right now I'm just hoping to survive.

Teachers with High Burnout Potential

Why is it that two teachers with the same number of years of teaching experience, who graduated from the same college, have taken the same inservice courses, who have worked in the same school, and whose out-of-school lives are comparable can have such different experiences as teachers? Why is it that one teacher (let's refer to him as Teacher A) can maintain his energy and enthusiasm in the classroom while another (Teacher B) feels drained and over-whelmed?

All teachers face considerable stress in their lives as educators. But as Hans Selye points out, stress can be felt as distress, which ultimately leads to burnout, or it can be used positively, leading to energy and enthusiasm.[4] The real difference resides not in the stressor but in the teacher's perception of it. For example, suppose Johnny calls you a "son-of-a-bitch." His remark creates stress, and you have two choices in responding. You can feel personally attacked by his comment and view him as an insulting, disrespectful brat (a majority view) in which case you will probably retaliate in some way, or you can view this as a challenge for contact that Johnny has just made and an opportunity to connect with him. Teacher A would view Johnny as threatening, and should the teacher's response to the threat not stop Johnny's misbehavior, "distress" would result. Teacher B sees Johnny as a challenge, and the challenge generates energy and excitement for contact that may even create a higher level of understanding and ultimately a more appropriate future response from him when angry.

A fitting analogy to this discussion is baseball. It is the bottom of the ninth inning of the last game of the World Series. Your team is behind by one run, there are two outs, the bases are loaded, and it's your turn to bat. You are under great pressure: stress! The "burnout" views the pressure as an opportunity to fail and most often will! By contrast, his counterpart sees the pressure as an opportunity to do well. For him it is a challenge that creates positive energy. While the outcome will not always turn out favorably, his positive energy increases the odds for success.

Teachers with high burnout probability generally fall into one of the following four categories.

Please Like Me

These teachers depend upon student approval and are often willing to ignore misbehavior to continue to feel liked. They apologetically set limits and rarely follow through with consequences when rules are broken. Such teachers prefer to give themselves headaches, back pains, and other forms of physical tension rather than feel guilty for acting "mean" to their students. Disruptive students see these teachers as weak and ineffective and take control of the classroom because the teachers are at their mercy.

Muscle Flexer

Muscle flexers adopt the attitude, "I don't care if they like me or not, but they'd better do as I want or else." They often resort to power-based methods, including open confrontation, that invite resistance, retaliation, and rebellion. These teachers are quick to write referrals and inevitably feel that the administration is too soft. Unless these teachers have a warm and caring support system outside of school, they are likely to receive so few positive strokes on the job that loss of enthusiasm and early burnout result.

Guilt Giver

The attitude of the guilt giver is, "Can't you see how miserable I feel when you misbehave—I *wish* you would stop," or "Look at all I'm doing for you, and look at how ungrateful you are!" These teachers lack self-confidence and resort to whining and complaining with hopes that students will come to their senses. Such teachers are personally hurt and angry when students misbehave, but they are unable to express this anger. And so limits are set through an appeal to guilt of students, which is thoroughly ineffective with students who feel no guilt. These teachers are often seen with clenched jaws and fists accompanied by a soft, submissive tone of voice. The students hear the message that they have the power to make the teacher angry, and the worst consequence will be complaining and whining. Such teachers are likely to have numerous interpersonal difficulties because of blocked feelings, which lead to high levels of stress and burnout.

Marine Sergeant

This is the tough and fair approach. "Everybody gets treated the same way in here, and there are no exceptions to the rule," is the prevailing attitude. Because of the rigidity inherent in this approach, pride often gets in the teacher's way of dealing with tough-to-reach students who read rigidity as an invitation to act out. These teachers are likely to be victims of fear and anxiety when disruptive students succeed at threatening their control.

Summary

It is our contention that these teacher types represent the most likely candidates for early burnout. They respond to misbehavior ineffectively, which leads to continuation or regression of the student's behavior. Faced with not knowing what to do, the teacher either holds in the tension or yields to explosive outbursts. If pattern continues, teacher burnout occurs.

Figure 7.1 illustrates the "discipline-burnout" cycle. It begins when a student acts in a way that interferes with the teaching-learning process. The teacher ineffectively responds by *denying* (pretending not to see or hear misbehavior), *rationalizing* ("I can't expect her to behave herself because of her home situation, history of school failure"), *blaming* ("I saw you do it, it's your fault"), or *provoking* ("I will test your limits as much or more than you test mine"). Each teacher type resorts to one or more of these ineffective methods (in some cases the cycle continues even when the teacher responds effectively, as with the out-of-control, incorrigible student). When the teacher's corrective response meets with a continuation or worsening of behavior, tension and frustration occur. When these feelings are allowed to

---

Figure 7.1
Discipline and Burnout Cycle

1. Student misbehavior
2. Ineffective teacher response
   a. blaming
   b. rationalizing
   c. provoking
   d. denying
   e. revenge (I must be in control, I'll get even)
3. No student improvement, or worsening
4. Teacher feels tension and frustration
5. Withdrawal or explosive outbursts by the teacher
6. Increased misbehavior by students
7. Burnout

---

accumulate and no relief is in sight, then the teacher responds either through withdrawal ("I don't want anything to do with you") or explosive outbursts ("You say that again, and I'll break your neck"). If the cycle becomes repetitive, then burnout is fast approaching.

Strategies for Reducing Stress

Generally speaking, burnout victims suffer from either mental, muscular, or visceral symptoms. Mental symptoms include fatigue, irritability, exhaustion, lack of motivation to go to work, and preoccupation with negative thoughts. Muscular symptoms include tension headaches, backaches, tension in shoulders, and tightness in limbs. Visceral symptoms include cardiovascular problems, gastrointestinal problems, high blood pressure, ulcers, and colitis.

Strategies for reducing stress can broadly be conceptualized in two categories. Lazarus speaks of these as *problem solving* and *emotion focused*.[5] *Problem-solving methods* attempt to change the situations or events that are viewed as stressful. Most of the strategies contained in this book have such an emphasis. Establishing social contracts, becoming aware of yourself and your students, and familiarizing yourself with various discipline theories help eliminate factors in the teaching environment that contribute to disruptive student behavior. Having effective consequences that are implemented with firm tone of voice, in close proximity to the acting-out student with good eye contact is designed to stop misbehavior when it occurs, providing you practice it consistently. Learning how to effectively resolve differences with "hard to reach" students through negotiation, understanding the art of paradoxical behavior, and using other strategies described in Chapter 8 (Creative Discipline) are designed to problem solve difficulties with particularly disruptive students.

Another category of stress reducers are "self-actualizing methods." There are times when we are aware of dreams unfulfilled and business unfinished. Stress associated with our need for self-actualization often pushes us through conflict and confusion toward a new awakening. It often manifests as risk-taking: trying a totally different grade level, going back to school, volunteering for a challenging committee assignment, or feeling free to try, experiment, or expand upon something with a student. It may even mean leaving education (despite tenure and security) or returning to education (even though it means less money).

Unfortunately, not all people or situations lend themselves to change. The fact is that in some circumstances, and with some students, no matter what you do or how effectively or consistently you do it, no improvement occurs. The stress that you feel either continues or worsens. It does not simply go away.

Emotion-focused methods provide opportunities for you to release tension and induce relaxation within yourself. Various techniques such as meditation, yoga, biofeedback, guided visualization, and neurolinguistic programming have been useful to many people in providing rapid relief to stress. Many teachers get support through psychotherapy or with groups of teachers who face similar problems.

Emotional relaxation involves the following:

- Becoming more aware of what you feel and what you may not be allowing yourself to feel. Withheld emotions may make parts of your body feel numb, dark, or heavy.
- Becoming more accepting, nourishing, and appreciative of yourself.
- Becoming aware of how you can manage your feelings through more adaptive thinking and imagining.
- Becoming able to release pent-up emotion in a safe way.

The following activities are stress-management techniques that are quick, effective ways of teaching yourself to relax both before problems arise and when students do not respond favorably to your efforts to stop their misbehavior. They provide a nondestructive relief from tension that may be felt as frustration, anger, or sadness when the teacher's corrective response is met with no behavioral improvement. There are several self-help books that describe in greater detail various relaxation methodologies that you may want to investigate. The activities in the next section provide a sampling of strategies and should not be construed as all-inclusive, although we trust that they will provide needed relief from stress.

We want to point out that these activities are not meant as substitutes for exercise or nutrition, which have been identified as important to low-stress living. They are intended to provide quick relief during a five-minute break between classes and can be done in your room, the bathroom, or any other location that is relatively distraction free. Many of these strategies can be learned by students. One contributing factor to disruptive behavior is heightened student stress. These strategies can increase the stress threshold for you and your students. Many of these strategies can also be effectively used with students so that one leading cause of disruptive behavior, agitation/tension, is reduced.

Breathing

When we are tense, our breathing often becomes shallow and irregular. Irregular breathing may constrict our blood vessels leading to insufficient blood flow and other problems. Frustration, sadness, and worry that contribute to visceral problems can often be alleviated through proper breathing. The following activities can help.

Breathing Activity #1

1. Sit in a comfortable chair.
2. Pay attention to how you breathe. Relaxed breathing is slow and deep.
3. Close your eyes and slowly breathe in through your nose, sending all the air deep into your lungs and stomach.
4. Slowly breathe out through your nose and mouth, and as you do, allow all of the tension (tightness, butterflies in your stomach) to leave your body through the breath that comes out.
5. Keep doing this for five minutes.

Breathing Activity #2

1. Close your eyes as you sit in a comfortable spot. As you breathe in through your nose, silently count from 1 to 5.
2. When you reach 5, hold your breath to the count of 5.
3. Now slowly breathe out as you silently count to 5.
4. After you reach 5, and all the air has been breathed out, count silently from 1 to 5 before you breathe in again.
5. Keep doing this for at least five minutes.

Breathing Activity #3

In *The Relaxation Response*, Herbert Benson found that when adults did a meditative exercise suggested in his book, they felt more relaxed and showed improved cardiovascular functioning. Benson recommends that the best results occur when the activity is done twice a day for 10 minutes each. The essence of this approach follows.

1. Sit in a comfortable chair in a quiet place where you won't be disturbed for 5 or 10 minutes.
2. Close your eyes and breathe in air through your nose.
3. As you breathe out, say silently to yourself the number "one."
4. Breathe in again, and, as before, each time you breathe out say the number "one."
5. After 5 or 10 minutes, end the activity by opening your eyes slowly, sitting in your chair calmly for another minute with your eyes open, and then slowly leaving your chair as you return to doing anything you want.

Many who do this (and most of the other quieting activities in this book) say that when they first start doing them, they have some trouble just concentrating on the number. When that happens, use your drifting thoughts as the cue to return to quietly saying "one."

Private Retreat[6]

This activity is done by yourself, requires approximately 5 to 10 minutes, and is most effective when done in anticipation of a stressful situation (before your cafeteria assignment, study hall, arrival of a particularly difficult class, the end of recess, and other tense times during the day that are easy to anticipate). The "private retreat" is designed to help you to remove yourself mentally from these realities so that when you return, you feel refreshed, alert, energized, and capable of dealing with the difficult situation. Read all steps before you do the activity.

1. Be in a place that is relatively free of distraction for the duration of the activity, for example, the library, an empty classroom, a free guidance counselor's office.
2. Find a comfortable position either seated or reclining.
3. Focus on your breathing . . . inhale . . . and as you exhale, quietly say "one." Repeat this five or six times. Close your eyes.

4. Remember a quiet, calm, serene setting that you have visited at least once. Most people return to the seashore, the mountains, the woods, or their own backyard. If you cannot recall such a time, then let yourself imagine what such a place would be like and where it would exist—let yourself be creative.

5. Now step into your picture and see all the colors and the sights . . . listen to the quiet, soothing sounds . . . notice all of the smells and aromas, and feel the texture of your surroundings . . . notice how you smoothly allow yourself to flow in this wonderfully peaceful place.

6. Stay for a few moments and realize how your mind and body are being renewed and refreshed.

7. After 5 to 10 minutes, let yourself slowly come back to where you are right now, taking with you the calm and peacefulness from your ideal place. In a few moments, some situations that can cause stress will be here again, but you will retain this feeling of relaxed alertness for as long as you like. You have the realization that you may instantly return to your private retreat whenever you wish.

8. Slowly open your eyes and stretch your body.

Smiling at Yourself

A group of scientists, including Robert Levenson of Indiana University, has found that when you express a negative emotion on your face, even if you *don't* mean it, your body actually experiences it.[7] Smiling, it is claimed, at least keeps you neutral. Imagine the implications if we began smiling through power struggles rather than yelling, pounding, threatening, or frowning. We recommend you try the following smiling activity.

1. Look into the mirror and put a happy smile on your face. It might help for you to think of something funny that has happened in the past that made you smile from your teeth to your toes.

2. Notice yourself smiling into the mirror as you think about this funny thing. (How do you feel as you smile? You can end the activity at this point if you're feeling good, or you can continue.)

3. Now go to your room or another quiet place where you won't be bothered. Either lay down or seat yourself in a comfortable spot.

4. Close your eyes and picture in your mind that happy smiling face from the mirror looking at your eyes. Now very slowly allow that smiling face to move itself down to your mouth. At this point, with your eyes still closed, you'll begin to notice your lips start to smile. Now let the smile work itself all the way through your throat and into your stomach. Notice how your stomach begins to feel tingly as if you want to laugh. Keep looking at that smiling face from the mirror move all the way through your stomach, to your legs, ankles, and toes. You begin to feel sparkly all over your body from the top of your head to the tips of your toes.

5. Keep enjoying this happy feeling. When you're ready, open your eyes and realize how much power you have to make yourself feel happy.

Laughing

Laughing from deep in your stomach up through your chest and out your mouth is one of the best things you can do to feel good. Norman Cousins' *Anatomy of an Illness* describes how he got rid of a serious illness by *laughing* after doctors told him there were no further treatments available to improve his chronic condition. Cousins, probably by accident, found that by watching a lot of funny movies he began to feel better and his medical condition showed remarkable improvement.

Now nobody is suggesting that you watch funny movies all day, but you need a *fun time* every day. This is a time that you *only* do things that make you feel good. Maybe it is telling jokes with a friend, listening to a funny tape, or just plain acting silly. Who are some people that make you laugh? You might want to spend more time with them. What is funny to you? What makes you laugh? Do you do a little of this every day?

Do you like the idea of having a *fun time* every day? If you're really stuck, observe some happy-go-lucky people and watch how they have fun. Some of us need to learn how to have fun, and we can do so by watching others who are skilled at it.

Sometimes it helps to blend improbable scenarios to laugh. For example, picture your spouse serving dinner while walking on his or her hands.

Reward Yourself

Think about all of the things that you do that you enjoy or feel good about. Some possibilities are watching favorite TV shows, going to the movies, taking a bike ride or a walk, planning a trip, playing sports, making love, going to a concert, building a project, getting new clothes, or telling yourself how proud you are of yourself.

These are your rewards. Treat yourself to at least one reward every day after you have finished work without judging whether or not you deserve one. Maybe you can do something extra special after reminding yourself of something you did that made you feel especially pleased.

Being Your Own Best Friend

What do you say or do for your friends when they make mistakes or get mad at themselves? How do you react to them when things just aren't real great in their lives? Most friends will say things like: don't worry—it's no big deal. Forget about it. You'll do better next time. Look, you gave it your best. Think of all the good you've done. Let's talk about it. It can't be as bad as you think. Let's go get a pizza.

Some friends might even buy a little gift for a pal who is feeling kind of low. What are some other things that you might do for a friend when things aren't going well? How about saying or doing some of these things to or for yourself when things aren't going great for you? You are the most important person there is, and you deserve to be at least as good to yourself as you might be to others. Just as you would say or do things to cheer up a friend, do the same for yourself.

Quick Release Exercises

Imagine having read every book on discipline, being thoroughly familiar with every approach, and being aware of what the experts say will effectively change a student's behavior. Such a teacher will clearly have more strategies and techniques available and, theoretically, will deal better with disruptive students. However, even our theoretically ideal teacher will no doubt encounter at least one or two students every year who defy even the most advanced strategies, and who persist in their anti-authority behavior at all costs. Such students can be punished, praised, verbally shamed, confronted, or have all privileges removed, and it just does not make any difference. Although the teacher is ultimately powerless to effect change, it is critically important that he recognize and safely express the tension generated by such a student.

Both of the following "quick release" activities are best done in the privacy of your home, office, car, or other place in which you will not think of or worry about other people's judgments.

Pillow Release

(5 minutes) Take a pillow and place it in front of you. Imagine that the pillow is really the "out-of-control" student. Now tell this student what you resent (Sammy, I resent _____). See if your body wants to say or do anything to Sammy. If you'd like to crack Sammy over the skull, then let him have it! (Don't hold back: Remember he's not really there.) Let yourself yell, scream, punch, or squeeze until you feel a lessening of tension.

Towel Twisting and Biting

(2-3 minutes) Because we believe that we have to walk on eggshells around the "out-of-control" student, we often keep our mouths shut to avoid escalating a power struggle. While this is sometimes the best direct method to use, repeated use causes tension to develop in the face (particularly the jaw) and upper torso. As a way of releasing this tension, take a towel and let the towel represent the student. Twist the towel (student) until it is taut, and keep twisting. Notice how your jaw and face become even more tense as you do this. Now take the twisted towel (student) and bite down, giving the towel all the tension that this student usually gives you . . . repeat a few times. Notice how a relaxed, tingling sensation replaces the tension that you felt just moments ago.

Changing Unpleasant Experiences

Bandler's work[8] shows that we develop either positive or negative feelings depending upon cues and associations that we make. For example, if we talk to ourselves with a slow, depressed tone of voice and we make long lists of our failures, then obviously we're going to feel sad, depressed, and hopeless. Bandler says that it really isn't all that difficult for us to change our associations. He might for example advise the depressed individual to picture a smiling, cheerful-sounding voice saying the same things. There are often different results. When we work with difficult students, negative associations begin soon after we have contact. We often give much more emphasis to the student than to other aspects of our work. It is as if the difficult student is on a huge movie screen, acting out in color stereo while positive aspects of either that student or other situations are relegated to the dimensions of a 2" black-and-white television. Try either or both of the following activities.

Activity One

1. Picture a difficult student saying or doing something that usually bugs you.
2. Keep looking at the student but begin to hear circus music in the background. Listen to the circus music right through to the end. (If circus music didn't work, try something else.)
3. Contrast your feelings with the difficult student in the presence and absence of the music. What does the music do to your feelings of tension/frustration?

Activity Two

1. Picture that difficult student saying or doing something that usually bugs you.
2. Imagine that picture first on a movie screen, colorful, lots of sound, big audience. Now watch it again, but this time on a color television set in an appliance store with the sound cut off. Finally, take a look on a 2" black and white.
3. Compare and contrast as in Activity One.
4. Begin to put more positive experiences, events, memories on the movie screen in your mind whenever you want.

Tension Awareness

Many teachers feel the effects of tension through the psychological and physical symptoms described earlier in this chapter, but have little idea of what causes the tension, how often during the day they are in stressful situations, and what events are most likely to create stress. Likewise, many teachers are unaware of the many activities that can relieve stress and give them positive energy.

The first step of this activity is to plan four specific times during the day to "log" your feelings and your activities. One should be just before the beginning of a class or activity, one just after the completion of a class or activity, another prior to a time when you know you will be involved with one or more difficult students, and the last one at the close of school. Take a few minutes at these times to answer the following questions:

Date _____ Time _____
Activity prior to log writing _____
Activity coming up (in the next few minutes) _____
_____
My two most positive (energy) feelings are _____
_____
My two most negative (energy) feelings are _____
_____

Keep the log for at least two weeks, preferably three weeks, and then review it by answering the following questions:

1. List all of the positive feelings, even if some are repeated.
2. Look at the activities that gave you these feelings. Are there any activities that always lead to them? Were there any activities that often lead to them?
3. Look at the situations that usually create tension. Did you experience any positive feelings during these times? What happened to generate these feelings? How can you recreate these feelings in other stressful situations?

Group Problem Solving and Support

Although teacher burnout is common in most schools, teachers generally have the feeling that they must face their tension alone. Teachers and administrators see stress, especially related to discipline, as a sign of weakness or failure. Unfortunately, many teachers feel they will be perceived as failures, or as weak, if they admit to their feelings. Thus, group problem solving and group support, two of the more effective strategies for coping with stress, are not available to most teachers. This strategy is designed to help reduce the obstacles by using a group to combat stress.

1. Invite teachers in your school who are interested in looking at stress in a group setting to participate. A good group size for this activity is between 6 and 15 (more participants indicate a need for a second or third group.)
2. Once the group is convened, each participant is to write anonymously on a piece of paper one problem that creates tension or stress on a regular basis.
3. All the papers are then collected. The group facilitator or a volunteer then reads each paper as if he were the person who wrote it.

4. Each group member then writes a short paragraph, which first states whether or not they have faced a similar situation, and if they had similar feelings. Then they write as many helpful suggestions as they can think of to solve the problem.
5. The leader then lets each participant read their response and, by asking questions, clarifies the answers, so that everyone in the group understands them.
6. Finally, all of the paragraphs are collected and titled. Once everyone has had their problem discussed, each teacher can collect his packet for experimenting in class. If there is not enough of them for everyone to finish, then plan several meetings, perhaps once a week, to give everyone an opportunity. Follow this activity up with another meeting in which teachers are only allowed to report which suggestions helped. Repeat as often as necessary, perhaps by scheduling a regular meeting each week or biweekly for the entire school year.

Guided Visualization (Blackboard Fantasy)[9]

1. Read all steps FIRST!
2. Close your eyes and take a few deep breaths. After you inhale, hold your breath for a moment before exhaling. Feel your body rise as you inhale and sink as you exhale. Continue doing this until you begin to feel some relaxation.
3. Picture yourself in front of a large blackboard with a piece of chalk in hand. Slowly write the number "10" in the upper left-hand corner.
4. Next to the number 10, slowly write the word "relax."
5. Now write the number 9, and slowly write the word "quiet."
6. Write the number 8, and slowly write the word "peaceful."
7. Write the number 7, and slowly write the word "tranquil."
8. Write the number 6, and slowly write the word "calm."
9. Write the number 5, and slowly write the word "serene."
10. Write the number 4, and slowly write the word "sleepy."
11. Write the number 3, and slowly write the words "very peaceful."
12. Write the number 2, and slowly write the words "very calm."
13. Write the number 1, and then slowly write the words "very relaxed."
14. Keep your eyes closed for another moment and silently count to 5 telling yourself that when you reach the number 5, you will open your eyes feeling relaxed, refreshed, and alert.

Guided Visualization: Troubles Balloon Fantasy

1. Do the same as steps 1 and 2 in the Blackboard Fantasy.
2. Picture a large helium balloon in front of you. It is a large balloon with a big basket attached at the bottom just like the one flown in *Around the World in Eighty Days*. The balloon can be any color you choose. Slowly walk toward the balloon and notice how much room there is inside the basket.

   Slowly begin to deposit all of your troubles in that basket. Place all of your disruptive students, annoying administrators, and all other hassles in that basket. Now slowly walk away from the balloon and seat yourself under a beautiful shady tree. Notice the balloon begin to rise slowly into the air. Keep watching it and all of your troubles getting higher and higher, further and further away from you. It is now so high that it looks no larger than a small dot in the sky . . . and now you can't see it at all anymore. You may realize that you can have these troubles back whenever you want, but for now just enjoy the calm and peacefulness that exists in you. Smell the freshly cut grass, hear the chirping sounds of birds, and watch the quietness of your peaceful surroundings.
3. When you feel ready, count to 5, telling yourself to open your eyes when you reach 5 feeling relaxed, refreshed, and alert.

Tightening and Releasing Muscles

Mental tension is often accompanied by a tightness in one or more of the muscle groups that manifests itself as tension headache, neck pains, shoulder tightness, lower back pain, or aching legs and feet. Releasing this muscular tension often leads to feelings of relaxation.

1. Do a body inventory by checking out each of your body parts to spot tension (some people find biofeedback to be an excellent aid in helping them to discover where they are manifesting tension).
2. Now tightly squeeze each body part that contains tension. If it is in the shoulders, then push the shoulders up towards your head and release; if in the neck, slowly roll your head back and forth and to each side; if in the head, squeeze your face and clench your teeth, then relax; if in the legs or feet, squeeze each leg and as you are doing this, make about five clockwise circles with each leg (foot), followed by five counterclockwise circles.

3. Now imagine yourself to be a tight, stiff, mechanized robot. Tighten your whole body and walk around for a few moments as this stiff robot.

4. Now imagine yourself to be a loose bouncing rag doll, or puppet on a string. Let your whole body sink towards the ground (don't fall down) and walk around for a few moments as this rag doll letting each body part flail about.

5. Take a few relaxing breaths (see previous activity).

For the Administrator

Stress, like discipline, is an intrinsic part of the teacher's everyday school experience; and like discipline, many teachers are reluctant to admit their feelings of stress because they do not want to be considered weak or ineffective. You can help your faculty by making it perfectly clear that you understand that job-related stress is predictable, natural, and manageable. Studies indicate very precisely that helping professionals experience stress and that it can be turned into a positive force.

Your main concern related to teacher stress is to accept it, provide strategies for dealing with it, and to help remove from your school as many creators of stress as possible.

Earlier we listed the combined stressors reported by teachers in our study. This list is a good starting point for examining your school for causes of teacher stress. However, every school has its unique sources of stress. We recommend that you do your own survey of school and classroom stressors. Ask your teachers to list (anonymously) the main causes of stress in their typical day, or use any of the standard stress surveys listed in the chapter. If you find that there is a common agreement on causes of stress, you can use faculty meetings or task forces to create ways to either eliminate or minimize the causes. You may find logistical or organizational ways of solving some of your stress problems with a minimum expenditure of resources. The Group Problem-Solving Activity lends itself very well to facilitation by a building administrator.

One school reduced stress by teaching its students how to use the open campus effectively. The instruction was enough to cut down on students interrupting classes by yelling and running through the halls during instructional time, which was identified as a major stressor by staff.

Another way you can help deal with the issue of teacher stress is to be particularly sensitive to teachers who seem overwhelmed. Use the descriptions in this chapter as a guide and pay attention to the way your teachers walk, talk, and behave in school. If you identify teachers who are highly stressed, take the time to offer guidance and comfort. Support them and see if there are ways you can help as an administrator. If the main cause of burnout for a particular teacher is discipline, as it is in so many cases, offer suggestions for improving discipline using the many suggestions in this book. These teachers might benefit from a reduction in responsibilities until they turn the corner and should be first on the list for some of the "better" assignments of classes and other responsibilities.

While all of your faculty will feel good if you greet them with a smile, your overstressed teachers will be especially appreciative. Offer to teach or take over a difficult class once in a while, and after the experience acknowledge the motivational and disciplinary difficulties posed by these kids before offering either advice or suggestions.

Worry less about assigning classes on seniority and more about meeting the real needs of your teaching faculty. When working with stressed teachers, encourage them to talk with you or with others about their problems and help them feel cared for by the school. Expect that they might need to unload and even try to project blame on you, the kids, parents, or anybody else before they take responsibility to do something different.

Teachers, like administrators, often feel ignored and unappreciated. Generous and sincere compliments can trigger weeks of enthusiasm. A positive, appreciative note for the personnel folder can make one feel special as can a Hershey kiss in the morning's mailbox. In many instances, all it takes to spur a sense of renewal among teachers is to be positively noticed and sincerely appreciated by their building administrator.

Another way you can help reduce distress is to provide a time and a place for your teachers to practice stress reduction activities. Activities such as meditation, fantasy, breathing correctly, improving body posture, and others should be considered healthy, not faddish, and you should do all you can to recognize publicly their legitimacy. Offer training and support groups for practicing yoga, meditation, dance, breathing, and all of the activities suggested in this chapter. Encourage staff members to share relaxation opportunities with their students.

Another way to deal with stress is through physical activity. Provide outlets for stress by opening the gymnasium and other facilities for faculty use. Help organize both formal and informal exercise groups, dance groups, basketball and volleyball games, jogging, frisbee, and other competitive and cooperative games. One school we know had monthly races with all teachers earning a tee shirt for finishing the race regardless of the time it took to finish. When setting up a program of physical stress reduction, emphasize enjoyment not competition. You might want to include your physical education staff to help develop a program similar to the one described here.

Finally, an important goal for all administrators is to take care of their own stress. Administrators have the difficult responsibility of being a buffer between teachers and the upper administration and policies of the school system, between students and teachers, and between parents and teachers. They must deal with parents and students in a myriad of ways that are often stressful. Be a role model for your entire faculty by dealing openly and effectively with your own stress. Give yourself permission to use the many stress strategies presented on these pages.

Endnotes

[1]B. Hendrickson, "Teacher Burnout: How to Recognize It, What to Do About It," *Learning* 7 (May 1979) 36-38.

[2]A. Mendler, "The Effects of a Combined Behavior Skills/Anxiety Management Program upon Teacher Stress and Disruptive Student Behavior" (doctoral diss., Union Graduate School, 1981).

[3]C.E. Thoresen, T. Alper, J.W. Hannum, J. Barrick, and R.N. Jacks, "Effects of Systematic Desensitization and Behavior Training with Elementary Teachers" (Stanford University, 1973).

[4]H. Selye, *Stress Without Distress* (New York: The New American Library Inc., 1974).

[5]R.S. Lazarus, *Patterns of Adjustment* (New York: McGraw-Hill, 1976).

[6]C. Howard, in *Stress and the Art of Biofeedback* by B. Brown (New York: Bantam Books, 1977), 257.

[7]This activity was introduced to us at a workshop with Edith Saiki sponsored by the Drug and Alcohol Council in Rochester, N.Y.

[8]R. Bandler, (1985), *Using Your Brain for a Change*, Utah: Real People Press.

[9]R. Levenson, (January 22, 1986), in "For a Strong Body, It's Mind Over Matter," by B. Jacob, *USA Today*.

8
Creative Discipline for Out-of-Control Students

I t seems that every year most teachers have a few students who will not become constructive members of the class. Instead, these students appear to enjoy setting up one power struggle after another as they disrupt the learning process. They are the students who loudly complain of the teacher's unfairness, who make various noises and sounds constantly, who show up to class unprepared, and who simply refuse to take responsibility for their actions. Their behavior is always somebody else's fault. The teacher finds himself at "wit's end" with these students and often proclaims, "Somebody's got to do something with that kid!" These students are likely to be referred for diagnostic services and often, although not always, turn out to be from homes where parental conflict is the norm. They often believe themselves to be inferior, inadequate, and unworthy, yet they hide this from themselves and others through destructive behaviors that make them feel in control. It is typical to find these students functioning well below grade level despite adequate intellectual potential. They have been identified as failures, believe this to be true, and try to live up to these expectations. They take comfort in surrounding themselves with others who mistake inadequacy for power.

Although factors outside of school are often at the foundation of such problems, these students generally find the school environment unresponsive to their needs. Because their lives are rooted in confusion and powerlessness, they resent a system that tells them what to do, how to do it, and how well they have done. When they come to school with their primary concern being how to belong with others and they are expected to do math, they become bored.

Some Alternatives Within the School System

We have found that the social contract process is very effective with many of these students because for the first time in their lives they are asked to shape the environment in which they live. And they are involved as members of a community that teaches them how to share decision making. They are often much more responsive to following the rules and accepting the consequences within this arrangement than they are when the teacher presents himself as an authority figure and demands compliance.

Some settings enable teachers and others to take greater control when working with chronically difficult children. It is quite common, for example, to find closely regulated behavior modification programs in most residential and correctional facilities. It is also very common to find kids pushing these limits so that many require interventions such as time-out or physical restraint. Even if such procedures were allowed in schools, the open campus of a traditional public school would lead most such students to simply stop attending. Therefore, these kinds of students who remain in a regular school setting require a teacher who mixes democracy with authority, is soft and warm as well as tough as nails, who responds immediately to untoward behavior, and who is both predictably consistent as well as loose and unpredictable. In short, working with chronic misbehavers and out-of-control students requires a broad repertoire of behavioral skills.

One of the problems in dealing with these students is that they know their own reputations. Because they have been successful in building these reputations (for some, over many years), they want to maintain and even enhance them. This is the one area of school where they misguidedly achieve a degree of success. Usually many methods have been attempted with these students, and for some, positive changes have occurred. Unfortunately, there are still some who have been actively listened to and who have been positively reinforced yet continue to misbehave. One solution for these students is to find another educational environment that will be more suited to their needs. We are firm believers in the principle that school is not for all students and that there are some students who need more than we can give. If it is possible, we urge you to work with your administration and mental health team to properly place such students in smaller, more individualized programs.

Unfortunately, many states and school systems are not as responsive to alternative placements as they need to be for helping difficult students. Complicated policies, bureaucratic red tape, and lack of resources all lead to delay and sometimes refusal to remove these students from your class. When this happens you are often left with little choice but to try to do your best and meet the needs of all students, including the most troublesome.

In addition to the extreme cases mentioned above, there are some students who act out enough to make you feel that they are totally uncontrollable, but, because of the nature of their misbehavior, or because it runs in cycles, you may believe that removal from class on a permanent basis is too radical. You just wish there was something you could do to keep those students under control more effectively.

Each of these student types is difficult to work with because of a history of locking into power struggles with teachers and other authority figures. They have already formed an established pattern of, "You do this, then I'll do that, and then when you try this, I'll escalate with that." The one positive aspect of teaching these students, and it is significant if you choose to feel its power, is that you have very little, if anything, to lose. Because all of the traditional methods have proven ineffective, you are free to try anything you want, within reason.

In spite of the freedom that difficult students allow, many times teachers continually try strategies they know from prior experience are ineffective. It is very difficult to abandon these unsuccessful methods because teachers are often unaware of other, more unusual options, and emotions often run high when teachers are confronted with these students. We know that students who challenge authority make teachers aware of many feelings that are difficult to accept: anger, frustration, sadness, failure, and helplessness. These feelings can make it difficult to try new strategies and behaviors. They are a manifestation of stress and reminders that it remains important to take care of ourselves. (See the activities in Chapter 7.)

As we have said, teachers have the most power to change their tactics in working with out-of-control students because they have nothing left to lose! They have tried all of the conventional methods and none of them worked, at least not for very long. Feeling defeated, their tendency is to grit their teeth and bear it, counting the days, hours, and minutes until Friday. Although there are no surefire ways to effectively manage the out-of-control student, there is an assortment of survival strategies that can build confidence and add excitement to the often draining process of attempting to control the behavior of a student who seems principally motivated to drive you crazy. Other chapters have described a comprehensive process for discipline prevention and effective actions to be taken when students break rules or refuse to accept consequences. But when these methods fail, it is time to try new, creative methods that have the potential to at least change the way you feel and respond, which can give you a new way to perceive your interactions with these difficult students.

The resolution dimension contains positive confrontation strategies that are negotiated between you and a student (sometimes one or more resource personnel, teachers, or parents are included) in an effort to make life more pleasant for both you and the student.

We also include programs with an instructional focus that aim to teach such students better social skills, problem solving, impulse control, and self-regulation. Educators need to be familiar with the more traditional methods of behavior modification as well as strategies we call "creative discipline." This refers to a series of methods that are less predictable, appear spontaneous, and are unfamiliar (at least initially) to students, which often creates at least a pause in a student's desire to begin or maintain a power struggle.

Positive Confrontational Strategies

The social contract, which involves the whole class in making rules and consequences, is often effective in preventing misbehavior among a large number of students who had previously created classroom disruption. However, there are some students who repeatedly violate the rules of the social contract. These students need individualized help to learn how to follow the classroom rules. Some of these students respond well with efforts to elicit their cooperation through negotiation. Positive student confrontation, the Family Intervention Process, and the Comprehensive Social Contract are three such negotiation methods.

Positive Student Confrontation

Positive confrontation involves setting aside some time to meet individually with the student and attempt to resolve differences through negotiation. It is patterned after processes of mediation that attempt to resolve disputes between management and workers. The idea is to find solutions that are good for both sides.

Although individual negotiation through positive confrontation can be accomplished by a meeting or series of meetings between the teacher and student, we recommend that a third person who is neutral to the conflict be called upon to help mediate a resolution of the conflict. This third party can be another teacher, a guidance counselor, an administrator, a resource person, or even another student. The important attributes of the third person are (1) being a good listener, (2) being neutral to the conflict, and (3) being able to remain calm when the going gets rough. We refer to the mediator as a "coach."

In individual negotiation, both the teacher and the student have an opportunity to state resentments or dislikes to each other ["What do you dislike about what Billy (Mrs. Smith) does?"]; to state appreciations or behaviors that are liked or appreciated ["What do you like about Billy (Mrs. Smith)?"]; or to make demands upon each other ["What do you want from Billy (Mrs. Smith)?" or "How do you want Billy (Mrs. Smith) to behave that is different from what he (she) is doing now?"].

After each person states resentments, the other is asked to repeat the statement to ensure understanding. This is done for each step in the process. After all of this information is presented, the teacher and student are requested to negotiate with each other ("Which of Mrs. Smith's demands are you willing to meet?" "Which of Billy's demands are you willing to meet?"). When a plan of action is settled upon through agreement, each person is requested to sign the contract and another meeting is scheduled to check how well the plan is working.

Individual negotiation requires the aggrieved teacher to be willing to (1) share directly with the student, (2) take the risk of hearing unpleasant things from the student, and (3) consider program modifications for the student.

The specific guidelines for positive student confrontation are as follows:

1. Coach describes the problem, process, and his or her role. ("I'm here to see if I can help each of you find a way to feel better about being together in the classroom.")
2. Teacher and student share feelings of dislike, resentment, anger, or frustration. ("Tell _____what you dislike about the way he/she behaves.") Each repeats or paraphrases the

other's statements so that an understanding of each other's concerns is encouraged. (Paraphrasing applies to subsequent steps as well.)

3. Teacher and student share appreciations. ("Tell what you like or appreciate about _____.")
4. Teacher and student make demands. ("Tell what you want __ to do differently from what he is doing right now.")
5. Teacher and student negotiate a solution. ("Tell what you are willing to do differently that you think could help solve this problem.")
6. Agreement is reached, put in writing, and, preferably, signed.
7. Evaluation responsibilities are established so that each side can keep track of how well the agreement is working.
8. A meeting for follow-up is scheduled.

The coach needs to be aware that each side usually comes with a list of complaints that feeds their frustrations. It is important in these cases that the coach ask each to list only the three or four things that they most want to see changed. This way things are more manageable and, if both sides can successfully agree to make small but clear changes during a session, that success can be used as a building block for future negotiation of remaining concerns.

Family Intervention Process

It is often desirable and sometimes necessary to involve parents as partners in helping their children become more responsible. The family intervention process is a collaborative effort where parents assist in defining concrete and reachable goals, defining positive or negative consequences contingent upon goal attainment and implementing the consequences. Goals must be specific, measurable, and attainable. They must focus primarily upon expecting improved effort. The steps are as follows.

1. Meet with parent. If a two-parent home, insist upon meeting with both. If a single parent, then meet alone or include any and all extended family who provide frequent child rearing. All people at the meeting are invited to be active problem-solving participants.
2. Be certain that the problem is lack of effort (i.e., student has the ability to do multiplication homework but doesn't do it; student has the ability to walk away from a fight but chooses instead to brawl). Decide which problem to tackle first.

3. Set a concrete goal that is measurable and can be reached in a short time (i.e., being in class on time, doing homework, having three days of no fighting).
4. Establish positive and negative consequences. Positive consequences are what the student wants for reaching the goal (i.e., personal attention, privileges, preferred activities, possibly material rewards, although only as a last resort). Negative consequences define what the student dislikes losing.
5. Consider making the plan into a written contract in which the student says what she agrees to do; what she will receive if successful; what she will lose if unsuccessful.
6. Decide on how you will monitor the student's progress and what kinds of follow up will be done. (Sending home daily or weekly reports; setting a date for the next meeting.)

The Daily Student Rating Card

The daily rating card (Figure 8.1) can be used to rate and monitor agreed upon behavior established through the family intervention process or the comprehensive social contract. The day is arranged by class period or subject, and the student is rated in relevant categories. Each rating is associated with a certain number of

---

Figure 8.1
Daily Student Rating Card
(from Barkely 1981)

NAME _____ DATE _____

PLEASE RATE THIS CHILD IN EACH OF THE AREAS LISTED BELOW USING RATINGS OF 1 TO 5. 1 = EXCELLENT, 2 = GOOD, 3 = FAIR, 4 = POOR, 5 = TERRIBLE OR DID NOT WORK

CLASS PERIODS/SUBJECTS

AREA	1	2	3	4	5	6	COMMENTS
PARTICIPATION							
CLASSWORK							
HANDED IN HOMEWORK							
INTERACTION W/OTHERS							
TEACHER'S INITIALS							

1 = +25 POINTS	4 = −15 POINTS	PARENT PROVIDES REINFOR-
2 = +15 POINTS	5 = −25 POINTS	CER. NOTEBOOK OF POINTS
3 = + 5 POINTS		& COST FOR PRIVILEGES (RE-
		WARDS) KEPT BY PARENT

---

points that can be accumulated and traded for rewards. The ratings are tallied, and positive or negative consequences are implemented at home depending upon point totals. There are obviously many variations on this theme, and it is possible to implement this system exclusively at school.

The following example of an individually negotiated contract at Morristown High School (New Jersey) provides an excellent view of how a well-integrated plan of action negotiated between home and school with a student's involvement can effectively deal with the problem of chronic class-cutting. Although not all schools have the good fortune of extensive resource services, the principles of involvement and responsibility are applicable to all situations. (The Morristown plan is called the Comprehensive Social Contract.)

The Comprehensive Social Contract*

The Comprehensive Social Contract is basically a resolution dimension contract between the student, school personnel, and the student's family.

The unique aspect of the Comprehensive Social Contract is that everyone claims ownership to the student's problem; specific tasks are outlined for each person to carry out to ensure a positive change in the student's behavior.

To effectively help a student, not only should his responsibilities be carefully outlined but also the responsibilities of all others involved in that student's life inside and outside of school.

The following guidelines should be an integral part of writing a Comprehensive Social Contract:

- Claim ownership to the problem (everyone, not only the student).
- Be honest and open with the student and his family.
- Focus on the feelings of the parents and student.
- Show faith in the ability of the student to correct his behavior.
- Present alternate plans if necessary.
- Set realistic goals for the student.
- Establish an ongoing communications system between home and school.

The Comprehensive Social Contract is being used at Morristown High School to deal with chronic class-cutting.

---

*We wish to thank Rocco Feravolo, principal of Morristown (N.J.) High School, for submitting this material.

An efficient attendance policy is one of the most important factors to an effective code of behavior for high school students. The attendance policy has been specifically designed to help students understand the importance of regular school attendance as the key to success in school.

The concept of the attendance team was developed several years ago and has proven successful. The attendance team consists of the teachers of the student, the guidance counselor, the attendance teacher, an attendance coordinator, a clerical assistant, and a class administrator.

The *classroom teacher* keeps accurate records of the students' attendance and counsels students who do not attend class regularly.

The *attendance teacher* is responsible for taking the official attendance for the day and is the first classroom teacher with whom the student is scheduled daily.

The *attendance coordinator* is a classroom teacher with no more than two teaching assignments—the balance of the school day being devoted to attendance matters.

The *clerical assistant* helps the attendance coordinator telephone parents and keep student records.

The *guidance counselor* is the person assigned to the student.

The *class administrator* is one who has been assigned to oversee the attendance for a particular grade level.

It is therefore a tenet of the Comprehensive Social Contract to involve all parties to a conflict in its resolution and to specify very clearly what each person is responsible for. Figures 8.2 and 8.3 illustrate these principles.

Instructional Methods

Many students who demonstrate frequent behavior problems may not have the skills to behave acceptably. For some, telling them to behave better is no different than telling the driven executive with frequent headaches and fatigue that all he needs to do to feel better is relax. Driven people often don't know how to relax and out-of-control students often don't know how to behave. Traditional behavior modification methods are often used when teaching new behavior. A target behavior is defined by somebody in authority as are rewards and punishments. Through the gradual shaping of desired behavior by reinforcing what approximates the final, desired behavior and punishing or not reinforcing that which does not, the targeted behavior finally takes hold. These basic principles of behavior modification

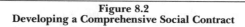

Figure 8.2
Developing a Comprehensive Social Contract

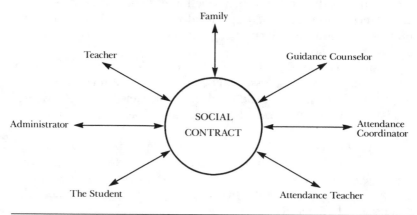

can be very useful in programs for the difficult child. Within the last decade or so, there has been an increasing emphasis on helping such students learn to more effectively control their own behavior in the absence of an authority who dispenses rewards and punishments.

Some Traditional Behavior Modification Methods

Positive Reinforcement is following a desired behavior with something that increases the probability that the behavior will occur again. School-based positive reinforcers include verbal praise and getting good grades. Positive reinforcement is the most effective method but rarely works immediately. Examples of positive reinforcement include sending positive notes home, making phone calls home after the child has been "good," sending notes of appreciation directly to the student, awarding coupons or tokens for desirable behavior that can be traded for favored rewards or privileges, and holding class pizza parties for meeting targeted behavior. One can also decide to reinforce the absence of undesirable behavior (i.e., 15 minutes of no shouting or talking out of turn earns something positive).

Punishment can be of two types. One involves the removal of a positive reinforcer. Time-out, detention, and in- or out-of-school suspension are some examples. Unfortunately, these may sometimes unintentionally strengthen a behavior one wants to eliminate. For example, if time out is to be effective, the classroom has to contain enough reinforcement that the child misses being there. Time-out areas should be free of attractive or distracting activities, and ele-

---

Figure 8.3
Jim's Comprehensive Social Contract

1. Jim agrees to attend his algebra class on a regular basis. If he feels that he wants to discuss his feelings about the class, he will make an appointment for a conference with Mr. Arthur, his algebra teacher.
2. Mr. Arthur agrees to help Jim during his free period with any of his assignments. Mr. Arthur will set the time and place for the extra help.
3. Mrs. March, Jim's guidance counselor, will arrange an appointment with Jim every Friday during the sixth period for the purpose of discussing the week's work with Jim.
4. Mrs. Koch, the attendance coordinator, will arrange a conference with Jim each Monday during the sixth period to review his week's responsibilities.
5. Mr. and Mrs. O'Brien, Jim's parents, will call Mrs. Koch, the attendance coordinator, every Friday at 1:30 P.M. to get a progress report on Jim's attendance during the week.
6. Mr. and Mrs. O'Brien will monitor Jim's homework period at home for the next two weeks to be certain that all assignments are complete.
7. Bill O'Brien, Jim's older brother, will check his algebra assignments to be certain that Jim is prepared for the next day's work.

_____
Student's Signature

_____
Attendance Coordinator's Signature

_____
Parent/Guardian's Signature

Social Contract Approved by

_____
Class Administrator

---

mentary students should rarely, if ever, stay there for more than 10 minutes. If the child hates the class, then time out provides an escape that is hardly punishing.

Response-cost programs are variations of punishment. The students in a response-cost program could, for example, lose points previously earned if they emitted negative behavior.

Negative Reinforcement involves ending an unpleasant situation after desired behavior has been given. For example, if a student hates math, he may be told that if he successfully completes the first three problems on the worksheet (targeted behavior), he won't have to do the remainder of the worksheet (escaping the unpleasant situation).

Extinction is the elimination of undesirable behavior through the systematic non-reinforcing of the behavior. Ignoring is the most frequently used method and can be effective with generally well behaved kids who occasionally emit undesirable behavior. It is almost never effective with the difficult child because even if you ignore it, others will acknowledge it and it will be reinforced. If it is your attention that is wanted, the individual will act even wilder to attract it. Ignoring may sometimes work when a more adaptive behavior is being reinforced. You might be able to reduce out-of-seat behavior through ignoring if there is a systematic method that reinforces the child when he is in his seat.

Most behavior modification programs require us to specifically target the behavior that we want to see change, identify reinforcers and possible negative consequences, and carefully monitor effectiveness. Keeping behavior charts is very important so that the teacher, student, and others can keep track of the gradual positive changes.

Self-Control Strategies

Some students who are difficult to reach have experienced failure that has snowballed to the point they believe they are incapable of changing their plight. As such, acting out becomes a viable option. Seligman (1981) and Dweck (1975) have shown that children's future success depends not on past success or failure but on what they attribute as its cause. Children who attribute their failure to lack of ability feel helpless to improve because ability is relatively impervious to change. By contrast, children who attribute failure to lack of effort see that they can improve their performance by putting forth greater effort. When problems are solvable (as many academic problems are), children need to be taught to make *internal* (I am responsible and in control)-*unstable* (effort is something that can change from day to day and I can control that)-*specific* (today I didn't work hard enough and I can work harder tomorrow) attributions for their failure.

Meichenbaum (1977) and others have described interventions that have come to be known as cognitive behavior modification. Here the emphasis is on teaching oneself to use verbalizations in a systematic way so that the self-talk mediates impulsive behavior. It seems that generally successful students learn to verbalize about their cognitive processes, and they use these verbalizations to guide their academic and social behaviors. By contrast, the child who is often in trouble may need specific help in learning how to use language before he behaves. As noted by Hallahan et al. (1983), self-instruction typically involves teaching the child to ask questions of himself about the nature of the problem, give himself instructions about performance of the task, and provide appropriate reinforcement and corrective feedback. Most self-instruction programs include turning over the responsibility for the monitoring and reinforcement directly to the student. There is usually a period of demonstration and modeling that is gradually reduced as the student takes charge. Let's take a look at some specific programs that provide some variation on the same theme.

"Think Aloud" (Camp, Blom, Herbert, and van Doorninck 1977). When encountering a problem, children are trained to ask themselves the following questions and provide an answer before asking the next question:

1. What is my problem?
2. What is my plan to solve the problem?
3. Am I using my plan?
4. How did I do?

"Problem-Solving" (Meichenbaum 1977). This approach includes the following questions:

1. What am I supposed to do?
2. I need to look at all possibilities.
3. I have to focus in and concentrate.
4. I have to make a choice.
5. How well did I do?

"Adolescent Anger Control" (Feindler and Ecton 1986).

1. Identify direct (provocations by another person) and indirect (thinking someone is being unfair or lying) anger triggers.
2. Identify physiological states related to anger (getting hot, sweating, hands clenched, tight facial muscles).
3. Relaxation methods (backward counting, meditation, deep breaths).
4. Cognitive behavioral methods. (Reminders such as chill out, take it easy, relax, I am in control of myself, just stay calm Assertion methods. Stopping and thinking of the consequences. If I lose control, get in trouble, suspended.)
5. Evaluation: How Did I do? (I did good, I kept in control. I did ok, I felt like killing him, and I only said ——— ——. I can do even better next time. I lost it. Next time this happens, I'll need to remind myself to ——————.

Assertion Techniques

Teaching students to substitute assertive behavior for aggressive behavior can be a turning point in gaining feelings of control and power. Many aggressive kids think that either you fight it out and prove your toughness or you turn the other cheek, which they believe only encourages others to victimize them. Feindler (1986) offers a graded series of assertive responses that can be taught to kids.

Broken Record (also described by Mendler and Curwin 1983)— "Please give me my book back" (repeated three times). If no success, *empathic assertion*: "I know you like that book, and it's probably a kick to teach me, but it belongs to me and I want it back." If no success, *escalated assertion*, progressive increase in assertiveness.

1. Please give me my book back.
2. I asked you to give me my book back.
3. I want my book back!
4. If you don't give me my book back, I'll tell staff and they'll get it back for me.

What Is Creative Discipline?

Our concept of creative discipline involves examining the transactions between the out-of-control student and the teacher. As we said earlier, this transaction is usually controlled by the student because he knows exactly how to "get the teacher." Teachers often relate to out-of-control students in very predictable ways because of limited options and strategies available to them. Thus, teacher and student are often trapped in their own little game, with no one winning in the long run. The main goal of creative discipline is to offer the teacher some ways to make those transactions less predictable. The idea is that when a disruptive student is faced with unfamiliar responses by the teacher, he might be willing to try to develop a new pattern. Many of the activities suggested here are designed with that goal in mind. Some strategies are helpful over a long period while others are for short-term use.

Creative discipline contains strategies that involve both a new way of perceiving classroom interactions and a series of strategies that do not fall into the normally accepted area of classroom management. Teachers who behave creatively with their out-of-control students are not as concerned about things not working out as they are with taking the risk of doing something new with the possibility, not certainty, that the situation will improve. They have exhausted their supply of traditional behavior management techniques and are not afraid to experiment with new ideas. They believe that there is little left to lose, and they are willing to explore the use of rather unusual and extreme techniques, which are needed to preserve the integrity of the classroom.

The goals of creative discipline are:
1. To stop a student's misbehavior so there is little interruption in the flow of the lesson.
2. To ensure that the out-of-control student is stopped from preventing others from learning what you have to offer.
3. To refuse the student's efforts at hooking you into a power struggle.
4. To defuse tense situations by using humor, including poking fun at yourself.
5. To define yourself as having the capability to remain calm in the face of "shocking behavior."
6. To occasionally say and do unusual things so that you are somewhat unpredictable to the student and may therefore be seen as somewhat different from the masses of other teachers whom the student views as the enemy.
7. To search for methods of communication that may lead to a new pattern of interaction between you and the student(s).
8. To offer the student substitute outlets for expressing feelings that interrupt the learning process.
9. To learn how to appreciate students who are intent upon driving you crazy.

Using creative discipline is not easy because it requires ways of being that most of us have had no experience or practice with.

Creative Discipline Techniques

School-Wide Inventory

Write out a situation or problem you face on a dittomaster and leave off the ending—like a mystery puzzle. Distribute copies to any of the teachers in the school you trust, or who you feel have a good reputation for dealing with out-of-control students. Include either the principal or vice-principal and one or two resource personnel, such as the school psychologist. Have each of them write in their ending, or how they would handle the situation. Ask them to be specific.

After you collect the responses, rank them in order of most to least preferable. Each time a situation similar to the one in your inventory occurs, try each of the trial solutions in order, until you have tried them all. Each time you have tried one, write at the bottom of the paper how you felt doing it and how successful the strategy was. It is important to try all of the suggestions without prejudgment.

Once you have gone through the entire list, eliminate any suggestions that didn't work or made you feel very uncomfortable. Review the blocks to creativity to see if you gave each suggestion as full opportunity to be successful. Refine and try again any strategy which either worked with the student or made you feel better.

Grafitti

A novel approach to the problem of subway grafitti was implemented by New York City with results that have exceeded everyone's expectations. Believing that grafitti artists are primarily motivated by attention, trains are washed, painted, and then rewashed and repainted several times so that each act of grafitti is visible for only a very brief time frame. When identities of the artists become known, they are approached by authorities, warned of a fine that will be levied if they are caught again, and perhaps best of all, are offered alternative, sanctioned places to draw and display their art. This approach illustrates some of the best principles of behavior management and could certainly be applied to problems with grafitti at school.

A related and more serious problem is school vandalism. We have found that entrusting suspected students with even greater school responsibilities has the paradoxical effect of decreased vandalism. In one school we worked with, this problem was addressed by the establishment of rotating committees of students to meet weekly with the building administrator to assess the current status of vandalism. Each committee included a cross-section of students. All repairs and clean-ups were done by the committee with the janitor supervising on Saturday mornings. When the identity of a vandal was known, that student was either turned over to legal authorities or a plan was developed for adequate restitution. Needless to say, incidents of vandalism plummeted!

The Discipline Institute

Imagine that you are the leader of the famed *Discipline Institute*, a creative institute dedicated to solving the most difficult discipline problems. In fact, you only accept severe cases, referring the more common problems and easily resolved ones to the local discipline expert. Your specialty is the most difficult cases the *Institute* accepts, and your caseload has as its number one priority your own biggest classroom problem. Write it up in an impersonal way as if it belonged to somebody else. Gather your *Institute* colleagues (friends or staff members at a team or faculty meeting), and role play your *Institute* staff meeting. Use the staff meeting to think of as many off-beat, seemingly crazy ideas as you can. Stay in your role as members of the *Discipline Institute* throughout the role play.

Once you have generated a list of solutions, imagine that you are the teacher client, and list all your objections to the suggested ideas. Now return to your role as the *Institute* leader and refute, in writing, all of the objections, and explain why the ideas will work. Try as many of the ideas as you can. Be certain to pick at least one that you are convinced is so extraordinary as to not be believable, and do it. The sooner you realize how little you really have to lose, the more quickly your creativity will flourish.

Role Reversal

The technique of allowing a student to play teacher for a short time has been used by many teachers. This strategy is designed to carry that concept one step further. Give the student the responsibility of teaching your class for a significant time period. Younger students might have 15 minutes, middle grade students an hour or two, and older students one-half or a full day (this is a lot of time to give up, but we feel that improvement with out-of-control students may well be worth it). You take the student's place and act the way the student usually does. After the experience, meet privately with the student to try to creatively solve your conflicts, but stay in your role reversal. In other words, you continue to play the student, and the student continues to play the teacher as you creatively try to find ways for both of you to resolve the conflict. Once agreement has been reached, honor it in your real roles.

Using Humor and Nonsense

Write down various jokes, phrases, sayings, and statements that you find funny or nonsensical. Try to include in your list some that are certain to get a rise from many of your students. At least once per day for one week when a student behaves disruptively, respond with one of your "funny" statements. For example, as Jack comes to class late for the third day in a row, tell him wryly, "Jack! Did you know that Peter Piper picked a peck of pickled peppers?" Contrast Jack's reaction to this with how things are when he's told, "Jack, where's your pass?"

While humor will neither defuse all explosive situations nor produce long-term behavioral change, it does set up possibilities for relationships to be formed that lessen the likelihood of power struggles. Moscowitz and Hayman found that those teachers rated "best" by inner-city high school students used more humor than did those rated "typical." Other characteristics of "best" teachers were discussing current events in class, not yelling while disciplining, and empathizing with students' feelings.[1]

Agree with the Putdown

You can deflect many nasty comments by agreeing that there is some truth in the accusation and then redirecting the conversation. For example, Sally calls Mrs. Lewis a "blind bat!" Instead of getting defensive, Mrs. Lewis says calmly, "There's a lot of truth to that. There are certainly times that I don't see very well. Thanks for pointing that out, and I'll again point out that your homework is due tomorrow." Also, you can train yourself to hear loaded comments with the same emotion that you would feel if someone called a "chair." This makes it much easier to think of a non-provocative way of defusing a potential power struggle.

Answering Improbably

Imagine telling a student that you've had enough and you're going to send him to the principal. The student looks you square in the eye in the middle of class and says he's not going, you can't make him, and concludes with, "What are you going to do about it?" Imagine saying, "I'm going to finish this lesson, hop on over to the airport and take the first flight to Tahiti!" How do you suppose he and the other students might react?

Behaving Paradoxically

Behaving paradoxically can be a very effective method with anti-authority students. It is based upon a psychotherapeutic technique developed by Victor Frankl.[2] Frankl found that some people resist changing even when they want to change. Because they resist change, they respond to suggestions for change by continuing to behave maladaptively. He discovered that many people can be helped by having somebody strongly suggest that the person continue to behave exactly as they have been and to even suggest that they exaggerate their maladaptive behavior. This is called "siding with a person's resistance."

For example, a therapist might suggest to a person who is afraid of the dark that tonight when it is dark they should be sure to feel extremely terrified and to make sure that their fear keeps them awake. Frankl found that for various reasons, this method can be highly effective in creating more adaptive behaviors for people. It is similar to the old-world adage of using reverse psychology (suggesting the opposite of what you want a person to do in order to have them do what you want). In a school situation, the message of the teacher is firmly, "I want you (student) to try to keep behaving exactly as you have been. You are just being yourself!" This is in contrast to, "The way you are behaving is unacceptable, and I expect or demand you to change." The former paradoxical message may have the effect of eliciting a challenge to the student who may then defy the teacher and behave in a desirable way. Consider the following typical and paradoxical messages:

Typical: "This is the third day that you have not done your homework. The consequence is that you will have to remain after school."

Paradoxical: "This is the third day that you have not done your homework. This is terrific! (genuine) Your assignment for tonight is to try hard to forget your homework tomorrow."

Typical: "Jane, I will tolerate no more swearing in this class. If you use those words again, you will not come with us on the field trip."

Paradoxical: "Jane, you said, '_____.' Tell me how you are defining that right now, and I will write the definition on the blackboard."

The contrasting styles are probably obvious to you. The *typical* responses will work with most students who respect the voice of authority. They do not work for anti-authority kids. The paradoxical message sets up a challenge to the student whose behavioral mode of functioning is contradictory to the message. If a student does the homework assignment in defiance of your instructions to him to forget it, then you have motivated him to do a valued school task. If he forgets it, then he has behaved appropriately according to your wishes. You can reward his compliance. Either way, you win! The same can be said for Larry. As an anti-authority youngster, the five minutes, or for that matter, five hours of time out will make no impact on his undesirable behavior. By acknowledging his ability to throw erasers as a strength, you have taken away this weapon of control and have challenged him to learn to talk as well as throw things. By telling him that he cannot talk, you have potentially motivated him to prove to you and himself that he can. "If that lousy authority figure thinks I cannot talk, well then, I will just have to show him that I can." The process involves setting up a situation where the student has to behave more appropriately as a way of defying your authority.

There are situations in which we would not advise this technique in a school setting. The most obvious is fighting or hard hitting (as opposed to the camaraderie shoving that most junior high school students use to express the combination of friendship and manhood). Obviously it is too dangerous for a teacher to encourage a student to hurt another student.

Sometimes, the other students will feel threatened and angry by the use of this technique. They may perceive their "out-of-control" peer as receiving preferential treatment and will experience more hostility toward the student and the teacher. It is often helpful to have a class discussion (when the identified student is not present) to explain the purpose of this "preferential treatment" to the class members. The concept of fair and not equal can be very useful in this process. This can also be a good time to enlist the support of students, particularly those who are not intimidated by the out-of-control student, to help you with your program.

Use of Nonverbal Messages

Most out-of-control students have been verbally reprimanded thousands of times every year. They eventually become immune to verbal messages, which are tuned out. Try using prearranged nonverbal signals to cue students to the fact that you've had enough. It can be any mutually prearranged signal such as a facial look or a gesture.

The Good Old-Fashioned Tantrum

Every so often, probably no more than three or four times a year, a well-timed tantrum in which you might yell, scream, stand on chairs, or even knock over a table or two can be wonderfully refreshing and renewing. It reminds kids that you, like all humans, have your limits, and that there are times when exceeding those limits leads to raw, visceral, nonviolent but poignant, gut-releasing emotion. They'll take notice unless this becomes a habit. Naturally, an excessive amount of this type of behavior will lead the kids to view you as out of control, and they'll enjoy pressing your buttons to watch the show.

Audio- or Videotaping Your Class

If you have access to a video recorder (preferable) or an audio recorder (acceptable) try taping your class for an entire period. Focus on those students who give you the most difficulty. After class, when you have captured an incident or a series of disruptions, meet with the students who are causing the problems. Show them or let them listen to the tape and discuss their feelings about the way they looked to themselves. When given a chance to actually see or hear themselves, students often gain an awareness of their negative impact and are willing to try something new. To help make this procedure more effective, it is helpful if you can also agree to try something new with these students. Your and your students' suggestions for change should be specific and manageable. Meet again in a couple of weeks to discuss how things are going.

Audio Playback

Some students are unfortunately committed to denying all responsibility for being disruptive. Furthermore, a phone call home may be greeted with a parent defending his child's actions. When you are confronted with such a situation, it can be helpful to tell the student that, "Beginning today, I will be keeping the tape recorder on record. Since I think that it is important for both you and your parents to understand the problems that we have here, I will make the tape available to your parents when we come together to discuss your school progress. Good luck!" This method has been extremely effective in curtailing a wide range of inappropriate behaviors (especially verbal abuse, put-downs, and swearing).

Using Older Students as Resources

Often older students who have been "in trouble" in school are wonderful resources for dealing with younger disruptive students. If you teach in a school that is close enough to a high school, try setting up a program for the disenfranchised high school students to work in your or other teachers' classes. Select those students who have been in trouble and need a healthy outlet for feeling good about themselves. The principal or school psychologist as well as high school teachers should be able to help you select the best candidates. Arrange for freeing up these students on a regular basis during the week. Short times work best because you do not want to give the student helpers too much of a rigid burden. An hour every week is sufficient.

Prior to coming to your class, meet with your student helpers and explain that you want their help in guiding some students who seem to be on the wrong track. The student helpers' job is to come to class and to work individually in a comfortable private spot with the troubled student. Work can include actual lessons in the form of tutoring, or they can focus on social issues. Try to provide a flexible structure so that the helper has an idea of what to do but is not required to deliver your lesson plans. It is important for the helper to feel like a worthwhile person who is given a special privilege to help another student. Meet with the helpers each month for an hour or so to help them get new ideas and listen to their observations and feelings.

Creative Limitations

We believe that there need to be limitations even with "creative" approaches. As mentioned previously, we believe that all students have a right to attend school so that their safety and security is guaranteed. Dangerous or violent behavior that includes fighting or carrying weapons cannot and must not be tolerated in a school setting. We feel strongly that fighting should be dealt with swiftly by excluding the student from school until such time as he can return with an action plan that specifies what he will do (other than fighting) the next time a similar situation presents itself. It is also a fact that carrying exposed or concealed weapons is a legal matter, and the solution to this problem should always include legal authorities.

A Fresh Start

The suggestions in this chapter are not going to work all the time for all people. Creative ideas are not designed to be perfect solutions but rather to begin an exciting new adventure into the unknown with the hope that both you and your students will learn more about yourselves and each other. By unblocking yourself and venturing into the unknown, you have the capability of changing old patterns and making an important difference in the lives of your most troubled students.

For the Administrator

There are usually a small percentage of students who can be legitimately called "out-of-control," but they require a large percentage of time—from the teacher, from the support personnel in the school, from other students, and from the administrator. The best role you can take is to help the student to be placed in the best educational environment possible. This might mean transfer to a special school or class either in or outside your district. Proper placement helps the teachers and students alike as well as freeing the teacher to spend more time and energy with the other students.

However, often the reality is that there are no special school or classes available, or that there is a long waiting list, or that there are no available funds for a given student. Even when special placement is a possibility, the time it takes to secure the placement because of red tape, paperwork, and due process requirements can involve many months. The teacher must still work with the out-of-control student during that time. Thus, in spite of your intentions to properly place students, you will have teachers in regular classes who must deal with chronic problem children.

Teachers need a lot of support when working with the "out-of-control" student. We propose the following ways to support your teachers' efforts.

1. When you have chronically disruptive students, their parents must be continually involved. Do not be afraid to call them at home and at work when you need to. If you have a student who must be sent home for disciplinary reasons, insist on parental support. If your teachers need a parent to come to school, intercede when there is a problem and use the weight of the school to get them in. If a parent claims that they cannot leave work for school, tell them that you are sure that their child is very sorry for the inconvenience and that he will be waiting in the hall in 20 minutes for pickup. Keep parents of disruptive students informed of their progress.

2. As the administrator, you can be a key person in facilitating the approaches requiring contracts. Don't hide from problems. For example, you can volunteer to be the "coach" in Positive Student Confrontation by offering to mediate a resolution to disputes between teachers and students. You can organize and lead the development of the Comprehensive Social Contract by calling together all of the parties and organizing the meeting.

    Acknowledge if need be that you don't know how to make a kid behave better, but that you'll keep being there to listen and try. Many teachers complain about the principal who is rarely seen or heard. Be visible. Be in places that are likely trouble spots so that your presence can prevent problems from happening and so that your faculty sees that you are there.

3. If there are problems involving several kids in a classroom that might have racial or gang overtones, you need to appeal directly to the families to assist with resolution. Go knocking on doors if need be to get parents to come to school. Once assembled, tell them about the problems in the classroom; let them know in no uncertain terms that you will not permit these problems to continue. Tell them what you are prepared to do (which might include involving other authorities or agencies) and, most importantly, elicit input and proposed solutions from them. Finally, when you have their support, invite their kids to join the meeting so that the kids hear their parents say that the problems will end.

4. Allow your teachers freedom in dealing with chronic problems. Remember that nothing has worked with these students for a long time. Teachers have nothing to lose when trying creative strategies, but they often fail to try creative strategies because they fear administrative non-support or disapproval. Let all your teachers know that you will support most of their plans that are nonpunitive and as long as the teacher shares them with you in advance.

5. Be vigilant with all follow up to any problem with a disruptive student. Keep teachers, parents, and students informed of all of your actions.

6. Working with difficult students is frustrating! You need to understand that when a teacher is calling a student names, is making demands of you for swift action, or is in some other way behaving "unprofessionally," that this is the time for support, not debate. You can help your teachers feel less frustrated by sharing information concerning the student *and* by being a good listener who can express empathy.

Endnotes

[1]E. Moscowitz and J.L. Hayman. "Interaction Patterns of First Year, Typical and 'Best' Teachers in Inner-City Schools," *Journal of Educational Research* 67 (1974): 224-230.

[2]V.E. Frankl, *Man's Search for Meaning: An Introduction to Logotherapy* (New York: Pocket Books, 1963).

9
Discipline and the Process of Teaching

Motivated students cause fewer discipline problems because they care about what they are learning. Enthusiastic teachers who present their material in stimulating, meaningful ways motivate students. When students are actively learning content that has personal meaning for them, they have neither the time nor the energy to create discipline problems. Conversely, when students feel that they are passive receptacles for irrelevant knowledge, they become bored, turned off, and find satisfaction in acting out.

The relationship between discipline and motivation is like heads and tails of the same coin. Teachers cannot motivate students when disruptions interfere with the learning process, when the classroom feels unsafe because the teacher cannot maintain control, or when a significant amount of time is lost to trying to keep order. On the other hand, teachers who discipline punitively, attack the dignity of students, and use methods that decrease internal locus of control have difficulty increasing student motivation regardless of how exciting the class content is.

Raymond Wlodkowski has made a significant contribution for systematically increasing student motivation in the classroom. Rather than leave motivation to chance or to trial and error, Wlodkowski has developed a highly effective method for motivational planning, which he calls the "time continuum model."[1] The model divides instructional units into three basic time phases: beginning, middle, and end. Each has its own motivational focus, structure, and activities.

Beginning

The motivational concerns at the beginning of instruction are *attitudes* and *needs*.

Attitudes. What can be done to develop a positive attitude toward the subject, the teacher, and the student's ability to be successful?

Needs. How can learning the subject meet the students' needs? Often teachers tell students that a particular lesson or course will help them in the future. But students define the future from the perspective of their stage of development, a perspective that can be very different than the teacher's. A teacher might mean that the course will help in college or in next year's sequential course. The student, depending on age, hears "future" and thinks of the next two months, two weeks, two days, or two minutes. When talking about needs, it is more motivating to choose a time frame that fits the students' perceptions.

This category is also concerned with needs related to the learning environment, such as companionship needs and feeling safe from embarrassment or threat.

Middle

The motivational concerns in the middle part of instruction are *stimulation* and *affect*.

Stimulation. What can be done to continually stimulate learners? Students today have been trained by television to be passive learners. They demand variety, a fast pace, a rock soundtrack, a comedian for a teacher, and virtually total control of the images before them. However, stimulating lessons requiring high-level thinking, working cooperatively, and creating products that evoke pride—and that encourage personal discovery—fill a great void created by television. Teachers can use this syndrome to great advantage by building lessons on what students need but don't get from television.

Affect. This refers to how the student's feelings about the lesson can be positive and how to use the affective domain in teaching.

End

The motivational concerns at the end of instruction are *competence* and *reinforcement*.

Competence. What can be done to help the student achieve a satisfactory level of competence in the subject, and how will the student recognize competence?

Reinforcement. How can the student be reinforced to desire to continue learning?

Wlodkowski emphasizes that motivating students to learn is difficult and does not commonly happen without planning.

> "[I suggest that] . . . each teacher develop a systematic approach to facilitating student motivation that as adequately as possible can be implemented on a daily basis in the classroom. Planning and systematization are the key elements here. Without them teaching becomes a stressful guessing game where trial and error become the dominant influences. Refinement, self correction, problem solving and what do I do next are issues that cannot be resolved relative to student motivation without some kind of systematic approach."[2]

Thirteen Strategies for Motivating Students

Borger, Carroll, and Schiller have examined motivation from the perspective of attribution theory. They define motivation with three facets: self-concept, achievement motivation, and locus of control. (Notice how these same factors are major concerns of effective discipline.) They offer 13 strategies for increasing motivation.[3]

1. Increase student response. Ask more low-risk, open-ended questions.
2. Monitor your behavior to see that low-ability students have an equal chance to respond. Make sure they are called on as often as high-achieving students.
3. Encourage students to persist with difficult problems and to finish projects.
4. Foster excitement about new ideas.
5. Assign more in-depth projects, activities, or independent studies.
6. Incorporate student self-evaluation in your grading system.
7. Involve students more in scheduling classroom learning.
8. Exhibit high expectations for your students.
9. Increase your students' readiness to learn. Begin lessons with intriguing questions. Use special objects or activities to help children focus on the concept.

10. Increase involvement and interest.
11. Cooperative assignments increase motivation, but you must also teach communication skills.
12. Audiences are great motivators. Invite the principal, parents, or other classes to activities.
13. Check to see that your low-ability students are "school wise." Do they need instruction on how to organize their desks, take down assignments, or memorize facts?

Lessons that are motivating share the following key elements:
1. Students are actively involved in their learning.
2. Teacher uses feedback more than judgmental evaluation.
3. Students control their own learning whenever possible.
4. Students are asked to use higher-level thinking skills.
5. Teacher uses cooperative learning structures.
6. Teacher keeps pace with the natural attention span of students.
7. Teacher integrates all domains of learning: cognitive, affective, and psychomotor.
8. Students feel a strong sense of purpose to the lesson.
9. The teacher uses competition carefully, stressing achievement more than winning, and does not have high negative consequences for the losers.
10. The teacher strives to create classes that are fun and validate a true sense of joy in learning.

Characteristics of a Healthy Classroom

Motivation permeates all aspects of teaching, either directly or indirectly. For example, it can be enhanced directly through motivational planning or indirectly through evaluation systems that maintain dignity for all students. Following are nine characteristics of a classroom with a healthy environment.

1. Trust is established. The learner trusts his abilities and his environment (including those who are helping him learn). Fear is minimized.
2. The learner perceives the benefits of changing his behavior. Learning is a change in behavior; if the learner does not perceive the need for change, then there is no reason to change.
3. The learner is aware of different options and is able to make a growth choice. This choice cannot be made for the learner. Education is structured to help the learner see different alter-

natives and to provide the opportunity to make choices that are real, meaningful, and significant.

4. The evaluation of learning actively engages the learner. Evaluation by others is effective when the learner perceives it as important to him. Both teacher and student share the responsibility for defining what is to be learned and how well it was learned. Mutual evaluation helps maintain the trusting environment. Because the goals of learning are personal, only the learner is truly capable of analyzing how well the goals are being met. The teacher lends his expertise in helping to define a level of outcome needed to ensure competence.

5. Learning facts and concepts are important but incomplete goals for the learner. They are not the final results of education. Personal meanings, uses, and understandings are the ends for which learning facts and concepts are means.

6. Learning is conceived as meaningful. Even in structured situations where the activities might be planned and the outcomes are left open for the learner to discover (uncover), effective learning takes place.

7. Learning is growth producing, actualizing, and therefore enjoyable. This does not mean that the learning is frivolous or light. Instead there is true joy that comes from knowing and being more complete than before the learning. True learning is genuinely pleasurable.

8. Learning is process- and people-oriented rather than product- and subject-oriented. True education helps students learn a process for successful living that applies to any situation. Product orientations are too limited and self-defeating to have any permanent useful effect.

9. Learning includes more than just the cognitive or affective domains. The separation of these two is artificial and unnatural. Feelings and thoughts should be incorporated for learning to have personal and lasting usefulness. One or the other exclusively is incomplete.

These characteristics of healthy classrooms are often difficult to translate into action. Lack of resources, rigid curriculum requirements of the state or school, and pressure from parents and administrators for high test scores all leave even the most enthusiastic teacher unable to teach creatively and manage students. Yet by setting up a preventive behavior program and changing the structure of the content in gradual, but significant, ways teachers can incorporate many of these characteristics into their everyday teaching. One of the biggest mistakes that the educational revolutionaries of the 1960s made was to assume that total freedom was not only possible but desirable. "Free" schools, which allowed students to do whatever they wanted, were doomed to failure because the students did not have the skills to handle what was asked of them, nor were they developmentally ready for that much freedom without responsibility. On the other hand, it is impossible for students to learn to be responsible unless they are free to make both good and bad choices. George Brown describes the main goal of his Ford Foundation Project:

> A goal we were striving for in our work was to help students become both *more free* and *more responsible*. We believed this could be done by increasing the student's sense of his own power to take responsibility for his behavior. Further, by providing experiences that made available ways to become free, followed by the actual experience of increasing freedom, we could help the student attain the personal satisfaction that is unique to feeling free.[4]

One way to provide opportunity for freedom and responsibility as part of the teaching process is to structure lessons in a way that not only delivers the content but also provides students the opportunity to learn about themselves and their environment.

Brophy and Porter have analyzed the research of teaching over 10 years. Their analysis shows that effective teachers:

1. Make clear their instructional goals.
2. Know their content and the strategies for teaching it.
3. Communicate to their students what is expected of them and why.
4. Use existing instructional material expertly to devote more time to practices that enrich and clarify content.
5. Know their students, adapt instruction to their needs, and anticipate misconceptions in their existing knowledge.
6. Teach students metacognitive strategies and give them opportunities to master them.
7. Address higher- as well as lower-level cognitive objectives.
8. Monitor students' understanding by offering regular, appropriate feedback.
9. Integrate their instruction with that in other subject areas.
10. Accept responsibility for student outcomes.
11. Reflect on their practice.[5]

Teaching and Learning Styles

Much research has been conducted in the last five years on styles of learning. A number of models purport to delineate several styles of learning, and a number of tests have been designed to measure variables that can define what type of learner a student is. The most important development is the notion that students who have a particular learning style have difficulty with incompatible teaching and instructional styles. The better the match between instruction, teacher, and student learning style, the better the student will learn. If there is a mismatch, students may become frustrated, confused, anxious, and likely candidates to act out in class.

It is beyond the scope of this book to review all of the literature on learning styles, but Figure 9.1 is a useful summary. It divides learning and teaching styles into three basic categories: dependent, collaborative, and independent. The figure also details what is needed by the student, the teacher's role, and teacher behavior is associated with each particular learning style.

While it is true that many people have a characteristic learning style, it is also true that learning styles vary for different topics. For example, Bill is a dependent learner when it comes to learning how to tune a car engine. He wants specific instructions from his teacher, who he wants to act as an authority. He also wants direct criticisms and specific assignments broken down into small, clear steps. When it comes to photography, Bill is more comfortable in a collaborative

Figure 9.1
Learning Styles Summary

Learner Style	Need	Teacher Role	Teacher Behavior
	information	expert	lectures
	approval		directions
Dependent	reinforcement	authority	assignments
(closed systems	esteem from		criticism
suggested)	authority		rewards
Collaborative	social accept-	co-leader	discussion
(mixed systems	ance		leader
suggested)	peer exchange	environment	resource
	varied ideas	setter	provider
	esteem from	feedback	sharer
	peers	giver	
Independent	ego needs	facilitator	resource
(open systems	self-esteem		
suggested)			

style. He likes taking pictures with his friends, comparing the photos, and learning from others.

Bill is also an avid reader of science fiction. For this activity he prefers to learn alone, reading his books and mulling over his new ideas, occasionally discussing them with others. He uses other people to suggest new books for him to read.

Dependent learners often are agitated and confused when put into a collaborative or independent situation. School-age children will act out if they are given more responsibility than they can handle. Students who are asked to be dependent when they are more natural in a collaborative or independent state either become easily bored or turned off to the structure. Thus, the most effective teachers are those who have a variety of activities that allow for differences in learning styles so students can learn in the mode most comfortable for them.

Dependent learners often need more closed structure (as described above) than collaborative or independent learners, who need more open structures. By developing activities that are both open and closed, and by matching or allowing your students to match themselves to the most appropriate styles, you will reach them more completely and eliminate many of the classroom-based causes for misbehavior.

Discipline and Teaching

We have found in our own teaching and in observing hundreds of classrooms that the attention span of students is a key ingredient in the extent of discipline problems. Teachers who easily flow from one method of teaching to another are better able to maintain a student's attention than teachers who do not. Many teachers unknowingly encourage minor classroom irritations such as out-of-seat behavior, foot stomping, pencil tapping, and talking by not varying the way information is presented. Frequently, the teacher is the focal point in the classroom because he stands in front and presents information to the students who are all seated facing him.

We forget how difficult it was to sit through a 50-minute lecture in college, looking for ways to distract ourselves from our aching behinds and the drone of the professor's voice. Most of us sat politely because it was more important to get a good grade and the college credit rather than to voice our dissatisfaction.

Students who are unmotivated by the good grade and who have little value for the importance of education are not so polite. Being referred to the principal for classroom misbehavior can be more rewarding than being bored by the teacher. When teachers shift from one mode of presentation to another, they are better able to maintain student interest than when instruction occurs in one fixed mode. More specifically, if you spend more than 10 minutes (elementary age children) or 15 minutes (junior high and high school students) in any one mode, you can count on a significant number of students becoming inattentive. The following teacher modes of instruction, when varied, lead to a rich learning experience for students and less hassle with discipline.

1. *Lecture.* This mode is most familiar to teachers. The teacher dispenses information to students and is the focal point of the lesson. All questions and student responses are teacher directed.

2. *Large-Group Discussion.* The teacher and all students participate in a discussion related to a topic. The topic may be defined by the teacher, but all students are invited to share their thoughts and ideas. Effective large-group discussion is directed toward soliciting opinions from the students by asking them to become immersed in the subject itself and to comment on its personal relevance.

3. *Small-Group Discussion.* Groups of two to six students are formed and are given a task to do or a topic to discuss. One student may be selected to summarize the group's discussion for the whole class.

4. *Independent Seat Work.* Following a teacher-directed or group discussion, each student is assigned a project to consider or work to be completed that is related to what preceded it.

5. *Student Support Teams.* All students are assigned to teams of four to six. Students are heterogeneously grouped so that each team contains dependent, collaborative, and independent learners. The teacher may assign either a group project or individual seatwork. If it is a group project, then all students are evaluated according to their group's performance. If it is an individual assignment, then students who are having trouble with their work must first solicit the help of team members before they can ask the teacher for assistance. Only then may a student approach the teacher for help. Marilyn Burns, a leading educator and classroom teacher, has reported extremely good results in using a method similar to this. She claims that she has more time to work with small instructional groups because she is interrupted far less frequently by students who don't know what to do.[6]

By varying your mode of presentation, you are far more likely to adequately address your students' different learning styles. When you are planning your lessons, consider how you can flow from one mode to another so that your instructional objectives are met.

Excitement and Enthusiasm

There can be little dispute that some students misbehave because of a mismatch between course content and individual learning needs. Yet, how the teacher presents material is more important than the content itself. It is not the teacher's job to entertain students like Abe Kotter or Big Bird, but it is essential that the teacher exude positive energy. If a teacher is bored with his subject, then he will do little more than go through the motions of presenting it. Bored teachers usually speak in a monotone, use few nonverbal hand and body gestures, and smile infrequently. They often resist self-reflection and refuse to consider that their boring way of being may be influential in generating disinterested learners. Perhaps saddest of all, they come to view the fringe benefits of teaching as the main reason for continuing in the classroom and feel little interest in pursuing professional growth experiences.

Solutions to the problem of teacher boredom are beyond the scope of this book. But there is a relationship between student boredom and teacher boredom. Boredom, like enthusiasm, is contagious! A teacher who smiles, loves his subject area, and communicates his excitement to students creates a stimulating environment in which acting out because of boredom becomes unnecessary.

There are many reasons why classrooms lack excitement. Art Combs lists 10 characteristics of the modern classroom that hinder learning:

1. Preoccupation with order, categorization, and classifying.
2. Overvaluing authority, support, evidence, and the "scientific method"—all the good answers are someone else's.
3. Exclusive emphasis on the historical view, implying that all the good things have been discovered already.
4. Cookbook approaches, filling in the blanks.
5. Solitary learning, with discouragement of communication.
6. The elimination of self from the classroom. Only what the book says is important, not what a student thinks.
7. Emphasis upon force, threat, or coercion; what diminishes the self diminishes creativity.
8. The idea that mistakes are sinful.

9. The idea that students are not to be trusted.
10. Lock-step organization.[7]

Students who are processed through a school like the one described above come to school with basic needs, such as identity, power, connectedness, and achievement. When students begin to see that their needs are subservient to the daily curriculum, the seeds for trouble have been sown.

Fostering Creativity in the Classroom

According to E. Paul Torrance, creativity is "the process of becoming sensitive to problems, deficiencies, gaps in knowledge, missing elements, disharmonies, and so on; identifying the difficulty; searching for solutions, making guesses, or formulating hypotheses about the deficiencies; testing and retesting these hypotheses and possibly modifying and retesting them; and finally communicating the results."[8] Torrance's definition can be used to write a curriculum that fosters creative behavior.

Savary and Ehlen-Miller believe, "Everyone has the potential for creativity. Some have more artistic outlets and special talents for expressing their creativity, but even the most 'unartistic' person can be creative."[9] They believe that creativity can be learned. "Creative learning involves not only the intuitive right-brain hemisphere, but also the analytical left hemisphere. . . . Creative learning, wherever it occurs, encourages use of the whole mind. Thinking out of your whole mind is most likely to lead you into a new world of creativity."[10]

Classroom activities that foster creativity are highly motivating. Many units are devoted especially to the development of creativity, such as problem solving, dramatics, and creative writing. Another and perhaps more effective way is to integrate activities that spark creativity into the "regular curriculum." This validates the creative process for use with everyday problems and expression rather than for special occasions for the artistically talented. The following questions can be used to review any lesson to see if it fosters creativity.

1. At what points were students asked to respond to something that had no *one* right answer?
2. In what circumstances were students required to deal with more than one possibility?
3. What activities required students to defer judgment?
4. How often was guessing and hypothesizing encouraged?
5. In what situations were students encouraged to try the unknown and take reasonable risks?

6. In what ways were students encouraged to think of new ideas?
7. What new experiences were provided?
8. In what ways were all of the senses used in the lesson?
9. How did the teacher model creativity?
10. How is students' creativity visibly apparent in the classroom?

Evaluation and Grading

Evaluation is a critical link between behavior and learning. Evaluation gives students information that can be used for self-understanding. We know that children who receive poor evaluations often become poor learners. Students who have had a history of failure in the public school will often prefer to drop out either physically or mentally and find other ways to be successful. One way students can turn failure into success is to succeed at becoming a behavior problem and to win approval through failing grades.

Mr. Andrews taught a 7th grade class of emotionally disturbed students. These students never received a higher grade than a C and their averages were closer to F+. As an experiment for the first quarter, the teacher gave every student an A or B in every subject regardless of "what they earned." Actually there was no way of knowing what they "earned" because of the nature of the curriculum and, more importantly, the problems of the students. Once report cards went home, many parents called to see whether it was their child or the teacher who was "sick." The teacher began the second quarter by telling the students that they could all maintain their A's by working just a little harder. This message was repeated the two next quarters, but the work required increased each time. Most students tried hard to keep the A's, a prize they had never known before.

This experiment highlights the need for students to receive positive feedback. Students who never receive good grades do no try for them because they know they are beyond reach. It is much more rewarding to be a nuisance than to try for an unattainable goal. On the other hand, once students feel that a good grade is achievable they have a lot more energy to maintain the good grades, even if it means more work. A system of evaluation that either forces students to compete with each other or maintains the same criteria for all students despite intellectual and academic differences is destined to produce winners and losers. The losers, more often than not, are tomorrow's discipline problems. They have learned that if they work hard, are well motivated, and do their best, then they are rewarded with a C or D that illuminates their mediocrity. Few of us can do our best for very long with such minimal validation. How many of us continue to paint pictures after we have discovered in elementary school the limited talent we have?

Discipline problems can be prevented by making it genuinely possible for all students to receive grades of "A." If you teach 8th grade math and have students who are functioning at the 4th grade level, then you can prevent discipline problems in two ways. You can try to have the child removed to a lower functioning classroom. If, however, the student is to remain in your class, then you must secure the necessary curriculums and staff resources to provide instruction at his level. And evaluation for him should be based upon effort and performance at *that* level. If you fail to provide instruction for students at their academic level, then they cannot be faulted for rebelling against a system that won't accept them as they are.

It is a good practice to have conferences periodically with children and provide them with statements concerning their assets and areas needing improvement. You might also consider asking them to describe how they feel about being in the class.

Performance contracting, which is similar to a self-contract, is an evaluation strategy especially useful with older students. A performance contract should specify what the teacher wants from the student, what the student wants to learn for himself, and how the final evaluation will be determined. Like a social contract, a performance contract may have a flag component, what the teacher must have for the contract to be valid, and a negotiable component, what the teacher and student can mutually agree to. Like a social contract, an effective performance contract should be reevaluated every two to three weeks to see that it is working and still appropriate. Many good performance contracts do not work because teachers and students think that once they are signed, they cannot be reevaluated. Flexibility is an important part of all phases of evaluation.

Performance contracting is not the only method of incorporating student input into your evaluation system. You can elicit test questions from students; you can incorporate student ideas as to what information should be on the test; you can have students test each other, write test questions for themselves, evaluate their own and each others' tests, use group projects as well as tests, and a host of other evaluative methods. The key to any evaluation method that will help minimize classroom discipline problems is that it provides as much responsibility for the student as possible, and that all students have a reasonable chance for success.

Grading Creative Assignments

Activities that foster creativity are hard to evaluate and even harder to grade. The best solution, of course, is not to grade them, but students learn to value what is graded. So, unless you are a non-graded system, it becomes a difficult dilemma. Here are some suggestions for grading creativity:

1. Establish criteria (define creativity assignment goals).
2. Prioritize and weigh.
3. Grade only the criteria.
4. Allow students to establish criteria.
5. Allow students to evaluate criteria.

Competition

Related to evaluation is the issue of competition in the classroom. There has been considerable debate over the value of competition in the learning process. Advocates claim competition is highly stimulating and motivates students to achieve their best. The strongest argument is that competition is a fact of life. Students will be unprepared for the real world if they do not experience competition in school.

Other educators claim that the world is competitive at times, but it is based more on cooperation. The foundations of society—the family, religion, love relationships, and even simple everyday procedures like driving—can be destroyed by competition. These educators advocate more cooperative learning opportunities with a minimum of attention given to competition. Students already know how to compete.

Our investigations of competition in classroom settings suggest that competition can be either a positive or negative learning experience. It is more important *how* rather than *whether* it is used. The two main variables are:

1. Is the competition voluntary?
2. Does the competition focus on ends or means?

Voluntary competition is chosen by the participant without direct pressure or indirect coercion. There are no hidden penalties for not competing. Under these conditions, children will take on challenges that are appropriate to their ability. If they take more than they can handle, they are emotionally prepared to understand that not succeeding does not equal failure. When students are forced to compete, they perform under fear or duress. Failure is perceived as personal, and negatively affects their dignity. Even success can be frightening if students fear being pushed to higher levels of competition.

When competition focuses on the means, or process, the results are rewarding and high levels of learning can be achieved. Teamwork is a positive experience. Winning is important, but not as important as playing. When the outcome is stressed, the result is often cheating or taking short cuts and the stress level is intense.

We advocate using competition in the learning process as long as students are given free choice whether or not to compete and are provided optional games that match their interest and ability.

Winning and losing is part of all competition, but the process of playing can always be stressed above the final score. In addition, there are many examples of non-competitive games and games without score that can supplement the more competitive activities.[11]

The teacher can change a negative competitive classroom into a positive one. The first step is to identify areas of competition in the classroom. Each classroom has its own unique competitive characteristics. The teacher can examine each competition, determine its nature, and assess its effects on the students. With the help of students and colleagues (including administrators), a teacher can determine ways to derive maximum benefits from competition.

It is up to the teacher to ensure that competitions are positive experiences for students. By choosing competitive structures that are voluntary and focus on process rather than outcomes, the teacher can, in effect, reap many of the rewards of competition while avoiding most of the pitfalls.

Students who are forced into negative competitive situations are likely candidates for behavior problems. By selecting competitive situations that are chosen by the student and which are means (process) emphasized, you will encourage student responsibility and minimize the student's need to break your social contract.

Time on Task

Increasing the students' time on task can be very helpful in improving classroom discipline. Students can't work at a school task and be disruptive at the same time. The more time students spend on task, the more likely they will achieve success, and the less likely they will act out to protect their dignity.

However, Art Combs asks the question, "Time on what task?" If the task is meaningless, tedious, unchallenging, too difficult, boring, or irrelevant, then spending time doing it is not beneficial to the student. Eventually, increasing a student's time on task will backfire and lead to misbehavior if the task is inappropriate or meaningless. The most beneficial way to increase time on task is to increase the student's desire to participate. Measuring time on task without considering the worth of the task is insufficient and can mask ineffective teaching.

Homework

In *A Nation At Risk*,[12] schools are criticized for not giving enough homework. In most other countries, especially the industrial and technological leaders like Japan and Germany, students have a great deal more homework than Americans. On the other hand, teachers complain that students don't do the homework given to them now; more homework will only result in more homework not completed.

Undone homework is one of the areas usually handled with a discipline technique. "Don't do your homework; get a consequence." On the surface this is appropriate. Teachers have a right and a responsibility to give homework, and students have a responsibility to do it.

Yet the problem is often more related to lack of motivation rather than a desire to break a rule. Students have a right to be given homework that will enhance their learning, and teachers have a responsibility give it to them. Homework works best when it:

1. *Is challenging.* Not because of its length or because it challenges the patience of students. Homework should give students a sense of pride or accomplishment when finished, not just a sense of relief.
2. *Is interesting.* Students don't need to love every assignment, and drill and practice certainly can be used as homework. But even drill and practice can be presented in a challenging or interesting way. Homework competes with the stereo, television, sleep, phone, friends, and family. The assignment needs a fighting chance if it is to get done.
3. *Is proportionate.* Homework should be the right length and intensity. Two hundred addition problems is out of scale, as is reading a paragraph a night of *A Tale of Two Cities*. Homework should not be assigned to fill time but to complete a learning objective.

4. *Is related to what is covered in class.* Homework collected and not integrated into class activities is perceived by students as a waste of time. Simply going over the homework in class is not enough. The learning gained by doing the homework should directly relate to other class activities.

5. *Is corrected quickly.* When homework is returned weeks after it was handed in, it is of little value to the students' learning. Homework can be returned faster if it is self-corrected or corrected by peers.

6. *Has choices.* Students are more receptive to assignments that offer some selection. If there are 10 questions at the end of a chapter, let the students select 6 to answer. The process of selection may be of more learning benefit than answering the questions.

7. *Is not written on unreadable dittos.* If dittos are used, make sure the challenge of the assignment isn't trying to read it.

8. *Is not always done alone.* Provide group projects and assignments whenever possible. In life outside of school, people more often work together than alone. Working together is more motivating and has a better chance of being done.

If students are not doing homework, they should receive an appropriate consequence. However, if homework does not measure up, then it needs to be changed or dropped.

Cooperative Learning

Cooperative learning strategies are becoming more popular as teachers see the power of working in groups. When done well, cooperative learning is highly motivating, produces achievement-oriented results, and minimizes students' needs to misbehave.

Research indicates that cooperative learning strategies increase self-esteem,[13] increase liking for school,[14] and increase academic achievement.[15] James Leming and John Hollifield examined hundreds of studies on cooperative learning and conclude:

> Using these processes, teachers have students work together in small groups in the classroom to master academic material. The small groups are carefully structured to include high and low achieving students, whites and minorities, and males and females. They work together to be rewarded as a team for what they accomplish, but they are also rewarded for their individual achievement. More than 100 research

studies in the last 20 years have found that students learn the material better in this kind of structure. In addition, they develop positive social attitudes and behavior. Students learn to get along better with students of other races and ethnic groups, to accept mainstreamed students into the classroom, and to show greater mutual concern for each other.[16]

Some of the fears about cooperative learning are that:
1. Some children will do most of the work while others will coast.
2. Some groups finish before others and get restless waiting for the rest of the class to finish.
3. It is hard to grade individuals when working in groups.
4. There is too much potential for students to get sidetracked from the group task and spend large amounts of time socializing.
5. It is too difficult to monitor each group.
6. It takes too much time. The same information can be presented in a fraction of the time with other instructional techniques.

Each is a genuine concern. However, with careful planning and monitoring of the activity, most of these fears can be eliminated or minimized. Special attention should be given to:
1. Ensuring that the size of the group matches the group task. Some students can get lost if the group is too large.
2. Allowing an appropriate time to complete the group task. Too little time is frustrating and minimizes the cooperative nature of the activity. The best students take over just to finish the project. Too much time leads to restlessness and boredom.
3. Giving clear directions. When students spend an inordinate amount of time trying to figure out what to do, they get frustrated and lose interest. Tasks take longer than expected to complete.
4. Ensuring that the activity leads to a product of some kind when completed. The product can be something the group made, a decision, an agreement, or a performance. Groups need some type of product to keep focused, to feel a sense of accomplishment, and to evaluate how well they did.
5. Discussing group process concerns. If the students are to learn communication and cooperation skills, the teacher should provide an opportunity for students to reflect and discuss them.

6. Integrating the cooperative learning activity with the curriculum. The reason for doing the activity should be clear in relation to what happened before it was used and what will happen after.

Technology

The technological revolution that many predicted would change the fabric of American education has not yet happened. Technology has had a greater impact in business than in schools. However, many inroads have been made, and, if the trend continues, the predictions for revolution may not be that far from happening. As of 1984, 85 percent of all public schools in the United States were using microcomputers. (Minnesota, Colorado, Utah, Oregon, and Arkansas were the top five respectively.[17])

Computer use is not limited to science and math. Courses in art, English, social sciences, music, and the industrial arts have all made use of computer technology. Technology is not limited to computers. The VCR has replaced filmstrips and 16 MM projectors.

The fusion of microcomputers and video is close at hand. "Hypermedia" is the label for interactive video that allows the participant to access hundreds of video images stored on laser discs. Interactive video allows students to follow progressions based on their choices to a final outcome. Prototypes have been developed in medicine that allow medical students to diagnose, provide treatment, and see what results without endangering fellow students or lab animals. Patricia Hanlon, an English teacher, and librarian Robert Cambell at Lowell High School in San Francisco have developed an interactive program to teach John Steinbeck's *The Grapes of Wrath*.

> Students read the novel, then sit down to a computer controlled videodisc player, loaded with Depression-era radio programs, photographs, film footage and magazine articles. They can use the system to study dozens of aspects of life in America during the 1930's. This is the ultimate research tool for a generation raised on television and stereo systems. "These students have been consumers of media," Hanlon says. "We want them to become manipulators of media."[18]

Eventually, computer access to stored information will replace libraries as we now know them. Students will be able to gather nearly any information they need from a home-based terminal. It is staggering to imagine the equivalent of the Library of Congress available to anyone with a computer terminal and an access code.

The effect of technology on discipline is obvious. A teacher in a training session on discipline announced proudly, "Last year I had so many discipline problems that I almost quit teaching. This year I have none." When asked how she made such a remarkable change, she replied, "Last year I taught math. This year, I am teaching computers." Students don't have time to disrupt when they are working with computers.

It is important to understand that technology can create lessons that could never be taught otherwise. It can increase motivation, stimulation, and participation. It can teach mastery learning or provide individual instruction with special tutorials for each step of the lesson. It brings to the class moving images that make books look like horse and buggies by comparison. But technology does not and cannot guarantee learning. Information is a far cry from wisdom. Students today have more information than any generation in history, but until they learn how to use it, that information will confuse as well as clarify the multitude of choices that confront them. When using technology as part of the instructional process, the following points should carefully be considered:

1. Technology excels at providing information. Teachers need to instruct students in how to process that information and how make decisions based on it.

2. Certain technologies, such as computer work stations, are often used by a single student. Extensive isolation is not healthy for children who need social interaction and communication as part of their educational experience. Cooperative learning strategies can easily be adapted to incorporate computers.

3. Students are media saturated at home. We have already mentioned the vast number of hours children spend watching television. Many children spend much of their free time playing computer and video games. We must be careful to provide students a balanced diet of instructional activities.

4. We doubt that technology can make students lazy, but it can teach them to be passive. Active learning is essential to the full development of the child.

Many students are more technologically oriented than their teachers. Many states require some form of computer literacy for receiving a teaching credential. School systems have been offering inservice training for a number of years in use of computers. As educators become more familiar with how to use the hardware (of all technology, not just computers), they will also be sensitive to using technology for achieving sound educational objectives.

Conclusion

In examining the relationship between effective teaching and discipline, significant attention must be given to the notion of student hope. As long as students believe that there is real hope for them to be successful, discipline plans can be successful. However, when hope is lost, so is the student. When students accept negative labels, when they believe that the curriculum is impossible to learn, when they believe that they will get in trouble no matter how hard they try to avoid it, no discipline plan can compensate. The nurturing of student hope must be at the core for teaching to be truly effective.

For the Administrator

You can be a valuable resource to teachers by sensitively offering your wisdom and experience, your knowledge of curriculum, and your broad view of your school's educational program. Most teachers feel more trapped by the demands of the curriculum than they need be. With your encouragement for experimentation and innovation and your support for curriculum modifications that meet student needs, your teachers will not only minimize discipline problems, but improve all aspects of their teaching. You can provide the leadership necessary for curriculum reform.

While it is critical for teachers to feel administrative support before innovation can occur, support alone is not sufficient. Teachers need examples of what can be done in concrete terms. They need release time to develop their ideas, and, most importantly, they need to feel safe so that they can learn from their failures as well as from their successes without penalty. Like many problems students, teachers often unnecessarily feel threatened by the administration. Provide more than lip service that alternative teaching styles are acceptable and desirable.

Because boredom is a major cause of classroom disruption, we suggest that you establish a task force to examine your curriculum. Update it so that it is relevant and focuses attention on more than facts. Encourage the task force members to actually take quizzes and tests, to participate in classroom activities, and to try workbook problems. If the curriculum is boring to adults it will most likely be boring to students. The goal of the task force should be to positively interact with teachers to minimize student boredom. Specific recommendations in the form of a report or summary at a faculty meeting can be most helpful.

You can also examine your evaluation systems and consider alternate ways of reporting student progress. Try to use methods that describe strengths and areas for improvement without judging them. All students should be able to achieve success in your school. Do your best to minimize competition in your school that pits student against student, and find as many ways as possible to encourage cooperation. When competition does exist, see that it is voluntary and focuses more on the process of learning than on winning. There should be at least some form of competition that every student can both participate in and win.

Have as one of your goals the development of teacher support groups. Teacher boredom can be minimized when a vital group of teachers learn to trust each other and to share methods, ideas, and lessons with each other. Help them learn how to observe each other non-judgmentally so that they may look to each other for inspirational support before the going gets rough.

Emphasize the importance to teachers of how varying one's process of teaching and methods of instruction can positively affect discipline problems in the classroom.

Endnotes

[1]Summarized from R. Wlodkowski, *Motivation and Teaching*, Washington, D.C.: National Education Association, 1980.

[2]R. Wlodkowski, "How to Help Teachers Reach the Turned Off Student," unpublished paper, 1978.

[3]J. Borger, M. Carroll, and D. Schiller, "Motivating Students."

[4]G. Brown, *Human Teaching for Human Learning: An Introduction to Confluent Education* (New York: Random House, 1971), 228.

[5]A. Porter, J. Brophy, "Highlights of Research on Good Teaching," *Educational Leadership* 45 (May 1988), 75.

[6]M. Burns, "Groups of Four: Solving the Management Problem," *Learning* 10 (1981), 46-51.

[7]A. Combs, *The Professional Education of Teachers* (Boston: Allyn & Bacon, 1965), 36.

[8]E.P. Torrance, "Scientific Vies of Creativity and Factors Affecting Its Growth," in *Creativity and Learning*, edited by J. Kagan (Boston: Beacon Press, 1970), 73.

[9]L.M. Savay and M. Ehlen-Miller, *Mindways: A Guide for Exploring Your Mind* (New York: Harper and Row, 1979), 84.

[10]*Ibid.*, 84.

[11]For a more detailed discussion on the factors of competition, see R. Curwin and P. DeMarte, "Making Classroom Competition Positive: A Facilitating Model," in *Degrading the Grading Myths: A Primer of Alternatives to Grades and Marks* (Alexandria, Va.: Association for Supervision and Curriculum Development, 1976), 14-19.

[12]The National Commission for Excellence in Education, "A Nation at Risk," 1983. Copies available from: Superintendent of Documents, U.S. Government Printing Office, Washington, DC 20402.

[13]R. Slavin, *Cooperative Learning* (New York: Longman [Research on Teaching Monograph Series], 1983).

[14]*Ibid.*

[15]D. Johnson et al., "Effects of Cooperative, Competitive and Individualistic Goal Structures on Achievement: A Meta-Analysis," *Psychological Bulletin* 89 (1981), 47-62.

[16]J. Leming and J. Hollifield, "Cooperative Learning: A Research Success Story," *Educational Researcher*, (March 1985), 14.

[17]USA Today Poll, *USA TODAY*, March 1985.

[18]"Hypermedia," *Newsweek*, October 3, 1988, 45.

10
Special Problems

Because Three-Dimensional Discipline is a flexible, eclectic process, it can be applied to any situation that involves teachers and students. However, we are frequently asked to discuss how to use Three-Dimensional Discipline for special problems. The most frequently asked questions deal with:

1. Working with handicapped students in a mainstreamed class.
2. Applying Three-Dimensional Discipline specifically to an inner-city school.
3. Minimizing drug and alcohol use in school.

The basic principles of Three-Dimensional Discipline were developed and field tested in inner-city environments. Teachers of mainstreamed classes who have used Three-Dimensional Discipline report that the model is effective with all students in their classes. Teachers of special education report similar results. Students who use drugs and alcohol should be dealt with in similar ways to any student who does not behave appropriately in class. Thus, each of the chapters and activities in this book can be used by teachers who teach in the inner city, who teach handicapped students in special education and mainstreamed classes, and who deal with students who use drugs and alcohol. We do not suggest that an entirely different approach be used in these special areas. Social contracts, consistent use of effective consequences, minimizing stress, using creative approaches for out-of-control students, and avoiding power struggles will help you take charge of your classroom whether you teach in an inner-city, suburban, or rural school; they will help you regardless of the type of students you teach.

However, each of the three special problems mentioned above is of sufficient importance to discuss in more depth; specific knowledge, awareness, and strategies might help you cope with discipline problems associated with these issues. In this chapter we explore additional activities and information that apply to these special situations.

Handicapped Children

Federal law PL 94-142 mandated that children with handicapping conditions receive the "most appropriate education" in the "least restrictive environment." The law is designed to prevent the indiscriminate dumping of children into special classes or schools. It is becoming common practice in most school districts to conduct extensive diagnostic evaluations that identify students for placement in special programs and establish individualized educational plans. Many school districts require rigorous arguments to be made in support of special services for fear of violating the "least restrictive environment" clause. This all means that it is more difficult and time-consuming to secure special placement and more likely that "handicapped" students who have previously received instruction in special classes will return either part-time or full-time to the mainstream. Whether you are ready or not, trained or untrained, you can expect more of these students to be in your class.

There are a variety of reasons why some students are referred to special classes: physical, emotional, behavioral, and learning disabilities. Because the educational and emotional needs of "handicapped" or disabled students vary so greatly, it is impossible to discuss how to set up an effective program of discipline for each potential problem. Moreover, many disabled children do not behave any differently than students considered to be normal. However, some disabled children have special behavior problems that make dealing with them doubly difficult.

Disabled children are often referred to special classes and remedial units because their behavior is unacceptable in the regular classroom. They may be viewed as hyperactive, distractible, argumentative, surly, rude, immature, or irresponsible. Youngsters enrolled in special education classes usually have many common characteristics. Except for those who are mentally retarded, they are generally of average intelligence or better (although some are slow learners) but experience learning problems in reading, spelling, writing, or arithmetic. They have either been retained in one of the early elementary school grades or referred for remedial services to supplement instruction in the regular class. At this early time in their school lives, teachers often use descriptions such as, "lazy," "could do better if he worked harder," "needs to develop good study skills," "seems unmotivated," "has better ability than he shows," "is bossy and can't share with others." From the 4th grade through the 8th grade, they usually have great difficulty competing with the rest of the class. The more difficulty they have, the more likely they are to act up in class. They lack enthusiasm, skip class, and become regular visitors to the office of the school disciplinarian.

For many, the experience of academic success is unattainable, and the special student seeks other methods of gratification. Excuse-making, failing to take responsibility for one's own actions, blaming others, and refusing to work or to follow guidelines for acceptable behavior are common. Without the help they need, such students often drop out of school, much to the silent relief of school guardians.

Disciplinary problems among handicapped students are therefore strongly associated with their inability to compete with others in class, to get the attention of other students, or to feel equal to them. Everyone, including handicapped students, needs to feel important, whether it is for acting up in class, for being the best swimmer on the team, for being a good musician, or for being a top-notch math student.

Since we are focusing our discussion on handicapped students who exhibit unacceptable behavior, changing that behavior needs to be one of the primary focal points in planning for the child's integration into a normal setting. If you work in a school that has the good fortune of extensive remedial and support services, then the major responsibility for preparing a student for life in the mainstream resides with the specialist. But if you do not, and you are a regular classroom teacher, then the burden of responsibility falls squarely on your shoulders. Like it or not, the student is in your class. Your choices are to continue teaching as if the student were not there, in which case the probability is high that inappropriate behavior will occur (or worsen). Or you can adapt your program to accommodate the child's special needs.

If you are teaching a special education class, or if you have handicapped students in a mainstreamed class, we suggest you set up a social contract with your students and follow the other guidelines outlined in this book. In addition, we offer the following suggestions that will help you both prevent discipline problems with special students and resolve them more easily when they occur.

Take Care of Yourself

The first step in working with special students who have behavior problems is to do some work with yourself. You need to be in touch with your feelings; you need to recognize them, acknowledge them, and find outlets for them. Teachers of learning-disabled or emotionally disturbed kids must be willing to give and give and give, and in return receive frustration, criticism, defeat, and failure. Despite many hours of extra planning and an inordinate amount of instructional time, complaints abound such as, "You never work with me like you do with the others." A good day in which the child behaves may be followed by two or three days of off-the-wall behavior. An "aha" experience in which Sammy finally "gets" subtraction is followed by a blank stare the next day that tells you it's back to step one. Inattentiveness, rudeness, messiness, and forgetfulness may be the norm for such a child. Some of the finest teachers resort to name-calling, acting like Marine sergeants, pleading, whining, or withdrawing as ways of dealing with such students. In short, these children can be a constant drain, depleting your energy reserves. If you have children such as this in your class, you need a support group of colleagues who understand your feelings and provide positive support.

Provide Responsibility

One common complaint from teachers of older handicapped students is that previous teachers, often in special classes and day or residential schools, did more for them than was needed in the long run. They tried to compensate for the disability by making sure that students got to class on time, had their work completed, and were dressed and washed properly. In general, they saw to it that the students experienced no failure, even if failure was a natural consequence of a choice they made. It is understandable why many special education teachers try to be overly protective. Their students need a boost to their self-image and need to live and learn in a positive, supportive environment. Furthermore, special education teachers, simply through the natural selection process, tend to be patient and humanistic and are trained to see that the child is more important than the subject matter and that even small gains in achievement are worthy of pride.

However, these qualities and values can be undermined when they lead the teacher to take responsibility for the child's behavior. Taking responsibility means that teachers (or administrators or parents) accept excuses that are not legitimate. They find solutions to the child's problems. They offer easy ways out of difficult situations that the child has created. They set expectations too low for both behavior and ability to learn, which often limits the child's potential. For example, some teachers do not follow through on agreed upon or previously stated consequences because the child uses a handicapping condition as a reason for not living up to realistic expectations. This situation often creates a vicious cycle when parents, stricken by the guilt associated with a disabled child, try to compensate for "apparent" behavior problems by doing too much for the child; in so doing they take responsibility away from the child and with that an opportunity for growth. By the time the child goes to school, he may not know how to take responsibility for himself. The next phase of the cycle is for his teachers to convert this diagnosis into a strategy, i.e., if a child cannot accept responsibility, then it might be harmful to thrust responsibility upon him. This confusion between a diagnosis and a strategy is common given the prevailing attitude of "take a child where he is, and help him grow from there." Unfortunately, this view can end up reinforcing the inability of the child to ever begin to take responsibility for himself. Obviously, age, ability to understand, maturity, and other social development factors are all important in determining how much responsibility a child can handle. It is important to teach responsibility by allowing students to live with their decisions.

We find that a great many of the behavior problems associated with disabled children come from the lack of responsibility these children have been given throughout their lives. We suggest you give students responsibility as soon as possible, without overwhelming them to the point of agitation. Begin by giving the child choices whenever possible. For example, allow him to select which reading book he wants that period. If the child needs to go to the lavatory, ask whether he wants three minutes now or next period. If the child wants to play a game, give him three choices. Once the child has made a choice, let him live with it. Don't come to his rescue if the choice does not work out. Give him the opportunity to learn from

bad choices within the limits of physical safety; allow natural consequences to occur, and ask evaluative questions such as:

1. How did it turn out for you?
2. What did you learn from that experience?
3. What other choice could you have made, which may have
   been better?
4. What will you do next time?

For those children who cannot make open-ended choices easily,
use close-ended choices. Do you want to read your book or review
your math problems? Do you want to play checkers or chess? Slowly
build up to more open-ended choices, but never stop giving as many
choices as possible.

The second part of teaching responsibility involves the same
principle upon which we based the whole notion of the social contract.
Set clear limits and expect the children to follow them. You might
need different limits in some cases with disabled students, but once
they are established and mutually understood, live by them. Excuses
and explanations are not acceptable reasons for failure to comply
with realistic and previously understood expectations. Using the
handicap as a reason or excuse for failure to meet expectations is one
of the most self-defeating concepts. The difference between a handicap and a disability is that a disability is a physical, emotional, or
behavioral impairment, while a handicap is other people's response
to that impairment. For example, deafness is a disability, but difficulty
in communication is a handicap. Be "kind and understanding" in
setting up realistic expectations that challenge, but don't overwhelm
the student. When it comes time to ensure that the expectations are
met, it is time for your more demanding self to take charge.

The third aspect of teaching responsibility is to encourage and
support problem solving and planning on the part of your students.
When they come to you with a problem or excuse, use that opportunity to help them gather information, identify alternatives, make
decisions, and analyze the consequence of those decisions. When they
behave inappropriately, ask them for a plan of action for changing
their behavior. Once they have thought of possible solutions and have
developed their plans, hold them accountable for doing them. Sometimes students will fail to behave according to plan. When this
happens, they sometimes need to experience an unpleasant, but nonpunitive, consequence and be re-directed to developing a new plan.
You can evaluate the plan to see that the student lived up to his part.
Then allow the student the opportunity for self-reflection by encour-

aging him to evaluate how successful the plan was in solving the problem. Self-evaluation of planning is a critical skill for increasing responsibility. You need a high tolerance for broken promises and misunderstanding as well as lots of patience!

Learn to Communicate with Handicapped Students Who Have Communication Difficulties

Many disabled students have communication problems. For example, hearing impaired, visually impaired, and learning-disabled children might be missing critical information that other students are receiving. Deaf students, for example, often miss much of the incidental information that most other students learn as a natural part of overhearing conversations in their environment. Much of this learning involves manners, social know-how, and implicit expectations of peers and teachers. Students who have communication problems might act out to express their confusion, anger, and disconnectedness with the group, or they may lack understanding about what constitutes appropriate behavior. They might also withdraw and try to avoid being noticed at all.

If you have students who you suspect have a communication problem, find out the extent and nature of the problem. Find out the ramifications of that problem for the child's ability to learn and his potential for picking up the subtle social cues of the classroom. Find out what you can do to learn how to reach the child and communicate directly with him. If you have support people in your class such as notetakers, interpreters, tutors, speech therapists, or readers, take the time to talk with them about their roles, about how you can work together to make both your jobs more successful, and about how to coordinate your functions to help the child.

Level with Them

Everyone has personal hang-ups and most people put out quite a lot of energy in hiding their "deficiencies" from others. The people who become intimate friends are those who appreciate successes and encourage strengths. They are also genuinely able to accept imperfections, which no longer have to be hidden. People who are close level with their friends by recognizing the balance of what they are: a person who has both strengths and limitations.

One reason that praise is differentially effective with handicapped students (or for that matter with anybody) is that it does not provide adequate balance to the complexities of the human condition.

It *only* emphasizes the positive and ignores the effectiveness of feedback that is holistic and balanced. Tom, a 5th grade student who was ultimately referred to a learning disabilities class, illustrates the limitations of *not* leveling with children in a balanced way. He was not completing assignments or doing his homework when his teacher and parents decided to praise any movement that he made in the desired direction. They were perplexed to discover that the more they praised, the worse he got. Despite their good intentions, they failed to recognize that Tom was afraid of praise because deep down he felt that he could not consistently meet their expectations. So he saw praise as a reminder of his inadequacy, which led to behavior that showed everybody just how inadequate he felt.

He needed honest feedback, which might include praise, but not praise *exclusively*. The fact is that students who are failures in school feel they have a big secret that needs to be hidden. You need to sensitively let them know that you know the secret and are prepared with a plan to provide needed remedial assistance as well as face-saving mechanisms to protect them from peers.

Don't Ask Why

If Billy fights, doesn't do his work, or makes excuses, don't ask him why he behaves the way he does unless you like to hear, "I don't know." Have a talk with him and list for him, using impersonal pronouns, the reasons why you think he does what he does. For example, you might say,

> Billy, I cannot accept your refusal to do your work. Although I don't know for sure what the problems are, *other* students who don't do their work may be feeling: (1) unable to do their work because they don't understand it, in which case I'm willing to offer extra help; (2) afraid to look stupid in front of their classmates, in which case I'm willing to call on you only when your hand is raised; (3) pressured to achieve by their parents or by me, and they don't work because they really feel angry, in which case you can write me a note that tells me how you feel or let me know after class or talk to the guidance counselor; (4) simply do not understand why they need to learn certain things, in which case you can ask me and I'll try to explain or offer you a different assignment that makes more sense to you.

Such an approach is generally far more effective in making contact with the troubled student than asking "why" questions. Although your hunches may be off-target, they do let the student know that you have an in-depth understanding of young people, which makes it more likely that you will see evidence of compliant behaviors. Students are more likely to consider the needs of others when they feel understood. As a way of concluding your talk with Billy, tell him, "Billy, I don't know if any of this is true for you, and what I want you to do is consider what I said, the choices that I offered, and let me know either through your words or actions, what you are planning to do to get your work done."

Adopt a "Friend"

Taking risks to explore new skills is both scary and essential to personal growth. It is even more difficult for the student who has grown accustomed to failure. But everyone, no matter how limited, can stand out in certain ways. Those who are more fortunate have a variety of mentors along the way who help to identify strengths and provide support in undertaking new and difficult learnings related to these strengths. This gives confidence and encourages risk taking.

Many educators are in a position to be mentors, but it is often the case that those selected are students who have already demonstrated their skills. Few want to be involved with children who do not (on the surface) appear to have much going for them.

We advise each of you to adopt one "friend" for a year and to make a commitment to real involvement with such a student to draw out a special talent. Expect more than your share of disappointments when your adoptee retreats to familiar territory such as poor motivation or antagonistic behavior.

Mr. McKane's relationship with Joe illustrates the immense possibilities for gratification. Joe was a repeating 7th grade student and he was identified as learning disabled; Mr. McKane was an industrial arts teacher. Early in the school year, Mr. McKane took Joe aside and told him that because he had already completed the 7th grade shop curriculum, he would be allowed to work on special industrial arts projects. Joe, who had demonstrated some prior talent (although nothing extraordinary), made a list of projects that he wanted to make, and Mr. McKane offered some of his time and help to participate with Joe in making these.

By mid-year, Joe had made a children's play table, a chair, and a small stool, and his work was placed on display in the window of the school library. Mr. McKane and Joe grew close to each other, which enabled Mr. McKane to discuss various problems that Joe had in other classes and made Joe receptive to considering other means of behavior. Joe's behavioral turnabout became the school's success story. Mr. McKane was both saddened and joyful to see his adoptee move on.

Permit Yourself to Make Mistakes

Disabled students have repeatedly experienced failure in school, which is one of the causes for their "handicap." They secretly see others as more worthy and competent than they so they often retreat to the safety of doing nothing as a way to avoid the risk of being wrong. You can help this child by allowing yourself permission to acknowledge your mistakes and by assuredly stating your lack of perfection loudly and publicly. By correcting your errors, you are also sending the message that mistakes are natural and are usually not permanent.

Provide Clear Structure

The learning-disabled student in particular is often disoriented in relation to time and space; he is inattentive and is more often than not hyperactive. As noted earlier, the social contract works well with such students because it specifically and clearly defines acceptable and unacceptable behavior. Your special needs students should be expected to follow the contract but may need some extra help from you in learning to do this.

Many special education students do best in environments that are structured and predictable. Because of their time and space disorientation, it may be insufficient to simply state a rule along with consequences. You may be enforcing rule violations all day! To help you and the student enhance your chances for mutual success, we offer the following tips:

1. If you have a hyperactive child in your class, keep him seated close to you and place masking tape on the floor around his desk that defines acceptable parameters of movement during "seatwork" time.
2. If you have a distractible child in your class and you want him to focus on a given task, have his desk face a wall to minimize classroom distractions, or, if feasible, arrange for one or more study carrels that block out visual distraction.

3. If the child responds excessively to auditory distraction when working at his desk, have him wear headphones to block out sound, or if you have the facilities, pipe in some soft, soothing music.

4. Provide a list of specific activities (hourly or less) to be done in class and tape this list to the child's desk. Make him responsible for placing a check mark next to each activity following completion.

5. Catch the child being good and formally acknowledge this through verbal reinforcement or, in more extreme cases, through activity or concrete reinforcement. You would do well to familiarize yourself with principles and practices of behavior modification, which have often been used with good classroom success for hard-to-reach students.

6. Use parents, volunteers, or other students (those with a high tolerance for frustration) as tutorial aides.

7. Accept that progress will be slow and find ways to show the student visible proof of his progress. Have him chart the number of times he raises his hand rather than blurting out an answer. Keep a monthly folder of the child's work so he can check his own progress. Keep a running record of all new spelling words learned, successful solutions to math problems, and other accomplishments.

8. Some of the characteristics of learning disabilities include poor memory and sequencing skills. Be sure to break down each task into its components because the child's lack of organizational ability prevents him from doing this himself. Each step of a task needs to be emphasized, such as:
   a. get your math book (pause)
   b. open to page 23 (pause)
   c. do problems 1, 2, and 3 (pause)
   d. raise your hand when you are finished
   If you give more than two or three steps at a time, the child is doomed to confusion, and you are on the path to greater frustration.

9. Find and acknowledge the child's strengths. When students are slow, disgruntled, or defiant, it is difficult to find ways to appreciate them by acknowledging their strengths. We are reminded of a time when one of the authors while teaching 7th grade was challenged to a game of chess by an L.D. student. The teacher was surprised by how slowly the game

proceeded, and was even more surprised when he lost. It was a good reminder that "slow" does not equate with "dumb." Some students who are slower thinkers are not necessarily inferior thinkers.

If you cannot see a person's strength, then there is no way for you to improve his weakness. Even behaviors that seem to defy appreciation can be appreciated. For example, fighting cannot and should not be encouraged in the classroom, and we are advocates of stiff consequences for such behavior. But consider the following two messages after Jason has punched Susie.

a. "Jason, I told you not to fight. Now go down to the principal's office at once."

b. "Jason, people are not for hitting. I can appreciate that you probably felt angry and fighting is one way that you know to stand up for yourself, but you have chosen to go to the principal's office. When you return, we can discuss other ways besides fighting that you can use to stand up for yourself."

Example b shows how an unacceptable action can be both appreciated as well as limited.

10. Learn and practice reflective listening skills. When students accuse you, swear at you, threaten you, or refuse your demands, active listening helps to defuse the emotional situation while maintaining good contact with the student.[1]

11. Give the student responsibility that he can handle and that meets with success. Jim, a 5th grade emotionally disturbed youngster, showed an affinity for younger children. He was sent to a kindergarten classroom to be a "helper," and this became the focal point of his day. It also provided much needed relief for his weary teacher.

12. When you do make special arrangements for a handicapped child, explain your purposes to the child. Students who are treated differently usually know they have a problem, and you will earn the respect and a connection with them when you let them know that some special considerations are being made. Explain the purposes of each special strategy.

13. Set up the classroom to be most advantageous for disabled students. Students with visual or hearing problems often need to sit in certain locations that maximize their ability to receive classroom information. Hyperactive students need

more room around their desks and more space at their worktables. Deaf students need to avoid looking at back-lighted subjects because they cannot see enough detail to see signs or to speechread (lipread). A very stimulating environment can be unsettling for emotionally disturbed and hyperactive children. The room and the walls should be colored in soft pastels. Objects should not be left on the floor where physically disabled students or blind students could fall over them. The aisles and areas between seats should be kept clear.

If you have a disabled student, take the time to contact the professional association associated with the disability. Ask questions about classroom arrangements that will provide the best possible learning environment for that student. You should also ask the student what special needs he may have. If you have support personnel in your district or in your class, be sure to confer with them about the most appropriate classroom arrangements.

Self-Injury/Physical Aggression

Many of the strategies offered in this book are ineffective when working with severe to profoundly retarded children who display self-injurious or aggressive behavior, and with autistic children. Most of the strategies that we've described require an understanding of language as well as an ability to use or process language so that problems can be solved. Children with severe intellectual limitations or sensory deficits generally lack the linguistic skills to benefit from these approaches. Behavior modification techniques that are combined into specific individualized programs have been the most frequently employed set of methods with the best overall results.

Most behavior programs for physical aggression or self-injury include an identification of positive reinforcers to use when either a more appropriate behavior occurs or the targeted behavior remains absent for a predefined time interval. Some programs contain aversive consequences (punishments such as physical restraint, a squirt of lemon juice in the mouth, mild electric shock) when the target behavior occurs. There are virtually always moral and ethical considerations in the development of such programs. Because there are very high frequencies of such behaviors in the most severe cases, careful measurement by charting change is a necessity.

There are many hypotheses regarding the reasons for self-injury and apparently "unprovoked" physical aggression. One is that aberrant behavior represents an individual's need to communicate, and lacking the standard communication skills, the child resorts to a behavior that appears aberrant to others. Many treatment programs and schools have developed alternate modes of communication such as communication boards or gestural/sign language for such individuals, sometimes with excellent results in behavior improvement. Another widely accepted idea is that such behavior represents a response to frustration and implies the need to simplify the environment.

In cases of severe self-injurious behavior, communication and simplification are necessary but usually insufficient. Foxx and Azrin[2] have developed programs called "Overcorrection," which feature positive practice and restitution. Programs are individually tailored after careful observation of the student in his natural surroundings. A program might work as follows: Bill slaps Sam. Bill is told to lie down on a mat or is guided by one or two staff members. His hands are held at his side for a predetermined time (5-10 minutes) and are released only after Bill has been calm for at least 30 seconds. Holding Bill's hands down for a time interval is an OVERcorrection for aggression. Bill is next guided to his feet where he PRACTICES more POSITIVE or less harmful arm movements. He might initially be guided by staff to reach up, out, and down with his arms (as one might while exercising) 40 times. Finally he might be told to apologize to the victim (if he can speak) or guided to approach the victim and touch the victim in a gentle manner. Overcorrection programs have reportedly been quite effective when more standard behavior modification programs don't work.

One current and exciting line of research is exploring the possibility that autistic children have a natural opioid level that is too high. When these children bite, gouge, or bang themselves, the overabundant opioids (also known as endorphins) may keep them from feeling the pain that would otherwise discourage such actions. Preliminary research in which naltroxene (an opioid blocker) was administered to such children yielded dramatic decreases in self-injury.[3] Some encouraging findings suggest that vigorous exercise programs may also be effective in reducing these difficult and perplexing behaviors.

Summary

Disabled students who are prone to behavior problems can drain your energy, create more work for you, and generate feelings of inadequacy and frustration. The students will demand, either implicitly or explicitly, that you employ skills you have not been trained for and that you devise both learning and behavioral strategies that might not have been created yet. You can improve your effectiveness by reducing the overall scope of the problem into smaller, more easily attainable goals.

Set clear limits for these students and expect them to follow them. Provide clear consequences and implement them consistently. Provide decision-making situations with clear and understandable choices. Appreciate the students as fully functioning human beings who are capable of joy and success. Above all, remember that both you and your special students have feelings, and these feelings are the most powerful motivators of behavior. Learn to express your feelings in helpful ways: the joys and frustrations. Teach your students to feel their feelings and provide acceptable outlets for expressing them.

The Inner City

Inner-city schools often lack many of the luxuries their more affluent neighbors consider necessities. Often, inner-city schools are older and scarred from the battles of 75 to 150 years of serving students. Many schools are overcrowded, with little of the needed space for students and teachers to feel comfortable. In some instances, the schools are located in neighborhoods that are threatening and hostile to the children who attend them. One school we visited had a problem because many of the 3rd and 4th grade students had their sneakers stolen off their feet on the way to school.

The visual and metaphorical picture of the inner-city school is bleak, reminiscent of the burned-out wasteland of a war-torn city. Once, when we were asked to assist an inner-city school in the New York area, the first words we heard as we entered the building were, "Move your car before it is stripped or stolen." No wonder many teachers would like to see their inner-city schools razed and rebuilt in a safer, more stable environment.

With the rapid increase in our immigrant population, the face of American cities is rapidly changing. Large numbers of peoples from diverse cultures continue to compete for sparse low-income housing, jobs, and other resources. Under conditions where there simply isn't enough to go around, tensions among groups naturally increase. City schools reflect the same tensions as the city itself. Each cultural group has its own standards and rights of passage. Different actions challenge pride and dignity for each group. There are many schools with English as a Second Language programs with up to 10 or 15 different languages spoken. Teachers who can speak such a wide variety of languages are rare.

At its best, the richness of each culture brings an energy and excitement that cannot be matched in suburban communities. Many immigrants place a high value on education. More and more smaller communities within the city are demanding and receiving resources for better schooling and demanding higher standards for their children. There is a trend among those who once fled the city to return. In most inner cities, there are neighborhoods of middle and upper middle-class professionals who have been lured back by the richness and diversity of city life. Although their children may attend private schools, their political clout is having an effect. People are beginning to believe that inner city schools can survive and flourish.

Once you get beyond the obvious environmental problems, inner-city schools can offer a rich, rewarding experience for teachers and students alike. The city offers a variety of resources that cannot be matched in the suburbs. The arts, business and industry, parks, museums, and a multitude of people are all within arms length of the creative inner-city teacher. For every turned off "street student," there are dozens of eager youngsters who want to learn. While the equal opportunities and education acts have not produced the results hoped for by their creators, more and more inner-city students believe that they can reach their potential, albeit with a struggle.

We were touched by an 8th grade class in a human relations course at an overcrowded school in a poor neighborhood in the Bronx. One student shared that her family had their extra money hidden under their living room rug. A classmate asked why this girl would reveal such confidential information. She replied, "But in this class you are all my friends; I trust you." The sigh from all her classmates indicated the closeness of the moment.

Differences in Dealing with Discipline

One of the biggest differences in dealing with discipline in the inner city is that the types of problems are more intense and destructive than their suburban counterparts. Violence, vandalism, drug use, thefts, and extortion are reported as part of the daily routine of many inner-city schools.

Another difference is that the culture of the students is very different from the culture of the teachers and administrators. Even city schools with a high percentage of minority teachers suffer from cultural clashes. Minority teachers and administrators who have "made it" and have graduated from college may be seen as different by the inner-city students who do not view college as part of their world.

A third difference is the overcrowded and older school buildings. Many of these schools look more like jails than places of learning. Students complain that they are prisoners, not students, and this attitude has a direct relationship to their physical environment. Further, these schools are often magnets for undesirable teenagers who are no longer in school and show up to cause trouble. Many schools have reported that their biggest problem with vandalism, drugs, physical abuse, and thefts are the result of teens who do not even attend school. It is difficult to learn and teach when physical safety is not ensured.

A fourth difference is the lack of trust that often permeates the school environment. The example of the trusting student described above is unfortunately not the norm. Students do not generally trust teachers or other students. Teachers fear many students, especially those who are bigger and have reputations for violence. Even parents can generate fear in teachers. One teacher in a Rochester, N.Y., school was hospitalized by an angry parent who came to school and attacked the teacher. Some teachers have been killed in their classrooms.

A fifth difference is the difficulty of a large number of students who do not speak English as a first language. Schools no longer have a mixture of two or three foreign languages, but possibly between 10 and 20.

While these problems are certainly imposing, they are not impossible to deal with. As we stated earlier, Three-Dimensional Discipline grew out of our initial work in the inner city.

Using Three-Dimensional Discipline

In 1980-81 we did a controlled study with inner-city elementary school teachers in Rochester, N.Y., which provided them with a 5-session, 10-hour Three-Dimensional Discipline program that attempted to reduce teaching stress associated with disruptive student behavior.[4] The finding from this study was that Three-Dimensional Discipline was effective in significantly reducing anxiety felt by teachers at the end of a school day, as well as reducing the stress associated with six areas (managing disruptive behavior, supervising behavior outside the classroom, target of verbal abuse, theft and destruction of teacher property, maintaining self-control when angry, threatened with personal injury).

These teachers generally found the social contract (because of its structure and flexibility) and the relaxation activities to be most effective in improving discipline and diminishing their negative feelings associated with disruptive student behavior. But perhaps more importantly, the training program provided a forum for teachers to share mutual concerns and learn how to become a support network for each other. Nowhere is this need greater than in the inner-city, where teachers are more often confronted with serious incidents of acting out and where they must have strong leadership, a high level of trust for each other, as well as skills to deal with student misbehavior. The 1979 New York State United Teachers' survey found that nearly three times as many inner-city teachers are experiencing high levels of stress as compared to those in suburbs and rural towns.[5]

Our experience in working with these teachers and other groups of inner-city teachers suggests that they often feel alone in tackling overwhelming problems, and that the communities in which they work are frequently lacking the values that lead to school success because of the problems described above. Violence is more likely to be viewed as an acceptable means to settle disputes, which may lead to a proliferation of fighting and, in more serious instances, stabbings and shootings.

It is unrealistic to expect major changes when we do battle with a society that theoretically provides equal opportunity for everybody, but in reality divides itself into the "haves" and "have nots." The net result of such a condition is the manifestation of intense anxiety and frustration among those in the lower socioeconomic classes. The anxiety and frustration is often expressed through violence, or apathy. Our responsibility is to provide a clear and firm policy of rules and consequences that provide safety for those students who want to learn, as well as many alternate nondestructive ways to express the negative emotions that are so much a part of many students' lives in the inner city.

Stereotyping the Inner-City Child

Teachers in the inner city must first be able to let go of the many stereotypes regarding the inner-city child. A series of studies (Hawkes and Koff 1970,[6] Hawkes and Furst, 1971,[7] Hawkes and Furst, 1973[8]) has elucidated the many misconceptions held by teachers regarding the inner-city child. Hawkes and Koff (1970) conducted a study in a large mid-western city, comparing the responses on anxiety scales by 249 children in the 5th and 6th grades of 1 inner-city elementary school to the responses of 211 children who were attending the 5th and 6th grades in a lab school connected with a large urban university. A content analysis was done of the responses to an anxiety questionnaire. It was concluded that the difference in the manifestation of anxiety was significant regardless of the type of anxiety being tapped. The inner-city child showed more concern than his suburban school peers on items that tapped objective fears, anxiety, general worry, concern about school work, and concerns of self-adequacy. Hawkes and Furst (1971) replicated these findings using as a sample 704 black 5th and 6th graders predominantly from the inner city and 495 white suburban children from public and private schools. This study was done on the eastern seaboard.

Hawkes and Furst (1973) studied the responses of 628 pre- and inservice teachers who were asked to respond to a 16-item questionnaire that was used in the two previous studies cited. The finding was that teachers significantly underestimate the anxiety levels of inner-city students and exaggerate the anxiety from upper middle class students. The authors (1973, p. 26) conclude that the following *inaccurate stereotype* is held by many teachers:

> The inner-city child who lives in a hazardous environment becomes accustomed to that environment, he reacts to that environment by becoming psychologically tough and resilient. He is unlikely to admit to fears and concerns about his daily existence, indeed he is unlikely to have such concerns. He doesn't care as much as his middle class peer does about getting ahead in life or school, his parents haven't trained him to care or be concerned about doing well in school, he doesn't mind being scolded by his teachers, he is not as likely as his middle class peer to worry, and he is unlikely to manifest symptoms of anxiety.

These investigations noted that teachers with three or more years of experience in teaching inner-city or suburban students were more accurate in their predictions, although still not predictive of the reality of the situation. This study raises the possibility that at least some classroom discipline problems result from the teacher's inability to recognize and address student anxiety. The teacher, thinking that his students are unmotivated, worry free, and unconcerned about their school work, fails to address these emotionally focused areas of student concern. Because the students' anxiety fails to be addressed in the classroom, they become unruly and disruptive in response to their anxiety. The teacher, faced with losing control of the classroom, may become dogmatic and inflexible in response to his increasing experience of stress. A real cause of discipline problems (high student anxiety and worry regarding school performance) is left unaddressed.

Specific Suggestions for the Inner-City Teacher

We suggest that the inner-city teacher use the processes of Three-Dimensional Discipline, as described in this book, by placing a strong emphasis upon prevention. The following 10 suggestions are offered to help the inner-city teacher deal with discipline:

1. Know Your Students and Let Your Students Know You

Because of the cultural differences between teachers and students and because of the potential for lack of trust in the inner-city school, we strongly suggest you know your students well before you begin to focus on content. You need to know how your students naturally communicate with you and with each other. Make sure that you are not offended by language that is natural for your students but may sound rough or uncouth to you. Learn your students' likes and dislikes. Find out what classroom privileges are meaningful to them and which are perceived as hokey or as undesirable chores. The more you learn about your students' interests, the more you should structure your instructional units around them. City students have a strong need for relevancy and meaningfulness in their school experience.

In addition, it is equally important for your students to know you. Many inexperienced inner-city teachers erroneously think that they must keep their guard up at all times. While it is a good idea to be on guard in a potentially hostile environment, doing so with your students will guarantee that your classroom will have walls between you and them. The more your students trust you, the less they will make unfounded assumptions about you. Research has pointed out time and time again that students learn best when they trust their teacher. Use open communication and establish an atmosphere of information sharing to build trust in your classroom.

2. State Your Rules and Consequences Clearly

Whether or not you use the entire social contract process, state your rules and consequences clearly to your students. Inner-city students come from a variety of family structures, some very tight with strong parental structure; others come from broken or single-parent homes. Trying to discipline 20 or more students with such a variety of school and family experiences is difficult at best. Start with a firm and clear structure that all students understand. Once you have firmly established your contract you may be flexible about changing it, but make your changes gradually. Your students will behave more appropriately when they always know what is expected.

3. Develop Consequences That Work

It is important that you develop consequences that work. Consequences should reflect the cultural values of the students receiving them. Be careful not to attack a culturally sensitive area for a student by attacking his dignity. Demanding eye contact, for example, is contrary to many Asian populations. Different cultures have different comfortable distances for proximity. Some countries in the Middle East are comfortable at very close distances, while many people with central European origins interpret closeness as a sign of aggression.

The best consequences are nonpunitive and relate to the students' lives as directly as possible. Ask other teachers and older students to help you think of the best consequences for your rules. Consequences that are too harsh will alienate and break down trust, while consequences that are too lenient will be seen as a sign of weakness. Your students must respect your ability to control your class, and effective consequences are a must. Once you have developed good consequences, it is crucial to implement them consistently. While occasional lapses of consequence implementation in the suburban or rural school may make a teacher's life more difficult, inconsistency in the inner city can spell disaster.

4. Provide Appropriate Outlets for Expressing Feelings for Both Yourself and Your Students

Many inner-city students believe that they must put on a "front." They try to appear cool and detached as if nothing bothers them. This is considered a sign of maturity and strength. But the reality is that inner-city students have feelings just like anyone else. And because these feelings are often hidden under the guise of "cool," they can and do intensify. Learn the language of "coolness" and provide acceptable outlets for feelings to be expressed. Make sharing a regular but optional part of each day. The use of anonymous techniques, like a gripe box, is especially useful.

Teaching in the inner city generates many feelings of inadequacy and fear. It is most important for the inner-city teacher to learn how to deal with his feelings and to learn strategies for reducing stress.

Our study showed that inner-city teachers can learn to minimize stress and feel better about teaching.

5. Capitalize on the Resources within the City

Working independently or with a group of other teachers, use the city itself as a teaching laboratory for experiences related to your content. Visit businesses, hospitals, the police station, museums, libraries, planetariums, historical landmarks, and other spots that are sometimes taken for granted. Arrange trips to the nearest rural areas whenever possible. Some city children never see a live cow until they are adults.

Bring city resources into your school if you cannot take your students out. One school made an arrangement with a local college to let its architectural students rebuild a hallway into an arboretum, another hallway into a library, and time-out areas in five classrooms. Both the school and the college students were enriched by the experience.

Many businesses and industries within the inner city are adopting schools. The sponsors provide resources in a variety of ways, including internships for students, supplies, expertise that can be applied to schools, fund raising, advisory groups, teacher-employee exchange programs, field trips, and sponsorships of special events. Oceana High School in Pacifica, Calif., had a relationship with a shopping mall. Students produced artwork for the mall that eventually went on a national tour that ended in Washington, D.C. The pride of those students was felt throughout the school community.

6. Improve Students' Reading Ability

All teachers, regardless of subject, are reading, writing, and English teachers. Make a point to improve every student's reading ability whether you teach math, science, or physical education. Lack of reading ability is directly associated with poor achievement and poor behavior. Find out what your students' reading abilities are and provide challenging reading and writing practice at their grade level. This should be a regular part of each class period. Continually reward efforts and improvements in reading and writing regardless of how small. Your students need to feel that they can and will become better readers.

7. Focus on the Positive

While it may sound hokey, we believe that all teachers of inner-city students must focus on the positive. If a student gets 2 right out of 10, tell him he got 2 right, not 8 wrong. Limit your corrections on writing assignments to one or two manageable corrections. Once the student has mastered the corrections noted, find one or two more improvements to work on. Continually build on success. Inner-city students need to feel that it is possible to be successful in school. They need to feel in a very direct way that the payoff at the end of the rainbow is potentially for them as well as their more affluent neighbors. Give them success every day as part of your teaching style.

Focus on the positive with your fellow teachers. Look for ways to make the school a better, safer place to be. It is better to suggest an improvement than it is to comment on what is wrong. By increasing the positive energy of the faculty and, most importantly, of yourself, you will reduce your own stress related to working in the inner city and make the school a better place for you and your students to live.

8. Develop Group Support with Other Teachers

Share your feelings openly. Teaching is traditionally done alone, with the teacher isolated from the rest of the faculty, except for informal discussions in faculty lounges or lunchrooms. Because of the intensity of the inner city, it is important to minimize isolation as much as possible. As we stated earlier, one of the most important reasons for the success of our inservice training programs is the process of teachers sharing with other teachers how they feel, what their problems are, and what can be done to make the school a better place.

9. Develop a Strong Working Relationship with Your Principal and Other Administrators

The Safe School Study indicated that the safest schools had a strong principal. Meet regularly with your principal and offer your support. Ask what you can do to make his job easier. Tell him what you need to be successful in your classroom. Problem solve together. The more your principal feels important to you and your students, the more he can support your efforts.

10. Enlist Community Leaders

Contact as many community leaders as you can and ask to meet with them on a regular basis. Every city has both formal and informal groups that try to help the community. Some examples might be the local YMCA, the NAACP, a church group, or a Mexican cultural center. These leaders take responsibility for improving the lives of the people they serve. Find out what their programs are, what support they can give you, and what support you can give them. Invite them into your class to talk with your children. Ask them to review your social contract and offer any suggestions for improvement. Use them to better understand the subculture of your students.

These 10 suggestions are offered to help make your teaching in the inner city a more positive and healthy experience for you and your students. It is not impossible to be successful in the inner city. You must feel that success is attainable for you if you expect your students to feel that success is attainable for them. The self-fulfilling prophesy works equally for teachers and students. Do not let your prophesy of your teaching experience be negative or you will ensure that it will be so. Many inner-city teachers would never change their environment. They feel that the energy, the challenge, and the needs of their students cannot be matched in any other environment.

Drug Abuse in School

Drug abuse in school is cited by teachers and administrators as one of their most difficult problems. The destructive effects of student drug use on learning are well documented. Even a few drug-enervated students in a classroom can change the learning climate for everyone. Baysner[9] found that young people are experimenting with drugs at earlier ages. According to Johnston, O'Malley, and Bachman[10] more than 9 out of 10 members of the high school class of 1985 had used alcohol. More than half had tried marijuana, and more than a quarter reported using it within the last month. One in six had used cocaine while one in eight had used hallucinogens. Although some studies have found that most categories of drug use peaked in 1979-1980, current drug use remains essentially at, near, or in some instances (such as cocaine) greater than those "peak" years.

Drug use is a complicated phenomenon full of facts and fiction; it evokes hysteria and fear, as well as economic and political concerns. Drug use creates a youth versus adult battle of ethical and legal concerns. Educators have trouble distinguishing between the use of drugs by school-age children from the drug problems of society as a whole.

Drugs affect student behavior in school. Some drugs act as stimulants, most notably amphetamines and cocaine, which dramatically increase restlessness, excitability, and hyperactivity. Others act as depressants, such as barbiturates and alcohol, which make students lethargic and apathetic. Angel dust and crack make behavior erratic and often dangerous, leading to sporadic outbursts of violence. Regardless of the drug, one thing is clear: Drug use in school blocks learning and creates either overt or hidden behavior problems for the teacher.

The problem of drug abuse in school is complicated because it is integrated with confusion and conflict in society as a whole. Students who take drugs do so for a host of reasons, only some of which are school related. In the discussion that follows we will first explore the relationship between the drug use of students and society's attitudes in general about drugs, and then discuss the relationship between drug use of students and school. Finally, we will explore what you, the teacher, can do in your school and classroom to deal with misbehavior associated with drug abuse, and we will suggest preventive strategies for minimizing drug use among your students.

William B. Hansen outlines the following reasons why children experiment with drugs:

1. Among the various factors that might cause drug use, the single best predictor of who will experiment with substances is use by a young person's close friends.

2. Children often misperceive the prevalence and acceptability of drugs; when adolescents are asked to estimate how many people their age use any given substance, they often think that the proportion is two to four times greater than it actually is.

3. Children use drugs to be rebellious. Those who are prone to risk taking, rebelliousness, and striving for independence are most likely to experiment with substances in a premature attempt to be "adult."

4. Youngsters who mature physiologically at a young age are more likely to use substances regularly than those whose development is normal or slow. The reason for this is not physiological per se. More likely, those who look more mature than their peers attempt to associate with older youth, who are more likely to use drugs.

5. Parent qualities affect drug use in children. Children whose parents use drugs are more likely to use them also.[11]

Drug Use in Society

The greatest contributor for drug abuse is the unrealistic, schizophrenic attitudes society has about them. Drugs are condemned and condoned. They are advertised and made illegal. People use them and criticize others for using them. Parents fear images of the pusher hanging around the schoolyard with an assortment of drugs in his trench coat, while the real pusher may be the good-looking kid next door, an older sibling, or a parent's liquor cabinet.

The image of the drug pusher is that of a Mephistophelian figure who poses a greater threat than did the communists in the mid-fifties. But the doctors who collectively write out 40 million prescriptions a year for valium are viewed as saviors for reducing tension and removing headaches. The mixed messages children receive even go beyond these images.

Professional athletes are cheered when they win, and people close their eyes to the amphetamines, steroids, and other wonder drugs that are a daily part of their lives. Parents hoot and holler when they see their children modeling their heroes by taking the same wonder pills. Athletes and rock stars, the two most powerful role models for our children, openly talk about cocaine use. Drugs are emphasized on our children's blasting stereos as they work on tomorrow's homework.

Society tries to explain rationally to children that marijuana is decriminalized in some states while at the same time other states are making it a crime to sell rolling papers and other drug paraphernalia. The results of these mixed messages are clear. Despite increasing efforts and media attention to the negative and even deadly effects of drugs, children don't believe that drugs are harmful. They see through the double messages. Statistical probability suggests that there are a significant number of teachers who are mandated to teach about the abuses of drugs who themselves are drug users. Ray Bird-whistell's research says that when a person is communicating, 70 percent of his message is sent by body language, 23 percent by the tone or inflection of his voice, and only 7 percent by the words he uses.[12] For example, if the teacher believes that marijuana use is not especially harmful, it is likely that between 70-93 percent of his message will be that marijuana is okay, while only 7 percent of his message will consist of the harmful aspects of marijuana use.

Each day after work, many "responsible" adults stop off at the local bar for a few moments to drug away the tensions of the day before they get into their cars with enough alcohol in their blood to be considered impaired or intoxicated. There are many educators who cannot function without that first or second cup of coffee in the morning, despite the well-documented harmful effects of caffeine intake. Psychotropic drugs by prescription have become an integral part of society. Drug companies spend billions of dollars yearly advertising pills to lose weight, pills for headaches, backaches, muscular tensions, and other stress-related conditions. The major networks could probably not afford to telecast sporting events without advertising dollars from the beer industry. The fact is that drugs are an inherent part of our culture. Groups that practice strict abstinence from drugs, such as Mormons, Jehovah Witnesses, Christian Scientists, Moonies, and Orthodox Jews, are viewed by some people as backward, extreme, and out of the mainstream of American life.

School Causes of Drug Use

In the preceding section we explored how society at large contributes to drug abuse by sending children confusing mixed messages about drugs. Children have learned to mistrust information that tells about the dangers of drugs. But these children believe their friends when they hear that getting high is an exciting, fun-filled way to reduce stress and feel good. In this section we will see how the structure of the typical school can contribute to the misuse of drugs.

All students need to feel that they are worthwhile, liked by, and important to someone who is important to them. They need to succeed at important tasks that are reinforced by their environment, and they need to feel that they have the power to influence the environment within which they live. Students who naturally feel good view themselves as important to others, capable of succesfully meeting challenging tasks, and in control of themselves and the world around them. They achieve a natural high when they are class monitor or helper because they feel important when their outstanding achievements are noticed and appreciated. They feel good when they can use and enhance their power by making decisions that affect their lives. When one or more of these basic needs are unaddressed, the seeds are sown for drug abuse. The students in class who seem bored, inattentive, daydreaming, poor achievers, or lacking friends are all receiving negative messages from their environment and may begin to feel inadequate, incapable, and incomplete. They are likely to turn to drugs as a way to escape recognition of a poor self-concept.

Some schools tell children that they are not as important as teachers, principals, and the curriculum. For six hours every day they are told where to go, what time to be there, how long they are allowed for even basic biological necessities, which learning is relevant, what to learn, and how well they have learned it. How often do the students decide what rules should exist in the school for themselves, for each other, or even for the teachers? How often are students consulted on what they want to learn, on how they should be evaluated, and on what activities they want to participate in? The answer is: not often enough! On the other hand, when students are given the opportunity to participate actively in the school, they are often given total unstructured freedom to do what they want rather than actively participating as part of the total school community.

One of the reasons for the frequent failure of the open school concept, which proliferated throughout the '60s and early '70s, was that most of the structure that children need (from a developmental perspective) was taken away. We feel that it is imperative for schools to give their students a say—a loud, clear voice in what happens in their school. The curriculums need to be examined so that they truly reflect the needs and concerns of students. School cannot afford to be a place that puts young minds to sleep with trivia, busy work, and boredom. At the same time, students need clearly defined structure, one which they have a part in developing, but one which is consistently adhered to, so that they feel that their school is safe and predictable and at the same time adaptable and concerned with their welfare.

Another way that schools contribute to students' need for drugs is through pressure. Students are pressured to perform, often to standards that they have had no say in developing. They are pressured to be like everyone else. They are pressured to like what teachers have decided is good for them. Tension in students is no less common than tension in adults, and for the same reasons. And as we stated earlier, students often reduce their tension in the same way parents reduce theirs—through drugs.

What Can Be Done about In-School Drug Abuse

Changing the drug picture requires an investment of time, energy, and money that has as its primary goal *prevention*. An effective drug program should begin in kindergarten and should address the underlying motives that are known to lead to drug abuse. Opportunities for experiencing "good" feelings need to be built into the curriculum daily and must emphasize units on decision making, problem solving, and stress reduction.

More importantly, drug prevention means:
1. Being aware of yourself and how you communicate yourself to students.

2. Being aware of students and setting the classroom climate that allows for feel-good, esteem-building experiences.
3. Teaching yourself and your students alternative ways to relax.
4. Teaching children how to assert themselves (especially how to say "no" and still save face with their peers).
5. Presenting accurate information on the effects of various drugs.
6. Avoiding the use of threats with children you suspect are using drugs and offering treatment instead.

An effective drug prevention program helps students learn that there are alternatives to drugs that are viable and can offer similar benefits. Schools cannot hope to eliminate societal drug abuse until we as a society decide to do so, and that has not happened since the birth of this nation. However, the use of drugs in, on, or near school grounds is a relatively recent phenomenon that needs to be addressed and probably can be changed. We concur with Hawley's[13] conclusion that "the school's commitment must be to become drug free."

The growth and support of Youth to Youth programs, Quest, and the school's sponsoring of drug free dances, parties, and proms are concrete, specific ways to achieve such a goal. As Hawley points out, changing the drug climate of a school begins with building a consensus among members of the faculty and staff. Provision of inservice training so that all staff become involved is necessary. Commitment to drug free also means that faculty and staff must limit their own drug use to what is lawful and consistent with effective performance. To do any less is to proliferate mixed, confusing messages.

The fact is that drug use is symptomatic of larger social problems our society still struggles with. Fixing blame has become a popular political issue that our leaders exploit at election time. Tough talk replaces any semblance of reasonable problem solving. Our leaders and those who desire to become our leaders talk about tougher prison sentences for drug pushers and even the death penalty. They promise to beef up patrols to intercept drug shipments at the border. In short, they promise to rescue a society from a problem that hasn't been arrested since the beginning of time. There is too little talk about what to substitute for the 14 year old who can earn $2,000 per week selling crack in the inner city or the depressed, hopeless feelings of kids who are all too willing to sacrifice the long-term goals they never developed for the 10-minute high offered by the next hit. It will take a major social effort that addresses the complexities of drug use for any significant impact to occur.

This impact can begin in the schools. Faculty, parents, and students can effectively define policy regarding drug use that is firm, consistent, and clear. A zero tolerance policy regarding use on school grounds should be the norm with clear consequences and drug treatment options offered to offenders. Fun activities that have nothing to do with drugs should be encouraged. Programs that help students learn how to be better decision makers and those that teach them how to effectively manage their tensions and anxieties can be a counterpoint to drug use. Helping students develop a positive self-image so that they can "just say no" to peer pressure is essential.

Encouraging Use of the Imagination

Because of the curriculum demands associated with emphasizing the 3-R's, we sometimes forget the importance of child's play and retreat into fantasy as a necessary and important development occurrence. And yet we often discourage the development and expression of fantasy ("stop daydreaming", "pay attention") in favor of the realism of cognitively defined classroom expectations. It is as if fantasy and imagination have no place in the world of the classroom.

As early as 1935, Griffiths' interviews of 50 five-year olds concluded that "fantasy or imagination provides the normal means for the solution of problems of development in early childhood."[14] Eric Klinger reminds us that most "normal" people spend between 30 and 40 percent of waking hours entertaining daydreams.[15]

Today's young child whose significant others criticize his daydreams and who is provided no outlet for the expression of his fantasy learns to mistrust his own perceptions. Although his fantasies often "feel good," the equation of fantasy being equal to wasting time valences negativism around what is and can continue to become a source of natural "high" for kids. Stripped of fantasy and not too successful with the reality demands of the classroom, the stage is set for drug use.

"Hey, Billy, want to toke-up?" becomes the cue for a return to the enjoyment of fantasy that had been earlier submerged to demands that attention be paid to "reality." There are many ways fantasy can be encouraged in the classroom and made consistent with other "reality-oriented" instructional goals. The following activities provide a sample of such methods.

Guided Fantasy. The teacher can select one of many fantasies from references such as *The Second Centering Book* (Hendrick and Roberts), *Mind Games* (Masters and Houston), or *Passages-Pilgrims to the Mind* (Andersen and Savery). After presenting a fantasy, it can be processed in a number of different ways including:

1. Encouraging students to share their fantasy verbally.
2. Having each student draw a picture of something from their fantasy.
3. Having students do a group drawing in which at least one aspect of each person's fantasy appears.
4. Writing a story based upon the fantasy and developing a class "book" of fantasies for all students to read.
5. Having one or more students act out or role play their fantasy.

Children's artwork and stories can be prominently displayed in the classroom.

Daydreams. In our task-oriented schools and other institutions, daydreaming is often thought to convey escapism or avoidance of the task at hand. Most teachers have at least a few children who are obvious "dreamers" who doodle, stare out the window, rest their heads on the desk, and "forget" directions. Less obvious are many more students who may be seated upright with hands folded on their desks, appearing attentive, nodding their heads up and down in apparent agreement and understanding of the material, but who, like their overt counterparts, are silently daydreaming. They are simply better at playing the "game" than their less fortunate classmates who are likely to receive reprimands for their inattentiveness.

Many of the same methods suggested in processing guided fantasy material can be used with daydreams. The wise teacher recognizes the nonverbal, body-language messages sent by children and modifies his style accordingly. If each question asked during a lesson is met with little or no participation, if students are seated upright with their heads straightened rather than slightly cocked to one side, if students are staring out the window, *stop* what you're doing and say, "My guess is that many of you are bored with the lesson. Probably you're thinking about other things. While your bodies are here it looks to me as if your minds are not. Your assignment for tomorrow is to write down all the places that your mind has been during this class. Tomorrow I'll collect your work and read each paper out loud. You don't have to put your name on your paper unless you would like others to know what you wrote."

As it is neither desirable nor possible to eliminate students' daydreams, it makes sense to legitimize this "misbehavior" by attending to it. Using open-ended questions that contain no right or wrong answers or using imagination instructionally such as, "If you were Christopher Columbus, Alice in Wonderland, et cetera, how would you have felt, what would you have done," are other methods that indirectly and clearly validate one's fantasy life. George Brown's work with confluent education provides many ways in which the teacher can effectively integrate instructional goals with the personal experience of each child.

Stress. We often forget that school for many children is a tension-prone, stressful experience. Academically successful children often feel pressured to continue their positive performance, middle-of-the-road students are often struggling to stand out in some way, and poorly performing children are often exhorted to work or try harder. The result is that the school experience for all children can become a key source of stress.

Recently, a parent of a 14-year-old boy was perplexed about why her straight A, exceptionally athletic son had dropped from the wrestling team and had plummeting grades. In further discussion it became clear that he had always put a lot of pressure on himself to excel in everything he did. Although his mother wasn't sure, Andy's red eyes, blank facial expression, lack of motivation, and flat, expressionless speech confirmed his use of marijuana. He had become sick and tired of living up to everybody's expectations of perfection.

Schools do not do enough to attend to student stress. It seems indisputable that the art of relaxation is a critically important skill for young people, and one that is not reflected in course curriculums. Schools are claimed to be expert at transmitting information and training intellectual skills, but we have for the most part failed to recognize the influence that tension, anxiety, and stress have in negating such training. If children arrive at school feeling tense about events occurring at home or on the streets or have developed a set of expectations about themselves that allow no room for failure, or who chronically receive a series of messages that reinforce their feelings of incompetence, then the energy and motivation for learning is diminished. A preventive drug program should teach children a variety of methods that they can use to induce relaxation and alleviate tension. Adopting widely known strategies such as meditation and body relaxation, and encouraging students to identify and express their feelings, may make drug use unnecessary.

Meditation. A study conducted by Joseph Morris in which he trained inner-city 3rd graders in how to meditate found a decrease in off-task behavior following training. Children had 2 20-minute weekly periods of meditation.[16] We recommend Benson's *The Relaxation Response* and Carrington's *Freedom in Meditation* as excellent guides for easily learning how to meditate and—by extension—how to teach your class to meditate.

Tension Relaxation. Many students who become involved with drugs are observed to be "anxious," "tense," "sitting on a powder keg," "aggressive," "hostile," and "hyperactive." As a way to help them drain off this tension, we offer the following activity.

> I'd like you each to find a comfortable seated position either on the floor (rug or mat if possible) or in your chair. Try to face away from each other. Let yourself relax and pay attention to your breathing. Listen to yourself breathing in and out. Now picture yourself in a very quiet, peaceful, happy place where you can do whatever you want. Nobody is going to tell you what to do unless you want somebody to do this. Close your eyes if you wish. What are you doing? Where are you? Just let yourself be wherever you are. Now again pay attention to your breathing.
>
> I would like you to think of one word that makes you feel very peaceful and relaxed. Friend, love, peace, quiet, and calm are but a few words that might be relaxing for you. Now choose your relaxing word. Take in a deep breath and as you let it out, say this word quietly to yourself. Now let yourself breathe naturally and each time you exhale say this word. Keep your eyes closed or, if you insist upon opening them, find a spot right in front of you and keep your eyes fixed on this spot. Continue breathing and quietly saying this word as you exhale. Keep doing this until I tell you to stop.

Some students will find both their eyes and minds wandering. Tell them that when this happens, to just let themselves wander. Then when they are ready to return their attention to their fixed spot, tell them to continue their breathing while quietly saying their word.

We suggest this as a daily activity, not to exceed 10 minutes with older children or 5 minutes with younger children.

Gripe Box

The purpose of this activity is to give an example of a method that provides an ongoing, daily account of difficulties and annoyances that students experience during each day. It is important that little daily annoyances and resentments are not allowed to accumulate but are dealt with each day. It is the accumulation of resentments, often minor, that may ultimately lead to drugs that make one feel "happier."

We suggest that you use a shoe box or cardboard box and decorate it with the words "gripe box." Explain to your students that each day various things happen that leave us feeling upset, sad, annoyed, or angry. These events can occur on the school bus, on the playground, in the cafeteria, or in the classroom. Explain that students may resent you, other students, hall monitors, security guards, or other people in the school. But from now on, when they think that they have been mistreated and they are feeling resentful, angry, sad, or upset, you would like them to write down on a piece of paper what happened and how they feel. After they have written this down, suggest that they put their gripe in the classroom "gripe box." Then explain that during a prearranged time you will read each gripe and together with them see if there are some things all of you can think of that would help the student with his or her problem. It is important that the teacher participate in this process as well and contribute annoyances to the "gripe box."

After you or a student has read each gripe, we suggest that you encourage your students to brainstorm as many solutions as possible. You might direct the discussion by saying, "Billy felt angry when Mr. Paulsen scolded him in the hall today. If you (class) were Billy, what are all the things that you could do to make yourself feel less angry?" We suggest that you list all proposed solutions on the blackboard (even the silly ones) and leave it to Billy to either publicly or privately choose those which best fit for him. It has been our experience that publicly stating a problem is often sufficient help for students. The empathy and concern they receive from their classmates helps them feel that they are not entirely alone with a problem and that the classroom can be a place to receive emotional support. If support is lacking, then this may indicate the need for you to devote time to helping build a stronger community spirit within the classroom.

Appreciations

Students who are prone to drug abuse often lack self-esteem. When a child feels uncared for and unappreciated, he learns not to care for himself and not to appreciate others. Particularly in the early elementary school years, it is important for all students to feel cared for and appreciated by both their teacher and their peer group. Students who do not get enough warmth will learn not to give and will gradually distance themselves emotionally from others. They may well resort to drugs to reinforce their protective shell. Following are some suggestions for appreciations.

1. *Appreciation day*. Place a picture of each of your students along with his name on a large sheet of newsprint. Explain to your students that each day one child's picture will be hanging on the bulletin board. Tell them that any time during the day (free time or play time might be preferred to minimize distractions) any student may go to the poster and write a statement beginning with "one thing I like about you is __," or to draw a picture expressing their caring and appreciation of this student. No put-down statements are allowed. Before the end of the school day, take a few minutes to allow students to file past the poster and encourage them to read each statement or describe a drawing that they made on the poster. When you have finished doing this, ask if there are any further expressions of appreciation. When the process is completed, put the child's poster away until his turn comes up again.

   After two rounds, allow the student the option of taking the poster home or displaying it in school.

2. *Self-appreciation*. We believe that one important desired outcome for students is to gradually shift their dependency on support from their environment to support within themselves. It is rare in our society for people to express genuine appreciation for each other, and unless one learns to value and appreciate his own worth, he will often bitterly wander from person to person seeking a sense of security.

   This activity can be done once a day, once a week, or several times each day. Have the students complete the following aloud: "Something I did, felt, or said today that I'm proud of is _____." "Something that I like about myself right now is _____.

3. *Expressing feelings through art.* Give the students crayons, paints, or thick pencils and tell them, "Right now I'd like you to draw or color in a way that expresses your feelings. If you feel sad, draw sad; if you feel angry, draw angry; if you feel happy, draw happy. These are your pictures and you may keep them when you're finished or show them to the class." Be sure to provide no more structure than this. The less structure you provide, the more likely the students are to express their true feelings.

Students may be given the option of displaying their work in the classroom. This can be done by having an "art gallery" in which all participating students hang up their work and then browse through the "gallery" to observe each other's work. Comments are encouraged by helping each commenting student to recognize his feelings. This is not a contest but an opportunity to facilitate a feeling discussion among the class. You might provide a little structure by suggesting that students say, "When I look at this drawing I feel (think, am reminded of, etc.) _____."

Feelings of competence can be enhanced through instructional use of Aronson's "jigsaw" technique" and other cooperative learning methods.[17] These techniques assign students to work with each other in small groups and makes each individual responsible for collaborating with others. All group members depend upon each other for the whole project and must work closely together for its completion. As an example, segments of a story may be assigned to each member of a group. Their task is to understand the story in its totality, to answer various questions that test comprehension, and to report their findings to the class. Students are thereby forced to interact with each other because they depend upon their partners for information. Pairing highly and poorly motivated students or skills proficient and deficient students together is effective at generating improved interpersonal skills and feelings of accomplishment and competence for all.

Accurate Information

We have an obligation to provide a balanced packet of information to students so that they get the facts. In efforts to stem the use of drugs, some curriculums have overemphasized their extreme effects. For example, we know that Len Bias was killed by snorting cocaine the first or second time, but to present cocaine as a drug that kills instantly is to ignore the fact that the majority of people who use this drug do not die from it (at least not immediately). If we want to maintain our credibility, we need to present the total picture. To do less is to make students disbelievers especially when they know a peer who has used a drug and who gives a different accounting of it's effects. Telling kids that people use drugs because it makes them feel good is an honest message. Providing them with the negative side effects as well as alternative ways to feel good without drugs furthers our credibility and increases the odds that students won't abuse drugs. Many schools have a chemical abuse coordinator who can help with curriculum planning as well as developing the necessary network of support, intervention, and treatment that is required when students are abusing.

Attending to Behaviors Associated with Drug Abuse

Students may or may not exhibit overt behaviors that will tell you they are taking drugs. Some signs of drug use are missed homework accompanied by a multitude of excuses and broken promises for improved behavior. A sudden or steady decline in achievement on tests, in class work, and in projects are other common symptoms of drug use. Students who take drugs often lack motivation and become passive in class. They appear to have many secrets to tell their friends and occasionally make drug jokes in class and snicker when words associated with drugs are mentioned. The suggestions above are designed to provide alternative options to taking drugs. But if you notice symptoms in some of your students, which indicate students are already using drugs, we suggest you try the following suggestions.

1. Do Not Accept Excuses

Do not accept excuses or empty promises when work is not completed. Demand that all work be done on time and done properly. At the same time, be sensitive to the needs that drug-using students might have to avoid pressure and tension. Offer suggestions for dealing with tension and pressure, listen carefully to your students' feelings, and offer them an opportunity to discuss their needs. Students need to learn that drug use cannot be explained away or that promises are not the equivalent of performance. The most natural consequence for drug abuse is the inability to complete work, and this consequence should be continually adhered to.

2. Point Out Changes in Behavior

Without making accusations, point out to the student, in descriptive language, what changes in behavior you have noticed. If you hear slurred speech or see red eyes more than occasionally, say something like the following (privately): "Mary, I notice you are having trouble saying your words and that your eyes are red." Merely pointing out the symptoms is enough to tell the student that the secret is out. Many students feel a false sense that nobody knows what they are up to. It is important not to accuse or make assumptions that may be false. Notice the difference in the statement above and the one which follows: "Mary you look stoned. What did you do, take a toke in the girls' room before class?" By reporting only the observable in descriptive terms you minimize the potential for diminishing trust, while at the same time, letting the student know that the secret is out.

3. Discuss Your Suspicions with the Student

If your suspicions are strong enough, and after you have communicated descriptively, you might take stronger action by stating that you are wondering whether or not the student is taking drugs. At this time it might help to let the student know that further action may be necessary. Notice the following message Mr. Calkins told Liza, a 10th grade student who he suspected of drug use in school.

"Liza, I have noticed that your homework has been missing for two weeks and that you have been daydreaming in class. When I call on you to answer, you have asked me to repeat the question and then you are still not sure what we are talking about. Last week your speech was slurred and you seemed to laugh in class for no apparent reason. I have been thinking that maybe you are becoming involved with drugs. It's not my place to demand that you tell me whether or not this is true, but I am concerned. So I am planning on telling you exactly what I need from you in class. I want you to do your homework, be attentive, talk normally, have clear eyes, and answer class questions. If you can do this then I will assume my feelings are incorrect, but if your current behavior continues, then I will think that I am correct and it will be time for me to share my suspicions with your parents and try to work with them to help you out."

In this statement Mr. Calkins might have alienated Liza if she was taking drugs, but he honestly shared his perceptions and outlined what he needed from Liza to be different. He gave Liza a chance to save face and stop using drugs, while letting her know that further action was pending. The key things he did were: (1) stated his observations, (2) offered choices, (3) stated consequences, (4) kept the demands related to classroom performance, not drug use, and (5) let the student know his suspicions without accusing her.

4. Confer with Other Teachers about the Student

Find out from other teachers and professionals in the school if the student you are concerned about has exhibited erratic behavior in other classes or school settings. If the student has, then set up a meeting with those involved as a team and discuss what the changes in behavior are and what you can do to help. In these meetings be sure that the student is not tried and convicted on circumstantial evidence. Many adolescents go through changes in behavior that are associated with growing up and not drugs. Keep your information-sharing descriptive and develop a plan to improve school and class-room behavior, not to eliminate drug use.

If your suspicions are strong enough, find one person in the group or in the school who has a good, trusting relationship with the student and who can try talking with him about his problem. Often a former or older student can be helpful in making contact. When meeting the student, the most important message to convey is that someone cares and is willing to listen. Accusations, threats, and punishments tend to push new drug users into a position of needing or wanting more drugs to deal with feelings of shame, alienation, or guilt.

5. Contact Parents and Share Your Concerns Regarding Achievement, Behavior, or Both, and Describe the Symptoms You Have Observed

Ask parents if they have noticed changes such as switching friends, emotional highs and lows, defiance of rules and regulations, becoming more secretive, withdrawal from family functions, excuses, missing items from home, weight changes, or verbal or physical abusive behavior. Tell them of the services offered by the school, and offer them a referral to someone who can help.

6. Don't Try to Be a Rule Enforcer for Impossible Rules

As a classroom teacher, you cannot enforce a rule that says students cannot take drugs unless you actually observe the illegal behavior. However, you can and should set limits that describe behavior. In other words, you can state clearly that students who come to class smelling of pot, with slurred speech, or who behave erratically will be sent to the nurse.

In the final analysis, schools and teachers can limit drug use by limiting negative behaviors associated with taking drugs; by offering a multitude of choices that help students to relax, feel good, energized, and excited; and by making school an interesting and exciting place where young minds and spirits come alive to the energy of feeling and learning. If you can give these experiences to your students and if they still take drugs, then that is a choice the student has made that is beyond your control to change. You need to appreciate that some students can and will choose destructive paths and your ability to help them rests solely on whether or not they want your help.

Conclusion

In this chapter we have explored three special problems related to discipline. As we have stated in the discussions, each of these problems is part of a larger social issue. But because of their impact on students, teachers must often deal with special behavior problems associated with handicapped students, the inner-city environment, and students who take drugs. Three-Dimensional Discipline is built on the foundation that prevention is far more effective than intervention. Many activities were suggested that help teachers to set up a preventive atmosphere related to each of the problems.

For the Administrator

Disabled Students

Aside from all of the paperwork involved in setting up special classes and special placement for disabled students, the administrator should see that the needs of the special student are met. This involves securing support services as necessary including interpreters, notetakers, readers, tutors, aides, psychological support, and physical support. Teachers need training in the use of support people. You should provide information about support people and a clarification of function.

In addition, teachers need training in methods of teaching students with disabilities. If there are special schools in your area that focus on a particular disability, arrangements can be made for visitations, exchanges, and information sharing. Local and national professional organizations are also helpful.

Be aware that teaching disabled students may create stress in both the teacher and other students. Be sure that each teacher who has either a special class or a mainstreamed class has regularly scheduled breaks during the day. Provide a place and time to practice stress reduction techniques, and make this practice legitimate. Many students and teachers might have irrational fears about interacting with a handicapped student. These fears need to be recognized and dealt with before positive interactions can occur.

When a disabled or emotionally disturbed child creates a discipline problem, it often requires the teacher to meet individually with the student to resolve the problem. You can help by providing either a substitute teacher for an hour, or by arranging for the teacher's class to be covered while the teacher works individually with the student. This might also be a good opportunity for you to teach. Use the list of suggestions cited earlier as a checklist for helping teachers deal with discipline problems related to their disabled students.

Above all, be ready to listen and understand the pressures and demands in working with special children. The rewards are hard to see and progress is slow, intermittent, and often goes backwards as equally as it goes forward. Encouragement and support from the administration can go a long way in making the year more rewarding.

Inner City

Like the teachers who teach in the inner city, it is most important for the administrators to know their students well. Knowing the students means understanding their culture, norms, and values and knowing the family history of each student. For those children who have a weak family structure, the school administrator often replaces the father or mother and becomes a parent figure. This responsibility must be taken into account when dealing with students, especially those who have broken the rules. When setting up school policy, it is important that the students have a voice in determining what their school will be like. Ownership of the rules and consequences is especially important in the inner city where most students feel powerless. However, once the contract has been established, it is critically important to consistently enforce every rule violation. Students must see order and learn that there are consequences for their actions.

One difficulty that administrators face in dealing with any discipline problem (which can be even more intense in the inner city) is whose side to take when the student and teacher are in disagreement. You can help both teachers and students by not taking sides when this happens but acting as a mediator and allowing the two to solve their own problems. Make it clear to all your teachers how you will handle referrals and what role you see yourself playing when a situation goes beyond what the teacher can handle. Have an emergency plan for those rare, but possible, situations when a student commits a violent act or threatens to commit a violent act in the classroom. Be prepared for situations in which the teacher demands that a potentially explosive student be removed from class, but the student refuses to leave. Your plan should have input from the faculty as a whole, and all teachers should know how to use it when necessary. This plan might never be used, but most teachers feel better knowing it exists.

Involve as many community resources in your school as possible. Invite parents, business people, local chapters of minority organizations, and others to be a regular part of your school community.

Encourage teachers who wish to use alternative teaching styles and who wish to use the city's resources as a learning environment.

One of the most helpful things that you can do is to set up support/discussion groups for teachers to share their concerns, feelings, and awareness about their jobs. We have found in our work in the inner city that teachers have a lot more strength and resources than they are aware of, and that they discover them when they can talk with their colleagues. Bull sessions are not particularly helpful, and neither are gossip sessions. The discussion should involve teachers exchanging ideas and taking responsibility for their own feelings.

Drug Abuse

A good program to curb illegal use of drugs involves two main parts: prevention and action. The prevention part should involve a variety of regularly scheduled stress reduction activities for students and activities that are fun. Fantasy and imagination should be a part of every class in one way or another. As the school administrator, you can legitimize this kind of program. Students who are turned off, bored, or stressed should be given individual attention before a problem with drugs is created. Special attention for the gifted, bright, and creative should be a regular part of the school programming.

When you set up a drug information program, be sure to emphasize that drugs are a part of society and avoid the scare tactics that often push kids toward drugs. Be rational and informative. Acknowledge the truth about drugs. Bring in ex-drug users to talk about their experiences. Ex-users have more credibility with youngsters than the police, doctors, or pharmacists.

When students are found to be drug users, refer them to the appropriate in- or out-of-school contact. Therapeutic and legal interventions are required. A visible administrative presence in the halls, corridors, bathroom, and outdoors will deter on-ground use.

If drugs are causing behavior problems, set limits and implement consequences based on misbehavior. Above all, don't accept excuses or empty promises as a way of avoiding consequences.

We recommend that you speak with the local law enforcement in your community and find out what your legal responsibilities and restrictions are in relation to drug use. Inform your faculty of this information. Then use the information as a base to set up a school-wide policy about students who are caught with drugs.

You can also set up a class or discussion group for parents, informing them of the symptoms of drug use and what they can do to be helpful to their children. Emphasize ways to prevent drug use and to help the child who has already started to experiment with drugs.

Endnotes

[1]T. Gordon, *Teacher Effectiveness Training* (New York: Peter H. Wyden, 1974).

[2]R. Foxx and Azrin, *Decreasing Negative Behaviors*.

[3]Reported by Barbara Herman, who is with the Brain Research Center at Children's Hospital in Washington, D.C., at the 1987 meeting of the Society for Neuroscience.

[4]A. Mendler, "The Effects of a Combined Behavior Skills/Anxiety Management Program upon Teacher Stress and Disruptive Student Behavior" (doctoral diss., 1981).

[5]"New York State United Teachers Stress Survey Information Bulletin," New York State United Teachers Research and Educational Services, 1979.

[6]T.H. Hawkes and R.H. Koff, "Differences in Anxiety of Private School and Inner-City Public Elementary School Children," *Psychology in the Schools* 7 (1970).

[7]T.H. Hawkes and N.F. Furst, "Research Note: Race, S.E.S., Achievement, I.Q. and Teachers' Ratings of Behavior as Factors Relating to Anxiety in Upper Elementary School Children," *Sociology of Education* 44 (1971).

[8]T.H. Hawkes and N.F. Furst, "An Investigation of the (mis)Conceptions of Pre and In-Service Teachers as to the Manifestations of Anxiety in Upper Elementary School Children from Different Racial-Socioeconomic Backgrounds," *Psychology in the Schools* 10 (1973).

[9]E.C. Baysner, "New Parental Push Against Marijuana," *New York Times Sunday Magazine*, August 1981.

[10]L. Johnston, P. O'Malley, and J. Bachman, "Drugs and the Nation's High School Students" as reported in "Schoolchildren and Drugs: The Fancy that Has Not Passed," by R. Hawley, *Phi Delta Kappan*, May 1987.

[11]L,. Johnston, P. O'Malley, and J. Bachman, "Drugs and the Nation's High School Students" as reported in "Schoolchildren and Drugs: The Fancy that Has Not Passed," by R. Hawley, *Phi Delta Kappan*, May 1987.

[12]R.L. Birdwhitsell, *Introduction to Kinesics* (Louisville, Ky.: University of Louisville Press, 1952).

[13]R. Hawley, "Schoolchildren and Drugs: The Fancy that Has Not Passed," *Phi Delta Kappan*, May 1987.

[14]R. Griffiths, *Imagination in Early Childhood* (Kegan Paul, 1935).

[15]E. Klinger, *Structure and Functions of Fantasy* (New York: Wiley-Interscience, 1971).

[16]J. Morris, "Meditation in the Classroom," *Learning* 5 (1976).

[17]E. Aronson, N. Blaney, C. Stephan, J. Sikes, and M. Snapp, *The Jigsaw Classroom* (Beverly Hills: Sage Publications Inc., 1978).

11
Twenty Questions

In this chapter, we address some of the most commonly asked questions that we receive in our workshops, seminars, and courses. To help organize the questions into a meaningful pattern, we have divided them into three categories, each representing one of three dimensions of discipline: prevention, action, and resolution.

Prevention

1. Question: There have been a number of thefts in my classroom. During the last few months, books, supplies, and games have been taken. I'm pretty sure I know who is responsible, but I have no actual proof. How can I handle this situation?

Answer: You are not an investigative detective, and if you are like most teachers, you probably won't enjoy playing policeman. Begin by having an open-ended class discussion in which you inform the class that various books, games, and other supplies are missing. Tell them that it makes you feel sad and upset when people take things that belong to you or to the students in the class. Ask the students if they have ever had anything of value taken from them. Allow enough time for a thorough discussion. It is wise to end the discussion by saying, "In this classroom, people have a right to their own belongings, and nobody may take what belongs to somebody else unless they have asked for and received permission." Make eye contact with and be in close physical proximity to the child that you suspect as you set this limit.

It is important to realize that at one time or another virtually every child steals. The child may have a need or desire to hoard or a desire for objects or money of which he feels he has been deprived; he may steal to demonstrate his generosity or courage by giving away the booty to others; or he may want revenge against perceived wrong-doings by peers or adults. Whatever the reasons, the child's reputation and integrity are crucial, and setting limits must be balanced with preserving self-concept.

Stealing can be combatted by setting up opportunities in class in which the child can be responsible. Such possibilities include making him the line leader, custodial helper, or class monitor. If you suspect that this is a deprived child, you might actually give him some paper or crayons that he can take home. You might also wish to encourage the class to make gifts to one another as a way of showing their caring and generosity. If the stealing persists following these actions, then it would be wise for you to refer the child to either a child guidance clinic or to the appropriate school mental health personnel for further evaluation.

2. Question: I'm a new teacher, and I was advised to use group punishment as an effective weapon for dealing with class problems. I don't like punishing the whole class for the violations of just a few, but I can't think of an alternative when I don't know who was the rule breaker. Can you help?

Answer: Group punishments are almost always ineffective. They generate resentment in the innocent students who learn to think that they might as well break the rules because they will be punished anyway, and they teach the rule violators that they will not have to take responsibilitiy for their actions.

We first suggest that you rid yourself of the idea that punishment and retribution will improve the behavior of rule violators. The "obedience model" fosters an external focus of control and hence promotes irresponsibility. Focus instead on teaching correct behavior through natural and logical consequences. Define your rules clearly and specifically before misbehavior occurs. Present your rules to your class and, if need be, suggest various privileges that the class can earn for each day that the rules are followed. You might even encourage students to brainstorm high-interest, rewarding activities that can be offered when class members behave. Encourage students, and permit yourself, to be as creative as possible in inventing ideas. Offering privileges will increase desirable behavior much more effectively than will group punishments.

You might also try brainstorming with your class possible consequences when someone breaks a rule and you don't know who did it. Offer some possibilities, and see what other alternatives you and your class can create. Use some consequences from this list when this situation occurs again. These strategies give your students some ownership and responsibility for the problem and provide you with far more flexible and creative options than group punishment.

3. Question: I am appalled at how little support I get from the principal and vice principal. I often feel put on the spot to justify a disciplinary referral, and, more often than not, I feel like I'm made out to be the "bad guy." To make matters worse, I see little improvement in students after they have returned from a meeting with the administrator.

Answer: Most administrators feel heavily burdened with the number of students referred. In many schools, the criteria for disciplinary referral is unclear. Insubordination, belligerence, and defiance are often mentioned as school rules that require some form of disciplinary action, but neither the rules nor the consequences for violation are made clear. Instead, teachers are expected to use discretion in defining when a student's behavior warrants a referral. The problem is that what may constitute "insubordination" to you may be viewed as "normal" behavior by the teacher next door or the administrator in your building. The result of unclear guidelines is often an overwhelming number of referrals for infractions ranging from refusal to pick up a piece of paper to physical assault. The administrator must then make judgments about which referrals are most worthy of his time.

Before you are faced with the next difficult situation, jot down which rule violations you believe to be worthy of administrative referral. Set up a time to meet with your administrator for a full discussion of your guidelines. If you have established a social contract with your class, then you can indicate which of your rules has a consequence of administrative referral that was agreed to by your classes. It is also useful to share the whole social contract so the administrators can have a complete picture of all classroom rules and consequences. Make sure you and your administration have a good idea when you will use the referral, and what you have tried prior to using it. Agree on your plan by compromising when necessary. Keep an open mind. The important point is to reach agreement prior to an incident when raging feelings make problem-solving difficult. Then follow your plan. If it doesn't work, discuss any modifications before changing the agreement on your own.

We suggest that you use referral as one of your last lines of defense. Follow-up the referral by contacting the administrator and asking what he decided to do with the student. Some students can be very convincing in pinning the blame on you and may elicit the sympathies of the administrator. To guard against this, try wherever possible to attend the meeting between the administrator and student so you will know what happened and may actually have some input into what will happen. If you find that a number of your colleagues feel as you do, then raise the issue of needing a clearer set of guidelines around disciplinary referrals. You may do this at a faculty meeting, in your yearly targets, or in another way that is relatively comfortable for you.

4. Question: There is another teacher in my school who teaches the same grade as I do. Her rules are much more liberal than mine, and when both our students discuss their classes, I come out looking more rigid and strict. When I discipline my students I always hear, "Mrs. Smith lets her class do it, why can't we?" This is driving me crazy.

Answer: First, check with Mrs. Smith and make sure that your students' statements are accurate. It might help to prepare a list of questions before meeting with her. If you find that her rules and consequences are very different from yours and that she allows for more freedom and privileges in her class, it might be helpful to discuss your differences in a nonthreatening way. See if you can find some points of agreement to generate some consistency between your two classrooms. But remember, you do not have to be like Mrs. Smith, and she doesn't have to be like you. Consistency can help, but you both must feel comfortable within your own style of teaching.

After your discussion with Mrs. Smith, set aside some time to discuss this matter with your class. Tell them that Mrs. Smith teaches her way and you teach yours. Not all classes are alike, just as not all homes are alike. Tell the class that you are willing to hear their suggestions for improving things in your class, but you are not Mrs. Smith and prefer not to be compared with her. Concern yourself with the validity of their gripes, listen to what they have to say, and act according to what you professionally believe.

5. Question: I think that being preventive is a great idea, but I'm not sure that I have enough problems to warrant doing so much work before problems actually occur. Can you explain why so much time is needed prior to discipline events?

Answer: We believe that prevention is necessary because most problems are much harder to solve after they have occurred. A power struggle, for example, is almost never adequately resolved without countless hours of work, worry, and luck. Yet, by practicing a few relatively simple procedures, many power struggles can be avoided. Many well-run classrooms get even better and have even fewer discipline problems when the focus is on prevention. And teachers who invest time in prevention are happier and experience less stress throughout the school year.

The prevention activities were designed with the joint goals of preventing misbehavior and setting a tone for a positive classroom atmosphere conducive to the business of learning. Perhaps more importantly, resolving conflicts with misbehaving students is less likely to generate hostility in an environment that has emphasized prevention.

6. Question: The biggest single problem that I have is lack of parent cooperation. Phone calls home are seldom returned, and some parents who want to help often have more problems controlling their child than I do. Any suggestions?

Answer: First of all, you have a perfect right to expect cooperation from parents. There are several ways to go about getting it. Be certain that each child's parents receive a copy of your classroom rules and consequences before a disruption occurs. One consequence for each broken rule should be a phone call home. This lets parents know that they will be called if their child's behavior warrants such an action. If another consequence is to retain the child after school, let the parents know in advance that *they* will be responsible for providing after-school transportation. If you receive no response in the mail, then try phoning the parents at home or call them at work. When a problem occurs—don't wait! Contact a parent as soon as you suspect a youngster's problem. Too often, parents complain that the teacher waited too long or never made them aware of the problem. So let them know early, and document your efforts at involvement.

It is also a sound and effective practice to send home "positive" notes when youngsters do as expected, praising their accomplishments, good behavior, or both. An occasional phone call home to share news of positive accomplishments or events related to that child may go a long way toward securing parental cooperation when needed. Setting a positive tone provides good modeling to be emulated by parents. If parents confide difficulty in managing their youngster's behavior, be prepared to suggest that they consult with the school guidance counselor, psychologist, or child guidance clinic for assistance.

7. Question: I teach a gym class, and I have a few students who are physically awkward. They are reluctant to try class activities, and the other students constantly make fun of them when they do try. Can you offer any suggestions?

Answer: We all vaguely remember how awkward it is to grow up, wondering whether or not our bodies will mature and whether or not others will find us attractive. There is no greater fear for a growing youngster than to look or feel foolish in front of his peers. Unfortunately, physical education classes show a student's clumsiness and physical vulnerabilities more overtly than English or math. There are some things that you can do to help improve the situation. First, examine your curriculum and see how competitive it is. Second, look to see how many choices are offered to your students. We believe that competitive activities should only be for those participants who choose them. Develop a number of noncompetitive activities for those not wishing to compete. These can include group activities such as frisbee, body spelling, people puzzles, dance, and the like. It is important that you allow awkward students to choose activities that they are good at or believe they can handle, and then slowly let them try new, more risky activities.

Action

8. Question: Amy and Gary are two students in my 4th grade class who pick on each other constantly. It seems that five minutes can't go by without a flair up between these two. Sometimes the most simple comment can create fireworks. I have tried having them negotiate between themselves and separating them from each other, but nothing works. They seem to gravitate toward each other, and then fight.

Answer: It sounds like the gravity pulling Amy and Gary towards each other is "love." Students at that age have few acceptable outlets for showing affection. Fourth graders usually frown upon "love" relationships. It might help to have another talk. But this time let them know that you are aware that they are fond of each other (in spite of their denials), and that they can work together on various projects providing they no longer disturb the class. You might offer them ways that they can interact that are more fun and less disturbing than fighting. In any case, encourage them to be aware of their feelings and to share them in ways that are more direct than fighting. Sharing feelings is a wonderful skill for students of all ages to learn.

9. Question: I have a student in my 2nd grade class who believes that as long as she tries, regardless of the results, her efforts will be rewarded. When I ask to see her work, she always has an excuse such as, "I can't do it," or "I did my best," or "I really tried hard but I didn't know how to do it." I think that she is being manipulative, but I don't know how to respond to her. Any suggestions?

Answer: Stop accepting her excuses. "Just try to do your best" is a message that persists with popularity, and some children misinterpret this to mean that as long as they tell somebody that they tried, all will go well for them. Children who become adept at trying and not doing have often found an effective manipulative method that usually results in "trying the nerves" of people around them.

Assuming that your student is developmentally capable of doing the assigned work, you can put an end to her manipulative excuses by refusing to accept her "trying" as an end product. Tell her that you want to see exactly how she tried and what she accomplished. Let her know that you will accept no more excuses and that if she doesn't understand how to do something, she is to ask for help. If she does not ask for help and if the assignment remains tried and not done, then tell her that she will have to miss recess or remain after school to show you exactly how hard she tries. Dreikurs has pointed out that some students seek attention through displays of inadequacy. You can teach your student how to feel adequate by rewarding her real effort, by actively refusing to accept her excuses, and by confronting her displays of inadequacy.

10. Question: When students misbehave in my class, I usually make them publicly apologize to either me or, when appropriate, to another student. This consequence seems to have little effect on their behavior. Do you think that public apologies are useful consequences?

Answer: Most public apologies, like writing someone's name on the blackboard, embarrass students; they see themselves as the object of ridicule much in the same way the 19th century felons did when they were in the public stockade. We have seen students who apologize to teachers while making obscene gestures behind their backs. Generally, public apologies evoke either embarrassment or anger, neither of which helps the student learn more acceptable behavior.

11. Question: What do you do with the child who habitually tattles?

Answer: Parents and teachers may unwittingly reinforce such behavior. "If Joey pushes you or Sally hits you or Freddy does mean things, then tell me," are examples of messages that are frequently communicated to children as alternatives to taking retaliatory actions when others say or do something that upsets the child. What we really want is for the child to tell us when he has observed something that is potentially dangerous and at the same time to learn how to be responsible for solving minor interpersonal hassles without telling the teacher.

Habitual tattlers have failed to learn the distinction between dangerous events that warrant teacher attention and those that do not. They have also learned to seek attention and approval from adults because they do not feel accepted by peers. It is almost certain that the tattler feels unnoticed and unappreciated and believes that the only way to stand out is at the expense of others. Treat the problem as symptomatic of the child's underlying feeling of detachment from and rejection by his peers. It is useful, as with all forms of disruptive behavior, to appreciate children when they are engaged in behavior that is incompatible with tattling. "Susie, I really like the way you are playing with Denise" and "Billy (privately), today I didn't hear you complain about any of the kids and that makes me feel really good" are a few examples of how this can be done. Other possibilities include classroom role playing in which one child is instructed to tattle on another followed by a class discussion, listing examples of tattling on the blackboard with students contributing), and then the teacher discussing those that warrant telling (the teacher) from those that don't; giving a satisfactory acknowledgment to the tattler such as "Thanks, when I see that happen I'll have a chat and now you can go back to your seat"; providing classroom activities that promote positive peer interaction. "Tattlers" may be really asking for some order and safety from continually being hassled by the disruptive children and in a way may be trying to put the responsibility for the chaos and disorder where it belongs—on the kids doing it and the teachers. If there is an abundance of tattling in your class it may well be a message that you need to provide more safety and security for the kids.

12. Question: In some classes, there is a large percentage of disruptive children. When they set the general tone for the class, how can you change the personality of the group (and do it without constantly lecturing to them about poor behavior)?

Answer: Because group problems are more complex than those involving only one student, effective resolution calls for considerable flexibility on your part. You may need to temporarily abandon your lesson plans to deal directly with the class. It is important for you to begin by specifically defining, first for yourself and then with your students, what you mean by "disruptive behavior." Encourage your students, either verbally or in writing, to let you know what they need to improve their behavior. Some of the more vocal students may register complaints about your style of teaching or personal attributes. It is important that you learn to "active listen" nondefensively to these complaints and to consider instructional or behavioral modification as a result. If you feel that you cannot or will not change your style, then explain your position. An open exchange of differences in which teacher and students experience no negative consequences for self-expression is sometimes sufficient to curb negative behaviors. Other possibilities include the following.

a. Meet with the ringleaders to acknowledge their leadership. You might say something like, "Most days, I have a very hard time teaching the class because of interruptions, fights, namecalling, etc. I'm tired of lecturing, yelling, and threatening, and I am hoping that maybe you can give me some advice as to how to stop this stuff."

b. Consider developing a social contract with your class in which both students and teacher develop a set of rules and consequences regarding classroom behavior. (For a complete discussion, see Chapter 4.)

c. Allow students to develop a "reward cookbook" of activities and privileges that they enjoy. Keep a daily or weekly record of classroom disruption and tell the students that each day (or week) that improvement is noted (be sure to define success criteria in advance), they will be able to choose one of the activities during a designated time.

d. Send a letter home to each child's parents letting them know of the disruptive classroom atmosphere. Be specific without personalizing, and request that they thoroughly discuss your concerns with their child.

e. Set up a "gripe box" in your classroom. Explain to your students that their misbehavior is telling you that they have gripes and complaints about you or the classroom or each other. Let them know that from now on the gripe box is the place to register all such complaints and that at a designated time you will read all gripes aloud. When you do this, be sure to involve your students in solving the complaint through brainstorming.

13. Question: Sometimes I find it necessary to let the rest of the class know how a particular problem was resolved with one particular student so the class understands that the student didn't get away with anything. Is it best to share with the rest of the class or just keep the incident between the student and myself?

Answer: By informing the entire class of the result of your incident with this student, you may let them know you "won," but you will also be telling them that you will use them as examples should the need arise and that they cannot trust you to keep your transactions with them private. These learnings will make it difficult for the class to feel safe with you and to interact normally with you. They will tend to keep their guard up.

We feel it is better for you to keep all interactions with individual students private and not to show publicly that you have won with a difficult student. It is better for your students to learn that you are in charge by seeing the improved behavior of the disruptive student. If the student's behavior hasn't changed as a result of your intervention, then you haven't "won" anyway.

Resolution

14. Question: Sam is in my 4th grade class and is constantly being a nuisance. Slamming his arm on the desk, dropping pencils, making noises in class, "accidentally" brushing up against others are but a few of his many behaviors that make me wish for his absence. Naturally, he has a perfect attendance record. When I correct him, either by telling him to stop or sending him to the principal's office, he becomes verbally abusive and puts me on the defensive. I don't know what else to do!

Answer: Sam sounds like a classic "uproar" player. He is determined to bug you until you finally blow up at him. If you ignore him, he'll continue to goad you until you lose control, and when you do, he'll complain to his friends, parents, principal, and anybody else who listens that you are unfair and out to get him. "All I did was tap my desk while I was looking for my book and she screamed at me" is a predictable outcry. Students like Sam have a way of choosing to forget the 50 or more incidents that preceded the blow-up by focusing on the minor event that in and of itself was relatively innocuous. His payoff is the perceived recognition and status that he achieves from his peers (although in reality they view him as a stupid schlemiel) for warring with the teacher.

You must develop a calm, firm, and consistent manner in dealing with Sam. Since Sam has strong needs for attention, be sure to catch him being good and to acknowledge any improvement in his behavior. Visiting him at a setting outside the classroom such as on the playground after school, taking him for an ice cream after a good day, and sending positive notes home are strategies that are likely to pay big dividends. Many of the activities in Chapter 8 are designed with kids like Sam in mind.

15. Question: I have a 3rd grade boy who continually wets his pants. Ronald's mother claims this never happens at home. We have tried putting him in the kindergarten as a helper to make him feel special. We have tried everything from embarrassing him to rewarding him with praise when he used the toilet. He does not seem bothered when he tells me that his pants are wet again. In fact, he seems rather proud. What can I do?

Answer: Stop trying so hard! You and his mother are unwittingly contributing to this problem because of all the special attention that he receives. Handle the matter in a low-key manner. Although it is unlikely that Ronald's problem is organically based (especially if confined to the school situation), be sure to have him checked by the school physician just in case.

Have a private meeting with Ronald and tell him that you want him to bring two pairs of clean underwear and two pairs of pants to school. Arrange for a place in which he can store these clothes and retrieve them by himself. Tell him that from now on, when he wets himself, he is to go directly to the prearranged place in which his clothes are stored. He is to put on clean underwear and clean pants. Should he wet himself more than twice in any day, then he will simply have to spend the remainder of the day in wet clothes. Before the end of the day, check Ronald's clothes supply. If he has fewer than two pairs of clothes for changing, then remind him to take home the dirty laundry and bring clean laundry for next day. Set aside a few minutes before day's end to ask Ronald how he did during the day. During your private chat, tell him that it is no longer necessary for him to tell you when he wets, but to simply take a supply of clean clothes and change. If he persists in telling you, then either ignore him or casually remind him that he knows what to do.

It is important that Ron's wetting does not become the centerpiece of your relationship with him. Be certain to provide a variety of positive reinforcers for appropriate classroom behavior. You may wish to explore with Ronald what he likes and does not like about school and to arrange things so that he may be doing more of what he likes. Ron's mother should be actively involved in the development of this plan.

16. Question: I'm having a bad time with one of my kids. Eric is hostile and resentful in class with a very low tolerance for frustration. He disrupts the other students and seems to use his outbursts to manipulate me. I suspect his hostility stems from a rocky home life. How can I reach this child?

Answer: Eric's hostility must not be allowed to interfere with your ability to teach and the other children to learn. As it is unlikely that Eric will easily give up his resentments, it is suggested that you meet with him when you and he are alone to balance your understanding of his problems with a strong and clear statement of limits. During this meeting it is important to provide more acceptable alternatives in which he can express his hostility. For example, "Eric, I will no longer tolerate your pushing or fighting (or whatever other specific behaviors it is that you wish to eliminate). When you feel angry in class you may write your angry thoughts on a piece of paper and rip it up, or you may go to the time-out area until you cool down, or you may leave the classroom until you feel better." You might also want to check out any other options that Eric can think of. When you observe him expressing his resentments more acceptably, be sure to let him know that you appreciate his effort. Children with a low frustration tolerance can often be helped by giving them challenging tasks in which success is practically guaranteed, by making them a teacher's helper, and by giving them the responsibility to work with younger students in a helper's role. As for the rocky home life you suspect, it might well be worth your effort to check this out during a parent conference or in consultation with colleagues or resource personnel. But remember, many teachers render themselves helpless to classroom disruption by attributing blame to an unsettled home. Effective action, with or without home support (preferably with), can and often does stop misbehavior.

17. Question: I have a 9-year-old boy in my class who does virtually no work, almost never turns in his homework, and spends most of his time daydreaming. I have cajoled him, threatened him, and had two parent conferences, all to no avail. He likes candy, and recently I offered him a candy bar for each day in which he completed two assignments and had his homework done. Result: he got even worse! What do I do now!

Answer: Refuse to give him any homework assignments and do *not* give him any books, papers, or other materials for classwork. The next time you give a class homework assignment, tell him privately that he has a special assignment. He is to make sure that he comes in with NO homework the following day. When you check the children's homework, ask him if he did his assignment. If he did his special assignment, then tell him matter-of-factly how glad you are that he remembered to do as told. Similarly, announce to him privately that from now on he may not use any books or papers in class. He may daydream all day if he would like! If he should decide that he would like to be treated like the rest of the children, then he must ask you for work. Emphasize that he still must follow all of the rules for behavior.

Your student sounds like a passive/aggressive child who is expressing his anger through refusal to do as expected. The more you threaten or praise him, the worse he will get. It is therefore wise for you to encourage him to continue to behave as he has been. If he does as told (nothing) then he has followed the rule. If he does his work to defy you (or his parents), then he has behaved in a socially acceptable way. Either way, you win!

It is also a good idea to refer him to your child study team for an intellectual and personality assessment. He may need more than you can offer him.

18. Question: Joey is in my 6th grade class and throws things around, fights with other students, and does not work. Whenever I discipline him, he grins, laughs, and refuses to obey my directive. Frankly, I'm afraid that he might turn on me and physically injure me. Any advice?

Answer: We suggest proceeding in the following way:

a. Be very clear and firm with Joey and tell him that you will no longer tolerate his fighting and throwing things.

b. Tell Joey exactly what you will do should this unacceptable behavior continue.

c. Let Joey know how he will be rewarded for each day (you might reduce this to a half-day or each hour) that passes without an incident.

d. Write his parents a letter that specifically details (1) Joey's misbehavior, (2) what you will do if this continues, and (3) how Joey will be rewarded if he decides to behave more acceptably. Follow this letter with a phone call and arrange for periodic conferences.

e. Catch Joey being good. If you realize that 15 minutes or a half-hour have passed and you haven't been aware of him, take time to notice and respond to him in a positive way.

f. Send home reports that specify Joey's progress. At first, daily reports are preferable, and you may later wish to move towards weekly reports. See if his parent(s) are willing to institute a home-based reward system that is contingent upon positive reports from school.

g. If no improvement is noted, approach a colleague or the principal and ask for help. It is advisable at this stage to find someone with an intimidating presence who is not beyond the use of tough talk. You want somebody who has no problem in firmly imposing his thoughts and values upon this youngster.

h. When you have gone through steps (a) through (g) on three or four occasions and still no change in behavior has occurred, then refer Joey to resource specialists for an evaluation to determine what kind of help he needs. Be certain to document your efforts so that others will have a complete picture of Joey's classroom disturbance with corrective steps taken.

19. Question: Billy is a handicapped student in my 5th grade class who is being mainstreamed for the first time. He desperately wants friends but doesn't know how to go about it. He is often boisterous and seems to unknowingly invite a negative reaction from his peers.

He complains that nobody likes him. What can I do to help him feel more positively involved with the class?

Answer: It sounds like your student needs some straight feedback, and don't be afraid to give it to him. Begin by focusing on his theme of "nobody likes me" with reflective or active listening skills. (For a thorough overview of this method we suggest Thomas Gordon's *Teacher Effectiveness Training*.) After he's had an opportunity to share his feelings, ask him if he is aware of anything that he says or does that might cause others to dislike him. If he is, then this may lead to a good discussion with some new ways for him to act or behave with his peers. If he says, "I don't know," then offer him your feedback. Tell him directly, "Billy, I sometimes notice that you talk very loudly and the other students are not used to this. Although I'm not positive, I think that this might be one reason why they aren't more friendly to you. Would you be willing for the next few days to speak more softly and see if their reaction to you changes?" You might then choose to do some role playing or modeling with him so that you are sure that he understands what you mean. This may also be a good time to let him know that for many students, he is their first encounter with somebody with a handicap, and they may be unsure of how to react to him.

Allow yourself to become acquainted with any special needs and problems that the student experiences in your classroom. Most handicapped individuals prefer to be treated the same as all other students, provided that their unique disability is addressed. After you have talked with this child, you might want to meet with the class—when Billy is not present—to provide information about the disability, allay anxiety in some children that they might "catch" the disability, explain that Billy's feelings get hurt just like everyone else, and answer any questions they may have. You may elicit a lot of support by asking a few willing classmates to pay some special attention for awhile to the special needs child. Most children and teenagers can be friendly, supportive, and encouraging once their own fears are placed in the proper perspective.

Summary

An adolescent in one of our workshops wrote the following.

My mother is a junior high school teacher who bitches all the time about how bad students are today. I hope that you print my letter so that teachers might realize that most of us kids care about school, and so that they can understand what it's like to be a kid. In most of my classes, the teacher gives us an endless amount of worksheets to keep us busy and they expect us to care about such boring assignments. Nobody ever asks us what we want to do or what is important to us. We're just supposed to sit in our hard seats all day and pay attention to what the teacher says. Us kids don't want to be compared to our brothers and sisters, we don't want to be made fun of when we don't know an answer, we don't want to be embarrassed by being yelled at in front of our friends, and we don't want teachers to call us names. We also don't like it when teachers play favorites.

Maybe if the teachers treated us with more respect then we would do the same and there would be less discipline problems. Maybe if teachers spent some time listening to our problems we wouldn't need to create problems in their class.

The few teachers I have liked treated us as people. They let us get to know them. They told us when they were having a bad day. They talked about their own ideas and feelings and listened to ours. They let us get to know them not only as teachers but also as people. They were tough when we acted up but didn't keep grudges. They enjoyed what they were doing and we enjoyed being with them. I wish that more teachers understood that school is a tense place for a lot of students. Maybe if they did, I wouldn't be thinking of dropping out!

12
Conclusion

I t is our heartfelt belief that schools are for children. Teachers carry on their lives and work there as do administrators and support personnel. And all that they do is for children. Students spend approximately 12,000 hours of their lives in school. Much of what they learn about adulthood happens in school. They learn by watching and interacting with those who teach them and those who discipline them. They learn how to relate to others and how to solve problems with people. They learn what happens when they stretch and sometimes break limits. They learn about their individuality and how they are perceived by others. They learn about the responsibility of being part of a group. They learn how to express the way they feel and the way they think.

These lessons are long lasting. That is why the way we manage student behavior cannot be viewed simplistically. There is too much at stake. Methods of discipline, when viewed from a holistic perspective, play an important role in development of self-concept, the ability to take responsibility for one's actions, the way children learn to communicate with others, and how they learn to work cooperatively with others.

It is our hope that the models, methods, and values expressed in this book will make a positive difference for teachers, administrators, and especially children.

Appendix A
Behavior Management Inventory

If you would like to see what you have learned after you finish reading this book, try this self-administered inventory. Respond to the questions in the survey, read the remainder of this book, and then answer the questions again. Compare your second set of answers with what we believe to be appropriate responses that are explained in the Behavior Management Survey. The changes in your answers will show you what you have learned.

These instruments may be used by teachers or schools without permission but may not be reproduced for distribution or included in any publication without written permission of the publisher.

Directions

1. Read each scenario. Close your eyes and picture the sequence of events as if they are happening to you. Try to see the scene in pictures rather than words; to actually feel what you would feel if you really were in the situation.

2. Write down what you would naturally do. List the steps briefly and in chronological order. Do not write complete sentences or paragraphs. The quicker you write, the better. Too much thought will most likely give an answer that sounds great, but might not be what

you would actually do if you had to respond without the benefit of reflection.

3. There are no wrong answers. Think less about how others might judge your answers than writing a response that reflects your authentic reaction to the situation.

Situation One: You are taking roll at the beginning of class and you notice Fred strolling in, one minute late. He slowly takes his seat in the back and begins talking with his friend.

Situation Two: You explain to Susan that the reason you asked her to meet with you later is that she has violated the "no passing papers during discussion" rule. She looks at you for a minute and says flatly, "It's not fair. I never heard of that rule."

Situation Three: Mathew never pays attention in your class. When you ask him why, he shrugs his shoulders and says, "I don't know. I guess I'm bored."

Situation Four: You are discussing with your students an important point about today's lesson. Two girls, who have been constantly whispering to each other all year, start to giggle for no apparent reason.

Situation Five: After you tell Vickie that she must see you later to discuss a rule she has just broken, she stands up and says loud enough for the whole class to hear, "Take a hike. I'm not coming and you can't make me!!"

Situation Six: Over one-half of your class is constantly asking, "Will this be on the test? How many pages does it have to be? Can I use a pencil? Does neatness count? Is it due at the beginning or at the end of class?" You set up a rule forbidding such questions, but they keep coming anyway.

Situation Seven: Micky hasn't done his homework in over six weeks. You have kept him after school, discussed the matter with both Micky and the vice principal, and have met with Micky and both his parents. Still the homework is never done.

Situation Eight: Rosie talks out of turn, daydreams constantly, sharpens her pencil without permission, is late by three minutes (never more) for two out of three classes, puts her makeup on during class discussion, and generally displays a "bad attitude" when dealing with you. After giving her three chances in the last hour, she takes out her lipstick and puts it on, right as you call on her to answer a discussion question.

Situation Nine: Your principal has asked you to critique the following punishments for use in your classroom.

1. Write offender's name on bulletin board.
2. The offender serves between one and five hours detention.
3. The offender is to be thrown out of the classroom and referred to the vice principal for further action.
4. Offender hears a lecture on the importance of the rule.
5. Offender must write why he did it, and why it is important never to do it again.
6. Offender must apologize to entire class.
7. Offender gets double homework for two nights.
8. Offender loses library privileges for one week.

Behavior Management Analysis

After most of the following suggested responses, you will find a chapter reference from *Discipline With Dignity* that offers more information about the situation and the suggested responses.

Situations One and Two relate to the Prevention Dimension or what can be done to prevent problems from happening before they start. Each of these situations could have been prevented from happening or have a built in method of response.

One: A rule is needed to stipulate behavior at the beginning of class. If none exists, then no rule has been broken, and therefore no consequence should be administered. The teacher can tell Fred that she disapproves of his behavior, but that's about all. If there is a rule for either coming in one minute late or talking during roll, then the teacher merely implements one of the consequences on the list. Don't get hooked on his "strolling" into class. It is very difficult and not worthwhile to attempt to regulate walking behavior. (Chapter 4)

Two: Playing "stupid" is a common game to avoid responsibility. But what if Susan is right? Is she responsible for a rule she didn't know? The common teacher response is that it was Susan's responsibility to know, and therefore her excuse is not valid. But why get into this mess in the first place? Give a test to all students on your rules and consequences. One-hundred percent is required for passing. In Situation Two, if Susan has passed the test, you will have a record of it, and you need not argue. She knows the rule and you both know that she knows the rule. If she has not taken the test, then her excuse is valid. Give her the test as quickly as possible. (Chapter 4)

Situations Four and Five relate to the Action Dimension, or what can be done when a rule is broken.

Four: The best response is to calmly walk over to the two girls and, speaking softly so only the two girls can hear you, tell them the rule and the consequence that you have selected for them from the list. Nothing else needs to be said or done. (Chapter 6)

Five: Vickie is trying to hook you into a power struggle. The only way to win is not to play. Calmly repeat back to her what you hear her say (active listening) without escalating the situation or excusing her from coming to see you. If she persists, use the "broken record" technique to let her know that this is not the time to argue. Later when both of you have cooled down, talk to her about a possible alternative consequence if she had a reasonable reason for not being able to come. If she simply doesn't show up, enforce the "insubordination" rule. (Chapter 6)

Situations Seven and Eight relate to the Resolution Dimension, or how to deal with chronic rule breakers.

Seven: This looks like a good case for the "paradoxical" method. Try setting it up for a one month period and see what happens. Another good strategy is the "Family Intervention." If the parents are willing to support you and honor the system, there might be some success. But always remember, there is no way you can ever make a child do something he refuses to do. (Chapter 8)

Eight: Rosie is clearly showing you that she doesn't like you. Further, she gets a lot of energy and attention by being a "bad actor." Use the "Positive Student Confrontation" strategy to gradually resolve the situation with Rosie. Remember to pick one or two things to work on at a time. Small steady success is better than rapid, major, unstable improvements. (Chapter 8)

Situations Three and Six are not really discipline problems, therefore a discipline intervention will not work and may make them worse. These are motivation problems and require a change in the way the teacher is teaching.

Three: Mathew is bored. Take him at his word. He needs an individualized learning program that matches his ability to the task, with a degree of challenge. If the motivation problem is not dealt with quickly, the situation will soon become a discipline problem, and in essence the teacher will have created most of it.

Six: This class is a group of finishers. The reasons might vary from previous school experiences to the teacher's lack of energy and enthusiasm for the subject. Rules and enforcement will not change the situation. The teacher must begin to stress the joy of learning with energy and enthusiasm. Assignments need to be interesting and internally motivating. Grades and other external rewards should be minimized, if mentioned at all. Give many assignments that are not to be graded at all. Use self grading.

The *Time Continuum Model of Motivation Planning* (Wlodkowski 1978) will help the teacher make specific plans to improve motivation in the classroom. Teacher needs to focus on attitudes, needs, stimulation, affect, and student competence. (Chapter 10)

Situation Nine is a request from your principal. Whether you answer or not, each of the punishments on the list are exactly that: **punishments.** They will not work in the long run, and will, in most cases, only make matters worse. They should be avoided. You could be helpful and supply a list of consequences that will work as well as the principles of what an effective consequence is. (Chapter 5)

- Clear and specific
- Has a range of alternatives
- Is related to rule
- Is not a punishment
- Is logical or natural

Appendix B
School Discipline Survey

Directions

1. Each participant responds to scales 1-9 (pp. 248-256).
2. Each participant fills the "Individual Data Summary" (p. 257).
3. The group leader collects the summary sheets and fills in the "Team Data Summary" sheet (p. 258).

Examine the results. See areas of agreement and disagreement. Discuss, interpret, and use for future faculty development activities.

These instruments may be used by teachers or schools without permission but may not be reproduced for distribution or included in any publication without written permission of the publisher.

Scale 1. Goal Clarity and Conflict

"Things about Discipline Procedures"

Read each statement and circle the response which best represents the situation in your school.

Statement I—I often wonder what is the basic procedure for school discipline here. There are people in the school (maybe even myself) who spend a lot of time and energy doing things that are not consistent with what I think our main objectives for discipline ought to be. They downplay or overlook important parts of our total objective or their time is directed at things I think aren't very important.

Statement II—The school's basic overall objectives re: Discipline Procedures are very clear to me. All of my and everyone else's efforts seem directly related to accomplishing these key goals. Whenever a question arises over what things need to be done, we are able to set priorities by referring to our basic objectives.

(circle one)
    a. Statement I
    b. More Statement I than II
    c. Between Statement I and II
    d. More Statement II than I
    e. Statement II

Example(s): In the space below describe one or more examples of situations in the school that illustrate your response on Scale 1.

Scale 2. Role Ambiguity

"Things about How My Job
Is Affected by Discipline"

Statement I—Often situations arise on the job when I'm not certain what I am supposed to do. Frequently, I'm not even sure if a discipline situation is my responsibility or someone else's. We never get together to discuss what each individual thinks he (she) and the others on the job can or should do to work together to do the best job.

Statement II—In almost every discipline situation I am very sure about what responsibilities I have and about what others in the school are supposed to be doing. These discipline responsibilities are often discussed by relevant members of the school, particularly when someone has a question about what he or someone else should be doing.

(circle one)   a. Statement I
                     b. More Statement I than II
                     c. Between Statement I and II
                     d. More Statement II than I
                     e. Statement II

Example(s):

Scale 3. Role Conflict

"Clarity of Expectations"

Statement I—Different people on the job expect different things from me in regard to working with students who misbehave. Often these get in the way of each other or there just isn't enough time to meet everyone's demand. My job makes me feel like a "juggler with too many balls."

Statement II—I have no trouble in doing the different things that the job and other people in school expect of me. I understand why I'm supposed to do things I do and it all seems to fit together. If I feel as though the demands people in the school make of me are getting too heavy or don't make sense, we resolve the problem with a discussion.

(circle one)

    a. Statement I
    b. More Statement I than II
    c. Between Statement I and II
    d. More Statement II than I
    e. Statement II

Example(s):

Scale 4. Participation/Influence

"How Staff Is Involved in Decision Making"

Statement I—When some people try to participate in a discussion of discipline methods, they often get cut off or their suggestions seem to die. People only seem to pay attention to some people and not others. Some people seem to do most of the talking while others don't participate very much.

Statement II—Everyone gets a chance to express themselves and to influence the group in discussions about discipline. We listen to every person's contributions and try to discuss the strong points in each. No one is ignored. Everyone is drawn into the discussion.

(circle one)
    a. Statement I
    b. More Statement I than II
    c. Between Statement I and II
    d. More Statement II than I
    e. Statement II

Example(s):

Scale 5. Commitment/Understanding

"How Discipline Decisions Get Made Around Here"

Directions: This scale is different from the previous ones. In this scale, read all the statements and circle the letter next to the one statement that most closely describes the general situation in your team.

When a disagreement arises among the faculty about a schoolwide discipline issue:

a. We assume it's probably best not to let it get personal, so we let it pass hoping it will cool down and eventually be forgotten. If it does start to ruffle feelings, we try to smooth the feelings and make the least of the disagreement (e.g., "Well, there is really no point in fighting about it, so let's forget it" or "We're all grown-ups; we shouldn't argue").

b. Often we end the disagreement when someone takes charge and makes a decision, or decides not to discuss it any further.

c. We try to come to an agreement somewhere between the two disagreeing positions. In other words, we compromise. That way everyone gets a little and everyone gives a little and the disagreement is taken care of.

d. We get the disagreeing parties together and have them talk to each other about their points of view until each party can see some logic in the other's ideas. Then we try to come to an agreement that makes sense to everyone.

Example(s):

Scale 6. Conflict Management

"How Discipline Affects What It's Like to Work Around Here"

Statement I—I often get the feeling that some people in the school don't think that some other people in the school have much of a contribution to make. Some faculty don't pay much attention to the problems or suggestions of others. People are often taken for granted, and many prefer to neither see nor hear discipline problems.

Statement II—Everyone recognizes that the job could not be done without the cooperation and contribution of everyone else. Each person, including myself, is treated as an important part of the school team. When you bring up an idea or a problem, people sit up and take notice. It makes you feel that you and your job are important. People are receptive to unpleasant feelings associated with discipline problems, and are eager to help each other.

(circle one)
    a. Statement I
    b. More Statement I than II
    c. Between Statement I and II
    d. More Statement II than I
    e. Statement II

Example(s):

Scale 7. Recognition/Involvement

"Style of Discipline"

Statement I—My style of discipline really gets me down. People do not seem concerned with helping each other get the job done. Everyone is pulling in opposite directions; everyone is out for himself. If you try to do something different, you get jumped on by people for being out of line, or if you make a mistake, you never hear the end of it.

Statement II—I really like my style of discipline, and I like working in this school. The team encourages you to take responsibility. You feel really appreciated by other staff members when you do a good job. When things aren't going well, people really make an effort to help each other. We really pull together on this team.

(circle one)
    a. Statement I
    b. More Statement I than II
    c. Between Statement I and II
    d. More Statement II and I
    e. Statement II

Example(s):

Scale 8. Support/Cohesiveness

"Clarity of Consequences"

Statement I—When students break school rules, they can never be sure of what will happen to them. The absence of consistently applied consequences for student misbehavior creates a chaotic school climate.

Statement II—Consequences of misbehavior are clearly understood by all students. When rules are broken, students know exactly what will happen to them. The school's discipline policy creates an orderly, organized school climate.

(circle one)
    a. Statement I
    b. More Statement I than II
    c. Between Statement I and II
    d. More Statement II than I
    e. Statement II

Example(s):

Scale 9. Consistency/Inconsistency

"What the Methods of Discipline
Are Around Here"

Statement I—I often get locked into power struggles with unruly students. I find myself saying and doing things that I know are ineffective or inappropriate, but I just haven't found any more effective alternatives.

Statement II—Discipline isn't really a problem for me, because my style and methods are usually effective in preventing and stopping student misbehavior. I believe that at least some of my methods could help other teachers that have greater problems in working with unruly students.

(circle one)
    a. Statement I
    b. More Statement I than II
    c. Between Statement I and II
    d. More Statement II than I
    e. Statement II

Example(s):

Individual Data Summary

Scales

1. Goal Clarity and Conflict   I _____ II

a   b   c   d   e

2. Role Ambiguity   I _____ II

a   b   c   d   e

3. Role Conflict   I _____ II

a   b   c   d   e

4. Participation/Influence   I _____ II

a   b   c   d   e

5. Commitment/Understanding   I _____ II

a   b   c   d   e

6. Conflict Management   I _____ II

a   b   c   d   e

7. Recognition/Involvement   I _____ II

a   b   c   d   e

8. Support/Cohesiveness   I _____ II

a   b   c   d   e

9. Consistency/Inconsistency   I _____ II

a   b   c   d   e

Team Data Summary

Scales

1. Goal Clarity and Conflict I _____ II
   a   b   c   d   e

2. Role Ambiguity I _____ II
   a   b   c   d   e

3. Role Conflict I _____ II
   a   b   c   d   e

4. Participation/Influence I _____ II
   a   b   c   d   e

5. Commitment/Understanding I _____ II
   a   b   c   d   e

6. Conflict Management I _____ II
   a   b   c   d   e

7. Recognition/Involvement I _____ II
   a   b   c   d   e

8. Support/Cohesiveness I _____ II
   a   b   c   d   e

9. Consistency/Inconsistency I _____ II
   a   b   c   d   e

Bibliography

Aronson, E., N. Blaney, C. Stephan, J. Sikes, and M. Snapp. (1978). *The Jigsaw Classroom*. Beverly Hills: Sage Publications Inc.

Bagley, W.C. (1910). *Classroom Management*. New York: Macmillan Co.

Bandler, R. (1985). *Using Your Brain for a Change*. Utah: Real People Press.

Baysher, E.C. (August 1981). "New Parental Push Against Marijuana." *New York Times Sunday Magazine*.

Bessell, H. (1970). *Methods in Human Development*. San Diego: Human Development Training Institute.

Birdwhistell, R.L. (1952). *Introduction to Kinesics*. Louisville, Ky.: University of Louisville Press.

Borger, J., M. Carroll, and D. Schiller. "Motivating Students."

Brown, G. (1971). *Human Teaching for Human Learning: An Introduction to Confluent Education*. New York: Random House.

Burns, M. (1981). "Groups of Four: Solving the Management Problem." *Learning* 10: 46-51.

"Can Public Learn from Private." *Time*, April 20, 1981, 50.

Combs, A. (1965). *The Professional Education of Teachers*. Boston: Allyn & Bacon.

Curwin, R.L., and B. Fuhrmann. (Sept. 1978). "Mirror Mirror on the Wall: Developing Teacher Congruency," *The Humanistic Education* 17: 34.

Curwin, R., and A. Mendler. (1980). *The Discipline Book: A Complete Guide to School and Classroom Management*. Reston, Va.: Reston Publishing Co.

Curwin, R. (Oct. 1980) "Are Your Students Addicted to Praise?" *Instructor* 90: 61-62.

Curwin, R., and P. DeMarte. (1976). "Making Classroom Competition Positive: A Facilitating Model." In *Degrading the Grading Myths: A Primer of Alternatives to Grades and Marks*. Alexandria, Va.: Association for Supervision and Curriculum Development.

Foxx, R., and Azrin. *Decreasing Negative Behaviors*.

Frankl, V.E. (1963). *Man's Search for Meaning: An Introduction to Logotherapy*. New York: Pocket Books.

Gordon, T. (1974). *Teacher Effectiveness Training*. New York: Peter H. Wyden.

Griffiths, R. (1935). *Imagination in Early Childhood*. Kegan Paul.

Hawkes, T.H., and R.H. Koff. (1970). "Differences in Anxiety of Private School and Inner-City Public Elementary School Children." *Psychology in the Schools* 7: 250-259.

Hawkes, T.H., and N.F. Furst. (1971). "Research Note: Race, S.E.S., Achievement, I.Q. and Teachers' Ratings of Behavior as Factors Relating to Anxiety in Upper Elementary School Children." *Sociology of Education* 44: 333-350.

Hawkes, T.H., and N.F. Furst. (1973). "An Investigation of the (mis)Conceptions of Pre and In-Service Teachers as to the Manifestations of Anxiety in Upper Elementary School Children from Different Racial Socioeconomic Backgrounds." *Psychology in the Schools* 10: 23-32.

Hawley, R. (May 1987). "Schoolchildren and Drugs: The Fancy that Has Not Passed." *Phi Delta Kappan*.

Hendrickson, B. (1979). "Teacher Burnout: How to Recognize It, What to Do About It." *Learning* 7: 36-38.

Howard, C. (1977). In *Stress and the Art of Biofeedback*, by B. Brown. New York: Bantam Books.

Johnson, D., et al. (1981). "Effects of Cooperative, Competitive and Individualistic Goal Structures on Achievement: A Meta-Analysis." *Psychological Bulletin* 89: 47-62.

Johnston, L., P. O'Malley, and J. Bachman. (May 1987). "Drugs and the Nation's High School Students." In "Schoolchildren and Drugs: The Fancy that Has Not Passed," by R. Hawley. *Phi Delta Kappan*.

Klinger, E. (1971). *Structure and Functions of Fantasy*. New York: Wiley-Interscience.

Lazarus, R.S. (1976). *Patterns of Adjustment*. New York: McGraw-Hill.

Leming, R.J., and J. Hollifield. (1985). "Cooperative Learning: A Research Success Story." *Educational Researcher* 14.

Levenson, R. Quoted in "For a Strong Body, It's Mind Over Matter" by Bonnie Jacob, *USA Today*, January 22, 1986.

Mendler, A., and R. Curwin. (1983). *Taking Charge in the Classroom*. Reston, Va.: Reston Publishing Co.

Mendler, A. (1981). "The Effects of a Combined Behavior Skills/ Anxiety Management Program Upon Teacher Stress and Disruptive Student Behavior." Doctoral diss., Union's Graduate School.

Morris, J. (1976). "Meditation in the Classroom." *Learning* 5: 22-25.

Moscowitz, E., and J.L. Hayman. (1974). "Interaction Patterns of First Year, Typical and 'Best' Teachers in Inner-City Schools." *Journal of Educational Research* 67: 224-230.

"New York State United Teachers Stress Survey Information Bulletin." (1979). New York State United Teachers Research and Educational Services.

Porter, A., and J. Brophy. (May 1988). "Highlights of Research on Good Teaching." *Educational Leadership* 45: 75.

Rubin, J. (March 1981). "The Psychology of Entrapment." *Psychology Today*, 58-59.

Rutter, M., B. Maughan, P. Mortimore, J. Ouston, and A. Smith. (1979). *Fifteen Thousand Hours*. Cambridge, Mass.: Harvard University Press.

Savay, L.M., and M. Ehlen-Miller. (1979). *Mindways: A Guide for Exploring Your Mind*. New York: Harper and Row.

Selye, H. (1974). *Stress Without Distress*. New York: The New American Library, Inc.

Slavin, R. (1983). *Cooperative Learning*. New York: Longman.

Squires, D., W. Huitt, and J. Segars. (1984). *Effective Schools and Classrooms: A Research Based Perspective*. Alexandria, Va.: Association for Supervision and Curriculum Development.

Thoresen, C.E., T. Alper, J.W. Hannum, J. Barrick, and R.N. Jacks. (1973). "Effects of Systematic Desensitization and Behavior Training with Elementary Teachers." Stanford University.

Torrance, E.P. (1970). "Scientific Views of Creativity and Factors Affecting Its Growth." In *Creativity and Learning*, edited by J. Kagan. Boston: Beacon Press.

United States Department of Health, Education and Welfare. "Violent Schools—Safe Schools. The Safe School Study Report to the Congress, 1978." (Eric Document Reproduction Service. No. Ed 149 464.).

White, R., and R. Lippitt. (1960). "Leader Behavior and Member Reaction in Three 'Social Climates'." In *Group Dynamics in Researched Theory*, 2d ed., edited by D. Cartwright and A. Zander. New York: Harper and Row.

Wlodkowski, R. (1978). *Motivation and Teaching: A Practical Guide*. Washington, D.C.: N.E.A. Publication.

Wlodkowski, R. "How to Help Teachers Reach the Turned Off Student." 1978.

Additional References

Abidin, R. (1976). *Parenting Skills: Trainer's Manual*. New York: Human Science Press.

Alschuler, A., D. Tabor, and J. McIntrye. (1971). *Teaching Achievement Motivation*. Middletown, Conn.: Education Ventures, Inc.

Bandura, A., and R.H. Walters. (1963). *Social Learning and Personality Development*. New York: Holt, Rinehart and Winston.

Barkley, R. (1981). *Hyperactive Children: A Handbook for Diagnosis and Treatment*. New York: Guilford Press.

Bar-Tal, D., and Y. Bar-Zohay. "The Relationship Between Perception of Locus of Control and Academic Achievement: Review and Some Educational Implications." Contemporary Educational Psychology: 181-199.

Becker, W.C. (1971). *Parents Are Teachers*. Champaign, Ill.: Research Press.

Benson, H. (1976). *The Relaxation Response*. New York: Avon.

Berne, E. (1964). *Games People Play*. New York: Grove Press.

Bloch, A.M. (1978). "Combat Neurosis in Inner-City Schools." *American Journal of Psychiatry* 135: 1189-1192.

Bolstad, O., and S. Johnson. (1972). "Self-Regulation in the Modification of Disruptive Classroom Behavior." *Journal of Applied Behavior Analysis*: 433-454.

Borton, T. (1970). *Reach, Touch, and Teach: Student Concerns and Process Education*. New York: McGraw-Hill.

Boyer, E. (1983). *High School*. New York: Harper Colophon Books.

Brophy, J., and T.L. Good. (1974). *Teacher-Student Relationships: Causes and Consequences*. New York: Holt, Rinehart and Winston.

Brutten, M., S.O. Richardson, and C. Mangel. (1973). *Something's Wrong with My Child*. New York: Harcourt Brace Jovanovich, Inc.

Buscaglia, L. (1972). *Love*. New York: Fawcett Crest.

Camp, B.W., G.E. Blom, F. Herbert, and W.J. van Doorninck. (1977). "Think Aloud: A Program for Developing Self-Control in Young Aggressive Boys." *Journal of Abnormal Child Psychology* 5.

Campbell, P. (1967). "School and Self Concept." *Educational Leadership* 24: 510-515.

Canfield, J., and J. Wells. (1976). *100 Ways to Enhance Self-Concept in the Classroom*. Englewood Cliffs, N.J.: Prentice Hall.

Carrington, P. (1978). *Freedom in Meditation*. Garden City, N.Y.: Anchor Books.

Cichon, D.J., and R.H. Kloff. (March 1978). "The Teaching Events Stress Inventory." Paper presented at the meeting of the American Educational Research Association, Toronto, Ontario. (Eric Document Reproduction Service, No. 16-662.)

Combs, A.W., D.L. Avila, and W.W. Purkey. (1971). *Helping Relationships: Basic Concepts for the Helping Professions*. Boston: Allyn & Bacon.

Coopersmith, S. (1967). *The Antecedents of Self Esteem*. San Francisco: W.H. Freedman.

Cousins, N. *Anatomy of an Illness*. New York.

Cowen, E.L., et al. (1975). *New Ways in School Mental Health*. New York: Human Science Press.

Curwin, R.L., and G. Curwin. (1974). *Developing Individual Values in the Classroom*. Palo Alto, Calif.: Learning Handbooks.

Curwin, G., R. Curwin, R. Kramer, M. Simmons, and K. Walsh. (1972). *Search for Values*. Dayton, Ohio: Pflaum/Standard.

Curwin, R.L., and B. Fuhrmann. (1975). *Discovering Your Teaching Self: Humanistic Approaches to Effective Teaching*. Englewood Cliffs, N.J.: Prentice-Hall.

Curwin, R.L., and A. Mendler. (1979). "Three-Dimensional Discipline: A New Approach to an Old Problem." *American Middle School Education* 1.

Curwin, R., and A. Mendler. (Fall 1981). "Discipline: Three Dimensions." *Partnership—A Journal for Leaders in Education* (Journal of the Center for Educational Leadership and Evaluation) 6.

Curwin, R., A. Mendler, and B. Culhane. (Feb. 1980). "Kids and Teachers Discipline One Another." *Learning Magazine* 8: 96-100.

deCharms, R. (1968). *Personal Causation: The Internal Affective Determinants of Behavior*. New York: Academic Press.

deCharms, R. (1968). *Personal Causation*. New York: Academic Press.

Deci, E. (1980). *The Psychology of Self Determination*. Lexington, Mass.: Heath.

Dillon, E.A. (1978). "Did We All Let Barry Die?" *Journal of Teacher Education* 29: 30.

Dodson, F. (1971). *How to Parent*. New York: New American Library.

Dodson, F. (1977). *How to Discipline with Love*. New York: Rawson Associates.

Dreikurs, R. (1964). *Children: The Challenge*. New York: Hawthorn Books, Inc.

Drew, W., A. Olds, and H. Olds, Jr. (1974). *Motivating Today's Students*. Palo Alto, Calif.: Learning Handbooks.

Driekurs, R., and P. Cassel. (1972). *Discipline without Tears: What to Do with Children Who Misbehave*. New York: Hawthorn Books.

Dweck, C.S. (1975). "The Role of Expectations and Attributions in the Alleviation of Learned Helplessness." *Journal of Personality and Social Psychology* 31: 674-685.

Epstein, C. (1979). *Classroom Management and Teaching*. Reston, Va.: Reston Publishing Co.

Erickson, E. (1968). *Identity, Youth and Crisis*. New York: W.W. Norton and Co.

Ernst, K. (1972). *Games Students Play*. Millbrae, Calif.: Celestial Arts.

Fantini, M.D., and G. Weinstein. (1968). *Making Urban Schools Work: Social Realities and the Urban School*. New York: Holt, Rinehart and Winston.

Feindler, E.L., and R.B. Ecton. (1986). *Adolescent Anger Control*. New York: Pergammon Press.

Furtwengler, W., and W. Konnert. (1982). *Improving School Discipline*. Boston: Allyn & Bacon.

Gailbraith, R.E., and T.M. Jones. (1976). *Moral Reasoning: A Teaching Handbook for Adapting Kohlberg to the Classroom*. Minneapolis, Minn.: Greenhaven Press Inc.

Ginott, H. (1972). *Teacher and Child*. New York: Macmillan.

Glasser, W. (1972). *The Identity Society*. New York: Harper and Row.

Glasser, W. (1965). *Reality Therapy*. New York: Harper and Row.

Glasser, W. (1969). *Schools Without Failure*. New York: Harper and Row.

Goldhammer, R. (1969). *Clinical Supervision: Special Methods for the Supervision of Teachers*. New York: Holt, Rinehart and Winston.

Hallahan, D.P., J.W. Lloyd, J.M. Kaufman, and A.B. Loper. (1983). "Academic Problems." In *The Practice of Child Therapy* by R. Morris and T. Kratochwill. New York: Pergammon Press.

Harris, T. (1967). *I'm OK—You're OK*. New York: Harper and Row.

Heisner, J. (1981). "The Ugly Side of the Urban Coin." *Instructor* 90: 20.

Hendricks, G., and T.B. Roberts. (1977). *The Second Centering Book*. Englewood Cliffs, N.J.: Prentice-Hall.

Holmes, M., D. Holmes, and J. Field. (1974). *The Therapeutic Classroom*. New York: James Aronson.

House, E., and S. Lapan. (1979). *Survival in the Classroom*. Abridged ed. Boston: Allyn & Bacon.

Howell, R., and P. Howell. (1979). *Discipline in the Classroom*. Reston, Va.: Reston Publishing Co.

Johnson, B., ed. (1982). *Dealing with Social Problems in the Classroom*. Dubuque, Iowa: Kendall/Hunt Publishing Co.

Jones, V., and L. Jones. (1981). *Responsible Classroom Discipline*. Boston: Allyn & Bacon.

Keirsey, D. (1969). "Systematic Exclusion: Eliminating Chronic Classroom Disruptions." In *Behavior Counseling: Case Studies and Techniques*, edited by J. Krumboltz and C. Thoresen. New York: Holt, Rinehart and Winston.

Kerman, S. (1979). "Teacher Expectation and Student Achievement." *Phi Delta Kappan*: 716-718.

Key, W.B. (1973). *Subliminal Seduction*. Englewood Cliffs, N.J.: Prentice-Hall.

Key, W.B. (1976). *Media Sexploitation*. Englewood Cliffs, N.J.: Prentice-Hall.

King-Stoops, J., and W. Meier. (January 1978). "Teacher Analysis of the Discipline Problem." *Phi Delta Kappan*: 354.

Kirschenbaum, H., S. Simon, and P. Napier. (1971). *Wadjaget, The Grading Game in American Education*. New York: Hart.

Kounin, J.S. (1970). *Discipline and Group Management in Classrooms*. New York: Holt, Rinehart and Winston.

Kyriacou, C., and J. Sutcliffe. (1978). "Teacher Stress: Prevalence, Sources and Symptoms." *British Journal of Educational Psychology* 48: 159-167.

Lerlech, J. (1979). *Classroom Management*. New York: Harper and Row.

Marquis, J.N., W.G. Morgan, and G.W. Piaget. (1971). *A Guidebook for Systematic Desensitization*. Palo Alto, Calif.: Veteran's Workshop.

Masden, C.H., Jr., and C.K. Masden. (1981). *Teaching Discipline: A Positive Approach for Educational Development.* 3d ed. Boston: Allyn & Bacon.

Maslow, A.H. (1968). *Toward a Psychology of Being.* 2d ed. New York: Van Nostrand Reinhold.

Maslow, A.H. (1970). *Motivation and Personality.* 2d ed. New York: Harper and Row.

Masters, R., and J. Houston. (1972). *Mind Games.* New York: Dell Publishing Co.

Meichenbaum, D. (1977). *Cognitive Behavior Modification.* New York: Plenum.

Neill, A.S. (1971.) *Summerhill: A Radical Approach to Child Rearing.* New York: Hart.

Nevin, E., S. Nevin, and E. Danzig. (1970). *Blocks to Creativity: Guide to Program.* Cleveland: Danzig-Nevin International Inc.

"Our Nation's Schools, A Report Card." (1975). Report of the Sub-committee to Investigate Juvenile Delinquency to the Committee on the Judiciary of the U.S. Senate. Washington, D.C.: U.S. Government Printing Office.

Postman, N., and C. Weingartner. (1969). *Teaching as a Subversive Activity.* New York: Delacorte.

Poteet, J. (1973). *Behavior Modification: A Practical Guide for Teachers.* Minneapolis: Burgess.

Raths, L.E., M. Harmin, and S.B. Simon. (1966). *Values and Teaching: Working with Values in the Classroom.* Columbus, Ohio: Charles E. Merrill.

"Report of Stress Conditions Within the Tacoma Public Schools." (May 1979). Prepared by I. Mazer for the Tacoma Association of Classroom Teachers.

Schein, E. (1969). *Process Consultation: Its Role in Organizational Development.* Reading, Mass.: Addison-Wesley.

Schrag, P., and D. Divoky. (1975). *The Myth of the Hyperactive Child.* New York: Pantheon Books.

Seligman, M.E.P. (1981). "A Learned Helplessness Point of View." In *Behavior Therapy for Depression.* New York: Academic Press.

Silberman, C.E. (1970). *Crisis in the Classroom.* New York: Random House.

Simon, S.B., L.W. Howe, and H. Kirschenbaum. (1972). *Values Clarification: A Handbook of Practical Strategies for Teachers and Students.* New York: Hart.

Simon, S., and L.J. Bellanca, eds. (1976). *Degrading the Grading Myths: A Primer of Alternatives to Grades and Marks.* Alexandria, Va.: Association for Supervision and Curriculum Development.

Sloane, H.M. (1976). *Classroom Management: Remediation and Prevention.* New York: John Wiley and Sons.

Syngg, D., and A.W. Combs. (1949). *Individual Behavior.* New York: Harper.

Stevens, J.O. (1973). *Awareness: Exploring, Experimenting, Experiencing.* New York: Bantam Books.

Tyrell, R., F. Johns, and F. McCarthy. (1977). *Growing Pains in the Classroom: A Guide for Teachers of Adolescents.* Reston, Va.: Reston Publishing Co.

Walker, H. (1979). *The Acting Out Child: Coping with Classroom Disruption.* Boston: Allyn & Bacon.

Weinstein, G., J. Hardin, and M. Weinstein. (1976). *Education of the Self.* Amherst, Mass.: Mandala.

Weinstein, G., and M.D. Fantini, eds. (1970). *Toward Humanistic Education: A Curriculum of Affect.* New York: Praeger.

Wlodkowski, R. (November 1982.) "Discipline: The Great False Hope." (Eric Document Reproduction Service. Ed. 224 780).

Wlodkowski, R. (1985). *Enhancing Adult Motivation to Learn.* San Francisco: Jossey-Bass.

Wolfgang, C., and C. Glickman. (1980). *Solving Discipline Problems.* Boston: Allyn & Bacon.

Wolpe, J., and A. Lazarus. (1966). *Behavior Therapy Techniques.* Oxford: Pergammon Press.